Access

Access:

MULTIPLE AVENUES
FOR DEAF PEOPLE

Doreen DeLuca,
Irene W. Leigh,
Kristin A. Lindgren,
and Donna Jo Napoli
Editors

Gallaudet University Press
Washington, D.C.

Gallaudet University Press
Washington, DC 20002

http://gupress.gallaudet.edu

© 2008 by Gallaudet University

Printed in the United States of America

Library of Congress Cataloging-in-Publication Data

Access : multiple avenues for deaf people / Doreen DeLuca . . . [et al.], editors.

    p. cm.

Includes index.

ISBN 978-1-56368-393-0 (alk. paper)

    1. Deaf—United States—Social conditions.   2. Deaf—Education—United States.   3. Deaf—Means of communication—United States. I. DeLuca, Doreen.

HV2545.A32 2008

362.4′20973—dc22

2008011300

∞ The paper used in this publication meets the minimum requirements of American National Standard for Information Sciences—Permanence of Paper for Printed Library Materials, ANSI Z39.48-1984.

Contents

Acknowledgments

This volume is a companion to the earlier Gallaudet University Press volume *Signs and Voices: Deaf Culture, Identity, Language, and Arts*. Both of them grew out of the Signs and Voices conference at Swarthmore, Haverford, and Bryn Mawr colleges in November 2004 and were enriched by additional contributions from experts in the field. The editors are grateful to the many individuals, departments, and offices at all three colleges who provided financial, logistical, and moral support. Without this support, neither the conference nor the books would have been possible. With respect to the present volume, we owe a special thanks to the Linguistics Department at Swarthmore, which generously offered help at many stages of the production. Additionally, we thank Karen Peltz Strauss for helpful comments on chapter 2 and, with regard to chapter 3, we thank Susan M. O'Reilly for Figures 1a–1c, the Med-El Corporation for Figure 2, and the Cochlear Corporation for Figure 3. For expert guidance at every stage, we thank Ivey Wallace at Gallaudet University Press. Since there are four editors, we now offer our individual thanks—beyond the gratitude we have to each other for all the good will and hard work we've shared.

Doreen DeLuca: Thank you to many in the Deaf community who have shared with me the richness of your language, the culture, and your lives. I thank Eileen Forestal and the late AlB for a wonderful foundation in ASL and your engaging stories. Thank you to my fellow contributors for all your hard work. A special thanks to Donna Jo Napoli for opening her heart to me eight years ago and, in turn, celebrating the lives of d/Deaf and hard of hearing people by sharing their works with so many in a variety of venues. To my good friend and colleague, Jai Wexler, thanks for sharing your passion and ongoing support. And to my family, thank you for your love.

Irene W. Leigh: I am grateful to all the authors who so willingly contributed to this book so that readers can better understand the access issues faced by deaf and hard of hearing individuals. It has been a pleasure collaborating with my co-editors. Having an understanding family makes it that much easier to do the work that goes into projects such as this one. Thanks!

Kristin A. Lindgren: I'm grateful to the colleagues in disability studies who first made me aware of the richness of d/Deaf history and culture and of the access issues faced by deaf, hard of hearing, and culturally Deaf people. Many thanks to my co-editors, who greatly furthered my understanding of these issues, and to the contributors, who generously shared their experience and expertise. My family has not only allowed me time and space to do this work but has also been willing to learn along with me.

Donna Jo Napoli: I thank Judy Kegl, who first introduced me to the linguistic analysis of ASL, and Shannon Allen, whose senior thesis on linguistics at Swarthmore College introduced me to issues in Deaf education and who has been constantly generous to me through the years with her knowledge and wisdom. I thank Doreen DeLuca for welcoming me into so many projects, always with that dazzling smile, and the contributors to this volume and the last, who give of themselves so heartily. And I thank my husband for staying by me through it all.

Introduction

DOREEN DELUCA, IRENE W. LEIGH,
KRISTIN A. LINDGREN, AND DONNA JO NAPOLI

The past half-century has seen major developments and attitude shifts—at the technological, institutional, societal, and personal levels—that have improved the lives of deaf, hard of hearing, and Deaf people. Nevertheless, there remain hurdles for deaf people to jump if they are to have full access to the rights and privileges enjoyed by the larger hearing society. And there remain hurdles for hearing people to jump if they are to respond to the need for equal access of all members of society. The essays in *Access: Multiple Avenues for Deaf People* address some of the practical and theoretical issues and advances in three major areas of access: assistive technologies, education, and civil rights.

Many of the essays and interviews in this volume grew out of the Signs and Voices conference, a four-day event in November 2004, which took place at Swarthmore, Haverford, and Bryn Mawr colleges. That conference was holistic, looking at multiple aspects of d/Deaf life, not just questions of access, and, accordingly, many works from that conference appear in a sister volume to the present one: *Signs and Voices: Deaf Culture, Identity, Language, and Arts.*[1] Other essays were written specifically for this volume at the invitation of the editors.

---

1. Following a convention first established by James Woodward, we use "deaf" to refer to individuals who are audiologically deaf and "Deaf" to refer to those who use sign as their primary language and identify with Deaf culture. Because these categories are overlapping and not always easy to tease apart, we also adopt the more recent practice of using "d/Deaf" to represent deaf and culturally Deaf people.

Taken together, the essays in *Access: Multiple Avenues for Deaf People* outline what is presently available and effective and what is still lacking or ineffective in the area of access. They give both personal and professional viewpoints, with an eye toward informing the reader regarding choices that must be made on the individual level as well as on the societal level. We hope that the volume will prove useful to scholars and teachers in a variety of fields, to their students, and, especially, to general readers, both d/Deaf and hearing, who are seeking information about access.

ASSISTIVE TECHNOLOGIES

Part One opens with Maggie Casteel's "Building New Ramps with Hearing Assistive Technology." The current explosion in communications technology provides increasing numbers of, and better quality access to, accommodations for deaf and hard of hearing people. Ms. Casteel points out that, to set the stage for assistive technology to be most effective, we must develop awareness on the part of society in general, and of families and employers in particular, of the communication needs of deaf and hard of hearing people. She has advice for hearing people dealing both with deaf and hard of hearing people who choose to be oral and deaf and hard of hearing people who choose to sign. She describes hearing assistive technology (HAT) that can improve awareness and accessibility to acoustic signals—from devices that convert sound into something else (light or vibration or text or sign language images), to those that enhance sound (including assistive listening systems such as FM, infrared, and induction loop, as well as personal listening systems, which may help with TV, radio, and stereo). She outlines the rights of deaf and hard of hearing people with regard to "reasonable accommodation" protected by the law and lists situations under which safety is threatened without HAT. Ms. Casteel goes step by step through each device so that the reader can be truly informed.

In the next chapter, Al Sonnenstrahl has a conversation with the editors about all aspects of telecommunications. Mr. Sonnenstrahl began his career in advocacy by convincing the U.S. Civil Service Commission to change their hiring rules and allow deaf engineers. After ten years as an engineer, he moved on to advocate for equal access for deaf people in multiple ways. He persuaded AT&T to provide operator services and directory assistance to deaf people. As the director of

Telecommunications for the Deaf, Inc., he worked with others to make sure that the draft of the Americans with Disabilities Act (ADA) addressed the needs of deaf people before it was passed. He gives details on the history of the development of communication devices and services, including video relay service and voice carry over, provides information about the choices available in visual communication services versus text and voice services over the phone line, and discusses the role of various agencies in ensuring access for deaf people. He stresses the need to maintain the text format in telecommunications and warns that we must not lose closed captioning as TVs turn digital. Further, he says, we must monitor developments to maintain interoperability and interconnectivity of different devices and systems, so they work together in tandem—Blackberry pagers communicating with Sidekick pagers and so on. And we must ensure that deaf people have access to 911 centers, not just through landlines, but with wireless systems and the Internet, where now, unfortunately, emergency centers are unable to identify caller locations.

In the final chapter in this section, "Cochlear Implants," the Alfred I. duPont Hospital for Children team of Robert C. O'Reilly, M.D., Amanda Mangiardi, rehabilitation therapist, and H. Timothy Bunnell, psychologist, offer a detailed description of how cochlear implants work and take us through every step of the process of receiving one— from determining whether someone is a suitable candidate, to the surgical process itself, to rehabilitation therapy following implantation. First, they describe auditory anatomy and physiology and explain how hearing occurs under ordinary circumstances. Next, they detail how cochlear implants deliver auditory information to the brain and give a complete picture of cochlear implant surgery. Determinations about the advisability of implantation are made by a team of professionals who educate and counsel parents as well. The source and severity of hearing loss, the amount of time between the onset of deafness and potential implantation, and the commitment of the child and family to rehabilitation therapy after implantation are factors that determine whether a child has a good chance of benefiting from implantation. For successful rehabilitation therapy, which works on both the perception and production of particular language sounds, parent participation is essential. Other factors that correlate with success are the child's nonverbal IQ and the quality of the implant device. And the best multichannel implants using the latest speech processing algorithms support better spoken language development. The article ends with a summary of the types of school environments typically offered to the child with an implant and comparative studies of their success.

EDUCATION AND LITERACY

The essays in Part Two explore approaches to educating deaf children, offering both research-based analyses and accounts of personal experience. In the first essay, "Civil Rights Issues in Deaf Education," Jami N. Fisher and Philip J. Mattiacci give a history of the legal acts which have aimed to ban discrimination against persons with disabilities and point out the need for legal recognition of the discrimination that d/Deaf individuals experience. In particular, they zoom in on the needs of culturally Deaf people as a linguistic minority within the educational setting. The mainstreaming of Deaf children has had disastrous effects for many children. In contrast, Deaf children educated in an environment which facilitates visual access that appropriately meets their linguistic needs have a better chance to achieve academically. The authors support this argument with a brief outline of the history of Deaf Americans from the early 1800s on. If Deaf children are viewed not in audiological terms, but in cultural terms, their needs can be recognized and, accordingly, met. Mixing Deaf children of various ages and cognitive skills in a classroom simply because of their English ability (a commonplace practice in mainstreaming programs) leads to social and emotional problems. Additionally, there is a crying need for teachers trained in American Sign Language (ASL) who are knowledgeable about the educational needs of Deaf children; for adequate support and training of parents of Deaf children, including early intervention programs; and for adult Deaf role models from whom Deaf children can learn cultural and linguistic awareness. Finally, Deaf children need access to extracurricular activities. The authors end with a list of recommendations for anyone involved in the education of Deaf children.

In "Inclusion and the Development of Deaf Identity," Michael Stinson discusses the choices available for d/Deaf children in their local public schools. He distinguishes between placing the child in a regular classroom and asking that the child adapt or be taken out of the regular classroom (mainstreaming), and placing the child in a classroom that adapts to the needs of that child (inclusion). In many mainstreaming environments, the child winds up in a special classroom for much of the day, with interpreters and other supports. Inclusion, therefore, theoretically has a better chance of welcoming the child, but only if teachers and students sincerely view the deaf child as a genuine member and, thus, use both ASL and English in an appropriate balance. Further, there needs to be a sufficient number of deaf children to make social interaction with deaf peers possible, interaction which is important for the development of a healthy identity. Additionally, the classroom needs good communication support, such as interpreters, notetakers, speech-to-text services, etc. Stinson describes patterns of identity among deaf people, from those whose culture is hearing, to those uncomfortable in both Deaf and hearing environments, to those whose culture is Deaf, to those who are bicultural. Research shows that deaf youths and adults who are culturally Deaf or bicultural report the greatest satisfaction with life. Inclusion programs that isolate deaf children within a hearing environment rarely provide the opportunity for learning about Deaf culture and, thus, developing a healthy identity. Mainstreaming, on the other hand, tends to group deaf children together, allowing for some Deaf acculturation, but far from enough to ensure good self-esteem. Stinson recommends that all programs include opportunities for Deaf children to interact with Deaf adults and peers and promote extracurricular Deaf activities.

Lisa Herbert shares with us her experiences growing up in "Deaf, Signing, and Oral: A Journey." She was born hearing into an Afro-Canadian family with Caribbean roots. At age four she became deaf as a result of meningitis. Within a year, it was clear hearing aids were not effective, so she was fitted with a cochlear implant. She had a variety of school environments, from being the only deaf child mainstreamed into all-hearing classes, to being in a school that had enough deaf children to put them in a discrete classroom. She made friends and once even represented her school at the regional spelling bee. When she had trouble speechreading, she learned to smile wide. The summer after ninth grade, she attended a camp where she learned ASL, loving how relaxed she could be in a visual environment. But then it was back to an oral environment, with class discussions that were too complex and fast to follow with speechreading and no interpreter. After eleventh grade, she headed off to Gallaudet University and faced the question of why she chose to have a cochlear implant. She wasn't using it at Gallaudet, so she stopped wearing it. Still, she didn't really fit in, so she transferred to the Rochester Institute of Technology. While there, her cochlear implant stopped functioning properly. It was old and only had a single channel anyway. Ms. Herbert describes the difficult decision she faced: whether to be re-implanted or not and facing all the repercussions that would mean to her identity. At the age of twenty, she was re-implanted. She finished college, worked for a while, and then attended Gallaudet University's graduate program in school psychology. She now works at the Indiana School for the Deaf, where she feels completely comfortable as a signing Deaf person who continues to use her cochlear implant.

The editors' conversation with Grace Walker, focusing on her personal experiences with a cochlear implant, ends this section. Ms. Walker grew up in a Deaf family and attended a residential school for deaf people from kindergarten through high school. She used an FM system and a hearing aid as a young girl at school. When she was 40 years old, she got a cochlear implant. She was judged a good candidate for surgery because her expectation that the implant would enable her to hear environmental sounds but not necessarily to decipher speech was realistic. Her family and friends at Gallaudet University, where she was working, had mixed reactions to her decision, but generally supported it. After the surgery, she experienced nausea for two weeks. She persisted, though, working hard at speech therapy for a year. The cochlear implant did allow her access to environmental noises, but it did not help her with language. A few years later, the nausea returned so severely, she had to be hospitalized. And a couple of years later, she had another attack of vertigo, even worse than the earlier ones. She took off the external apparatus of the implant, but for a year she experienced mild vertigo almost all the time. After that, it came sporadically. Now, if she experiences the dizziness, she battles it with yoga and medication. She no longer uses her cochlear implant and has been vertigo-free for years. She does not regret getting the implant, despite the vertigo.

Civil Rights

Part Three consists of essays and conversations that address the civil rights of d/Deaf people in the workplace, in settings where they receive education about and treatment for HIV/AIDS, and in telecommunications. We begin with the editors' conversation with Christy Hennessey, focusing on rights in the workplace. Ms. Hennessey grew up with parents who were proactive in her education, relocating the whole family so that she could attend a school for deaf people and then working to change the school curriculum to better meet the needs of the children. Their advocacy work influenced her career choice: She now instructs

Deaf people on how to advocate for themselves. She teaches Deaf clients how to write a résumé and gives practice interviews for jobs. Once on the job, if people have problems, she helps assess what their needs and rights are, particularly with respect to the ADA. She urges them to inform employers that they are entitled to reasonable accommodations, including interpreters at staff meetings and other events as well as technology such as videophones. Sometimes employers benefit from the sensitivity training workshops that she runs. In most cases, once an employer understands what a deaf person needs in order to work effectively in a safe and friendly environment, the employer is cooperative. But if problems persist, Ms. Hennessey will advise an employee about how to file a complaint with the Equal Employment Opportunity Commission. Ms. Hennessey gives practical advice while adding a historical perspective to the issue of employment since the passage of the ADA. Her services are free, and similar services are available in many urban areas.

Our next editors' conversation is with Tony Saccente, focusing on HIV/AIDS counseling. Mr. Saccente worked for Housing Works, in New York City, which helps provide housing health care, job training, and other vital services to homeless people with HIV/AIDS. Mr. Saccente did Deaf outreach, particularly to the gay community. He describes a survey conducted in 2000 by the National Development and Research Institutes, Inc., which showed that the percentage of HIV-positive Deaf people in NYC, relative to the Deaf population of NYC as a whole, is three times that for hearing people. Part of Mr. Saccente's work was educating the Deaf public, since social factors and language barriers (in the case of immigrants) inhibit access to information. He trained interpreters to use frank language about sexual activities to avoid misunderstandings and to give explicit directions about what people should do if they are infected or think they might be infected. He trained peer education groups, so that his students, in turn, could go out into their communities and educate. While the Deaf community in NYC is close-knit, it has subgroups (e.g., Asian Americans, Latinos, African Americans, and gay Americans), and Mr. Saccente worked to find ways to communicate sexual, social, and medical information that was culturally acceptable to these subgroups. His workshops used visual aids and role-playing to deal with emotional matters such as anger management (people feel "why me?") as well as medical matters. One of his goals is to inform the public about testing options; people are more likely to wait for results if tests are reliable and quick—and it is imperative that people know their own health status if they are to behave appropriately.

In "HIV/AIDS in the United States Deaf Community," Leila Monaghan reviews recent studies of Deaf attitudes toward HIV/AIDS. Repeatedly, Deaf people display knowledge about AIDS-related maladies but seem to know little about how to practice safer sex to avoid transmission. This information gap is due, in part, to the difficulty Deaf people experience in reading medical material. But when medical material is presented in ASL, people understand readily. Deaf people want accessible information so they can protect themselves. Interactive group presentations, workshops, peer information networks, and straightforward, but culturally sensitive, presentations of information from outreach groups at d/Deaf events were particularly well received by the respondents. The interviews revealed hesitancy to seek information about HIV because of stigmas attached both to being gay and to being HIV-positive. Because Deaf communities are small, fear of lack of confidentiality is intense. Unfortunately, information on the extent of HIV/AIDS among deaf people is hard to come by, since most states do not collect information on the hearing status of people being tested for HIV. But the information we do have is unsettling: Deaf people are significantly more likely than hearing people to be HIV-positive, and in the youngest age groups, deaf people are over four times more likely to test positive—a difference that parallels the knowledge gap between deaf and hearing people. Deaf people feel clueless about where to go for testing. Even if they locate a testing site through the Internet, they do not know if ASL services are provided. Once a person is diagnosed HIV-positive, sometimes no further support is offered. AIDS in the Deaf community is epidemic, and information that can reduce risk is essential, particularly because health care is not easily accessed. Yet limited funding threatens the very programs that help the most.

We close this volume with "DPN and Civil Rights" by Gregory Hlibok, who grew up in a Deaf family passionately involved in advocacy. As a child, he protested whenever he met communication barriers. So as a student at Gallaudet University, it was natural for him to lead the Deaf President Now (DPN) movement that resulted in the selection of the university's first Deaf president. Subsequently, student body governments across the country asked for his protest "tool kit." But Mr. Hlibok couldn't supply one; the protest succeeded because the students involved had grown up oppressed, and, according to him, that made them ready to fight more effectively for their rights than any hearing person could have. With the DPN protest, Deaf people took control of their destiny, and hearing people became aware of their capabilities. In the years following the protest, demand for ASL courses increased, as did job opportunities for Deaf people. Mr. Hlibok testified in support of the ADA and then saw the passage of the TV Decoder Circuitry Act, and later, the Telecommunications Act. By 2001, he was working at the Federal Communications Commission as an attorney who advises in regulating telecommunication relay service matters and captioning. Laws requiring "functional equivalency" for Deaf and hearing people with respect to technologies must be interpreted as having moving goals, so that providers constantly ensure availability to the deaf consumer and improvements whenever new technology enables a higher level of functionality. Targeted laws often have unexpected benefits; closed captioning benefits anyone trying to learn to read English, not only Deaf people. Changes such as the instituting of closed captioning helped to raise awareness on the part of the hearing public of deaf people's needs. We must applaud technological innovations, but stay vigilant in seeking and protecting equal opportunities and accessibility for all.

The essays in this final section highlight both the tremendous advances in protecting the civil rights of d/Deaf people and the work that remains to be done to educate everyone about d/Deaf and hard of hearing people's rights and to ensure the ongoing protection of these rights.

Part One
Assistive Technologies

1 Building New Ramps with Hearing Assistive Technology

MAGGIE CASTEEL

Hearing loss has undoubtedly existed since the beginning of time. Consider our distant ancestor, Og, managing his hearing loss through those long winter months spent in the cave—poor lighting, lousy acoustics, someone constantly pounding something (or someone) in the background. Of course, Og may have had the advantage of living in a society where a standard form of sign language was widely used and understood among all people. Imagine it: an ongoing prehistoric charades depicting cave life, including everything from carving mastodons to fire building to idle gossip. A system where everyone was able to communicate on the same level and no one was judged or excluded for lacking seamless verbal communication abilities. Or perhaps even then, Og was forced to rely upon intense visual observation or cupping his hand behind his ear while trying to converse in the cave. Perhaps he felt the need to bluff appropriate grunting responses so as not to appear foolish among his fellow troglodytes. ("Ah, stupid Og!" "Eh, foolish, worthless, Og!" "Forget about him. He never knows what's going on anyway!") Some of us are still relying on that ploy for the same reasons. Not being able to participate in dialogue isolates one from other people. Not being able to communicate imposes societal judgment and can lead to implications of inferior intelligence and a lack of education and sophistication. Nobody wants to bluff his way through life; no one wants to feel like Og in the cave.

Despite disability legislation guaranteeing all Americans with disabilities equal and effective access to information and services, persons who are D/deaf, Deaf Blind, hard of hearing, and late deafened have remained part of a largely ramp-less society. Until very recently, making the connection with the hearing world seemed a logistical impossibility. We can all summon visions of early assistive technology—bespectacled men in powdered wigs holding ear-horns and leaning intently toward the speaker. We also know that the spectacles were functioning more effectively as assistive devices than the ear-horn!

Thanks in part to the current explosion in communications technology, access accommodation for persons with hearing loss is now a matter of endless possibility. The range of visual and auditory solutions increases and improves daily. By promoting awareness, developing strategies, supporting empowerment and self-advocacy, and exercising civil rights, the hearing loss community can now begin building new ramps toward equal access. We can finally leave Og, and his world, stuffed and in the museum where he belongs!

BEGIN AT THE BEGINNING: HOW DOES THE EAR WORK?

A simple description of the function of the ear in hearing helps in understanding the role of hearing assistive technology (HAT). (Interested readers are referred to the O'Reilly, Mangiardi, and Bunnell article in this volume for a much more detailed description.) The outer ear really does do more than hold our earrings and sunglasses. It serves as a sort of net to help gather sound waves and funnel them down the ear canal. These waves then buffet against the eardrum, which vibrates like the woofer on a stereo speaker. This motion jiggles three bones—the hammer, anvil, and stirrup—further amplifying the sound signals. Next, the stirrup plunges against the opening to the inner ear (or cochlea), creating waves of liquid motion that are detected by sensory cells in the cochlea. Cells in different places detect distinct sound tones, allowing our brains to distinguish among them. Any variance or malfunction in this process at any level can be a cause of hearing loss.

When referring to persons with hearing loss, self-identification rules. It is an individual choice and may not have direct relevance to level of loss or clinical diagnosis. People who choose to self-identify as Deaf share a common language (American Sign Language) and a common culture (the Deaf culture). Those who choose to self-identify as deaf may tend to rely more on written or spoken English and identify with the hearing culture. People whose identity lies with the hearing culture generally identify as hard of hearing and try to function in the hearing world by maximizing their residual hearing. Persons who are Deaf Blind are aware of their unique identity and affiliate where they are most comfortable. This is not to say that there is no crossover among groups, also determined by choice and comfort level.

Developing Effective Approaches to Communication with Persons with Hearing Loss

Persons with hearing loss want to be fully involved with their families and friends, their work, their familiar world. They want the continued opportunity for self-fulfillment in all its manifestations. Achieving this goal requires

- Acknowledging the universal and situational needs of those with hearing loss
- Developing communication skills that are respectful of individual choices and needs
- Optimizing device options to achieve a smooth and expressive flow of communication
- Learning simple and direct solutions to modes of communication, including dealing with language barriers
- Developing an awareness of, and learning the operation of, assistive technology
- Developing awareness of sign language or speechreading skills
- Recognizing the direct need for assistive technology

While all of us sometimes struggle to communicate effectively, people who have a hearing loss face an even greater challenge. If you have a friend, family member, or coworker who has a hearing loss, you may find yourself having difficulty with even the simplest communications. Most dialogues can be immediately improved by following a few fundamental strategies, sometimes referred to as "Clear Speech" (Gilbert 2000). Clear Speech can be used with persons who are oral deaf, those who speechread, and those with some level of residual hearing. Those of us who share our lives with persons with hearing loss can make this challenge less difficult and probably find ourselves communicating more effectively with everyone around us by implementing these Clear Speech strategies and becoming more aware of sign language basics.

Clear Speech Strategies

- Speak at a slightly louder level. Do not shout.

- Speak at a normal rate, but not too rapidly.

- Do not speak unless your face is visible to the person with hearing loss.

- Do not speak when there is a great deal of environmental noise.

- Never speak directly into the person's ear. The listener cannot make use of visual cues.

- Rephrase rather than repeat.

- Separate words, but do not over-articulate, which causes distortion of the sounds of speech.

- Include the person in all discussions about him or her.

- Treat the person as an adult.

Sign Language

Sign language is a strategy for people who choose visual communication. It includes several systems of manual expression, ranging from American Sign Language (ASL) to several varieties of signed English. These systems have the common advantage that they do not rely on hearing as a basis for communication. They have the common disadvantage that the systems are of value only if the person with whom you are communicating can use the system, and learning them demands a sustained and intense commitment. However, learning this visual form of communication has great reward and efficacy in communicating with the deaf people who use sign language and those with speech disorders. It is important to note that sign language systems are not universal, and, in fact, there are many differences in the language systems among regions, countries, and even generations of people. So if you say "toe-may-toe," and I say "toe-mah-toe," please allow for the accent before you call the whole thing off.

Additionally, a person who is Deaf may utilize other nontechnical forms of communication such as writing, drawing, and speaking. They may also require a certified interpreter for interface with the hearing community. If a person has a hearing loss and chooses a certified interpreter as the primary means of communication, it is imperative that this request be respected and that communication in other forms not be forced. Conversely, it cannot be assumed that an interpreter will satisfy the needs of all persons with hearing loss. Every person has a right to equal and effective access to information and services being offered, and the most important consideration in implementing these options is choice. The individual with hearing loss always gets the first choice for personal accommodation.

Building Bridges with HAT

Historically, communicating with persons with hearing loss has been inhibited by a lack of awareness, sensitivity to cultural nuance, and appropriate methodology. Beyond the simple Clear Speech and sign language communications courtesies just mentioned, there were no bridges. The implementation of HAT is the most important way for persons with hearing loss to achieve equal and effective access.

HAT refers to devices, programs, and services that help persons at all levels of hearing loss live more independently. Devices can improve awareness and accessibility to acoustic signals, either through substitution (i.e., converting sound into light, vibration, or text) or sound enhancement (e.g., a personal FM or TV listening system). HAT functions by helping to mitigate the effects of the distance between the listener and the sound source, competing noise in the environment, and poor room acoustics (Hearing Loss Association of America 2005).

As Easy as 1-2-3, a Plan of Action

How does this process begin? Ideally, those with hearing loss are introduced to augmentative equipment and services through their total hearing-care team—which may include an audiologist and an assistive device consultant. An OVR (Office of Vocational Rehabilitation) counselor or other rehabilitation professional may also be quite helpful in this process. Centers for Independent Living, or CILs, exist everywhere and are capable of offering information on assistive technology. These centers can be located in phone books and through Internet searches.

The Internet and device catalogs are extremely useful tools in learning about technology. Hopefully, by making yourself aware of your options and your rights, you will gain the confidence to pursue communications improvements on your own behalf.

Appropriate communications solutions are empowering, but given the preponderance of options, and the rapidity of change and improvement in HAT, the consumer may feel overwhelmed, perhaps even paralyzed by the number and range of choices. Many potential improvements for communications are never addressed, simply because the path to choice and acquisition seems overwhelming. Even this overview cannot be comprehensive, but will offer a fundamental understanding of some of the options and a simple plan of action for becoming a better consumer.

Additionally, the consumer may be deterred by prior negative experiences and the burden of bearing the cost for devices and services that are ineffective. Many devices are labeled as failures because they were poorly chosen and ultimately remain in the box! Device dollars are dear and compromises must be made, so failures are absolutely unacceptable. It is important for persons with hearing loss to be involved in any solution selection process, even if someone else is purchasing it for them. They may already have a preference regarding what to select. It is always recommended that the person with hearing loss test the product in all the environments for which it is intended before it is purchased. Assistive technology was never designed to fill drawers.

Note: According to the laws listed at the end of the chapter, providing reasonable accommodation in public places involves shared responsibility. The person with hearing loss must request accommodation at least two weeks prior to any scheduled meeting, stating preference. The professional or agency in question is then responsible by law for providing reasonable accommodation, a term open to interpretation and discussion.

It is important to establish priorities for acquiring appropriate and effective solutions before beginning the task of implementing technological support. First, it is necessary to determine a person's communication needs at home, on the job, and during recreational, social, and religious activities. Other situations unique to the individual, such as travel for business or pleasure, should also be considered. The following three considerations make the gathering of preliminary information useful to the outcome—easy as 1-2-3.

It is essential to determine the person's choices (i.e., basics about how people who are D/deaf, hard of hearing and Deaf Blind "hear"—visual or auditory—or a combination of both).

- Is your primary choice for "hearing" visual or auditory, or a combination of both?

A "needs assessment" is valuable for identifying what strategies may be useful to pursue.

- In what situations do you have difficulty hearing?
- What is the extent of your hearing loss?
- Do you wear hearing aids? A cochlear implant?
- Do the hearing aids or cochlear implant have a T-switch or direct audio input?
- Do you use assistive technology?

Determine viable sources for acquisition of supportive technology.

- What financial resources are available to you for acquiring HAT?

Having determined these preliminaries, for purposes of clarity and efficacy it is then helpful to break HAT into three sometimes-overlapping areas that address communication needs in order of urgency. The next step then becomes making a list of needs in order of primacy. Again, easy as 1-2-3.

Priority #1: Safety First! Devices and Services We Need to Be Safe.

Everyone has the right to be safe and must have the ability to summon and access emergency services within the same time frame as persons using traditional 911 procedures. This includes devices appropriate to our hearing function for alerting us to fire, intruders, and auto-related signals, and a system for enabling us to summon help in an emergency.

Alerting device checklist—Do you know when:

- The smoke alarm goes off?
- The phone rings?

- Someone is at the door?

- Someone (baby, parent, spouse, child, employer) needs you?

Priority #2: Getting the Job Done! Devices We Must Have to Allow Us to Carry Out Our Work and Responsibilities to the Optimum of Our Abilities.

We all have ongoing responsibilities that require our best efforts. We have a right to the tools necessary to carry out ongoing responsibilities related to our job, education, or caregiving of another or of ourselves through use of appropriate telecommunication devices and other technologies—vibrating alarm clocks and watches, super-ringers, flashing lights, personal listening systems, teletypewriters (TTYs), wireless pagers, video relay systems . . . whatever it takes.

Priority #3: Life Is for Everyone! Devices We Should Have to Enhance the Quality of Our Lives.

These may include voice-to-text systems, CART (computer assisted realtime) transcription, assistive listening systems (ALSs) for public places, appropriate travel and leisure aids, and any and all devices and accommodations that allow us to enjoy the same level of participation as persons without communication challenges. After establishing this list of priorities, it is then possible to move on to exploring the particulars of possibility, choice, and implementation.

Hearing Aids and Cochlear Implants

Hearing aids have long been considered the most effective and potent noninvasive therapeutic tool available for the vast majority of people with hearing loss. They can be a crucial and necessary component in any effort designed to address the consequences of a hearing loss.

Cochlear implants (CIs) represent surgical technology for profound hearing loss. The process begins by being deemed eligible for implantation by an ear, nose, and throat physician specializing in implantation. This selection process is highly particular about eligibility parameters. One cannot just choose to be implanted. First, one must be eligible.

The evolution of the cochlear implant has introduced severe to profoundly hearing impaired people to the everyday world and all of its noise. The addition of assistive technology for hearing aid users has expanded to the cochlear implant user as well. As the cochlear implant device has brought the recipients into the noisy world of the normal listeners, the ability to filter out extraneous or unwanted noise is more difficult for the hearing impaired. The factors of reverberation and background noise in a room increase the frustration of a hearing impaired person. The current models of cochlear implant processors may include a telephone coil or T-mic to improved telephone communication, as well as lapel microphones or TV/stereo direct input wiring to improve the signal to noise ratio for their various listening situations. This allows a cochlear implant recipient to experience direct and selected sound through their cochlear implant processor. The use of assistive technology has allowed a hearing impaired individual, even a cochlear implant recipient to be more focused on the signal of choice with the competing background noises selectively reduced. The successful use of any hearing device is complemented with the additional use of assistive technology.

—*Kathleen Gilmartin, AuD, CCC-A, Clinical Audiologist*
UPMC-Eye and Ear Institute of Pittsburgh

How Hearing Aids Work

Hearing aids are electronic devices that pick up and amplify sound. Sounds that the wearer normally would not hear are increased in volume and therefore better communicated.

All hearing aids contain certain basic components. A microphone picks up sound waves that are converted into a tiny electrical current. This current is then amplified and changed back into sound by the hearing aid receiver. (More than one microphone collects sound from different areas.) An amplifier increases the strength of the impulses. A receiver transforms the electrical impulses back into sound waves and redirects them into the ear of the wearer. It is located in some form of BTE (behind the ear) or in the canal housing. And finally, a battery supplies the energy source.

Other components are found in some, but not all, hearing aids. A computer chip is found in programmable hearing aids. Some aids have switches that turn the device on or off, allow for phone usage, or provide the ability to control volume. Some aids have multiple programs which offer different settings for a variety of listening environments.

As an example, one program may be for conversations, another for the telephone, and a third for noisy situations. An aid can come with numerous programs, and the wearer may manually change back and forth between different programs, while some aids switch automatically.

Hearing Aids: Telecoils and Direct Audio Input

The best way to conceptualize a telecoil is as a microphone, but one that responds to a varying electromagnetic field rather than to sound waves. Not all hearing aids are equipped with telecoils. This is a great disservice to the user. A hearing aid without a telecoil lacks the ability to directly connect with assistive technology.

Direct audio input hearing aids are hearing aids with audio input connections which can be connected to TV, stereo, tape, and radio as well as to microphones, auditory trainers, personal FM systems, and other assistive devices.

How Cochlear Implants Work

A cochlear implant is a small, complex prosthetic replacement for the inner ear (cochlea). The first implants in the United States occurred in 1961 at House Ear Institute (Christiansen and Leigh 2002, 16). The details of how cochlear implants work are handled in chapter 3 in this volume. Here only the briefest description is offered.

A cochlear implant is very different from a hearing aid. Hearing aids amplify sound. Cochlear implants compensate for damaged or nonworking parts of the inner ear. The cochlear implant system consists of two parts (Ross n.d.). The internal part is composed of wires that are surgically implanted into the cochlea through the skull and behind the ear. The transmitter that sends the coded signals to an implanted receiver is just under the skin. The external part connects to the internal parts via a connecting cable and magnets that join the processor with the implant. The processor consists of a microphone and a speech processing computer that analyzes and digitizes the sound signals and sends them to a transmitter worn on the head just behind the ear. The speech processor may be housed with the microphone behind the ear, or it may be a small "box" worn in a chest pocket. Hearing through an implant may sound different from normal hearing, but it allows many people to communicate fully with oral communication in person and over the phone.

Hearing assistive technology can be used with or without hearing aids or cochlear implants, though these devices may serve as the first link in the device chain.

Types of HAT: Auditory and Visual

There are three primary categories of hearing assistive technology devices:

- Alerting devices
- Listening devices
- Telecommunications devices

Alerting Devices

Alerting devices can be simple or complex, visual or auditory. They may consist of single freestanding devices or be part of a facility- or house-wide hard-wired system. Alerting devices can indicate the presence of any sound in the environment through any of three different ways: louder sound, light flash, or vibration (National Association of the Deaf 2005).

Examples include

- *Special alarm clocks* that have exceptionally loud, volume-controlled rings designed for people who are D/deaf or hard of hearing. Some also have frequency controls so you can choose a frequency you can hear well and options to flash a light on your night table or even shake the bed.

- *A baby crier* that lets you know by flashing lights or vibrating that the baby is crying, or that someone needs your attention or aid. A transmitter is put near the baby (e.g., in a room where the baby is sleeping), and any noise triggers the alert in another room, where you can see it or feel it.

- *A door knocker* that transmits a signal to a flashing light or vibrator so that a person with a hearing loss knows that someone is at the door. Some door knockers may also be set up to recognize that the doorbell is ringing.

- *Fire alarms* that consist of audible and visible signaling products are engineered to emit a high-intensity flashing light (strobe) when the smoke or fire alarm is triggered.

Vibrators are usually small, handheld, or clip-on radio receivers that receive signals from sensors capable of detecting various sounds or events. The sensors include a transmitter that signals to the receiver that they have detected the sound or event they were designed to detect. For example, you might wear the small receiver and strategically place sensor/transmitters around your house to alert you to a phone ringing, a baby crying, a doorbell ringing, someone knocking at your door, or other events, like a car in the driveway or an oven beeping. When one of the sensor/transmitters is triggered, it sends a radio signal to the receiver that then vibrates in a pattern that lets you know which signal was triggered. Some receivers also have lights that indicate which signal was triggered (Signal Source 2005).

Assistance dogs for deaf and disabled Americans are trained to assist people who are D/deaf and/or physically disabled in leading more independent lives at work, at home, and at school. These assistance dogs become an extension of their owners and bring security, freedom, independence, and relief from social isolation to their human partners (Dogs for Deaf and Disabled Americans 2005).

Assistive Listening Devices

Assistive listening devices (ALDs) are primarily auditory solutions. The basic function of an ALD is to improve the "signal-to-noise ratio" for the listener. Listening in groups, meetings, restaurants, lectures, theaters, or in one-on-one conversations is not only affected by noise but also by the distance between the speaker and the listener. This means that desired sounds (signal) are amplified, and undesirable sounds (noise) are minimized (Barr Productions 2005).

ALDs are used by persons with residual hearing and can be thought of as binoculars for the ears. They increase the loudness of specific sounds by bringing sound directly into the hearing aid, cochlear implant, or ear. ALDs are designed to help people hear better in a variety of difficult listening situations. This category may include personal, FM, infrared, and induction loop systems. All are capable of working well, can work with or without hearing aids, and are available in wide-area or personal versions.

- *FM ALSs* use a specific radio frequency (generally 72–76 MHz) to carry sound from the transmitter to the receiver. The sound source can be either a microphone or audio input. FM systems are the most versatile because they are portable. Both the user and speaker have complete mobility, so these systems are ideal for classrooms and meetings.

- *Infrared ALSs* use invisible infrared light waves to carry sound from the transmitter to the receiver. Infrared systems are considered to be line-of-sight devices often used in theaters, courtrooms, and meetings. The infrared system uses a single transmitter and one or more receivers, which must be on the same channel (95 KHz, 250 KHz, and 2.3 MHz). The receiver converts the infrared light waves back into sound, which then can be amplified.

- *Induction loop ALSs* use a wire antenna "loop" that physically surrounds a room. A transmitter circulates a signal through the loop wire, creating a magnetic field. Hearing aid users who have switched to "t-coil" will pick up the signal coming through the system's microphone when they are within the "looped" area. No receivers are necessary for hearing aid wearers with a telecoil (the telecoil itself is the receiver). Loop receivers can be provided for people who do not have telecoils. Loops are often permanently installed.

- *Personal listening systems* are designed to carry sound from the speaker (or other source) directly to the listener and to minimize or eliminate environmental noises. Personal FM systems and personal amplifiers are especially helpful for one-on-one conversations in places such as automobiles, meeting rooms, and restaurants (New Jersey Speech and Hearing Association 2005).

- *Large-area ALSs* consist of a transmitting system that uses one of the varieties of methods described above to send sound signals to an individual receiver. Some systems must be used with a hearing aid or cochlear implant; other systems can be used with or without a hearing aid (Assistech Special Needs 2005). Many major auditoriums and theaters, churches, synagogues, and other public places are equipped with special sound systems for people with hearing loss.

- *TV listening systems* are designed for listening to TV, radio, or stereo without interference from surrounding noise or the need to use very high volume. Models are available for use with or without hearing aids (Hearing Loss Association of North Carolina 2005).

Transmitters contain built-in microphones and have the ability to operate on an omnidirectional, directional, and/or super-directional setting.

Microphone issues play a vital role in the effectiveness of an ALS and need to be selected carefully in order to obtain the best sound possible for the circumstances. Professional audio sound contractors may be needed to perform an assessment. Sometimes consumers cannot set up an effective ALS using parts obtained from catalogs for residential use. Microphones (and mixers) are often the most expensive part of a wide-area system (Barr Productions 2005).

A variety of coupling devices are available to bring the sound into the ear. Some listening attachments are more appropriate or effective than others. Coupling devices may include the neckloop telecoil that is placed over your head and around your neck and converts audio signals into magnetic signals that can be received by a hearing aid equipped with a T-coil; ear buds that fit in the outer part of the ears and will provide sound to one or both ears and are designed for mild to moderate hearing loss without hearing aid; silhouettes that are placed directly between a hearing aid and the head and are attached to the device with a cord; and direct input couplers that are attached directly to hearing aids or cochlear implant processors.

> In providing communication access to deaf and hard-of-hearing people, we should not overlook the fact that hard-of-hearing people require auditory access as much as, and for the same reason, as Deaf people require visual access. Such access can be provided in public places with large area Infrared, FM, or Induction Loop systems. These systems will permit hard-of-hearing people to employ their residual hearing for the fullest benefit it can provide them. It should be recognized, however, that in these situations hard-of-hearing people often still require such measures as CART (Computer Assisted Real Time) transcription, which is of value to both deaf and hard-of-hearing people.
>
> —*Mark Ross, Ph.D., Professor Emeritus*
> *University of Connecticut*

Visual Solutions

While common visual solutions include fax and Internet chat, visual access device solutions include the rapidly evolving area of HAT. (It is impossible to list all the possibilities, especially as they relate to specific manufacturer products. This information is available on the Internet.) Visual access device solutions may comprise text and sign language images that offer the D/deaf and hard of hearing user equal access via a broad range of services, devices, and programs while being respectful of individual choice. These devices may include a component of human interface as well as a broad range of computer devices and software. Many forms of these programs exist under various manufacturer and program names.

- *Voice-to-text* technologies include automatic speech recognition (ASR), which can be defined as the independent, computer-driven transcription of spoken language into readable text in real time (Naturale 2005).

- *Videoconferencing* generally supports two-way video and audio communication. This means that two or more people at different locations can see and hear each other at the same time. Therefore, parties can utilize sign language systems to communicate and interpret from remote locations. A videoconferencing system must have audiovisual equipment (e.g., monitor, camera, microphone, and speaker) as well as a means of transmitting information between locations.

- *C Print* is a version of CAN—computer assisted notetaking—in which the associated software converts the input text to an outline format for D/deaf and hard of hearing persons who may not desire a word for word transcription

- *iCommunicator system* is a multisensory voice-to-text computer device that provides both text and a signing human image simultaneously, allowing for better comprehension of spoken language and speech skills.

- *Instant captioning* provides live captions or transcriptions to assist during conversations, meetings, or lectures.

- *Personal captioning systems* use wireless radio transmission (FM signals) and provide easy-to-read text captioning anywhere within a venue.

- *CART,* also known as communication access realtime translation, is the instant translation of the spoken word into English text using a specially trained transcriptionist with a stenotype machine, notebook computer, and real-time software. The text appears on a computer monitor or other display. The Americans with Disabilities Act (ADA) specifically recognizes CART as an assistive technology, which affords "effective communication access." Thus communication access more aptly describes a CART provider's role and distinguishes CART from real-time reporting in a traditional litigation setting (Barr Productions 2005).

TELECOMMUNICATIONS: VISUAL AND AUDITORY

Telecommunications issues are an essential concern for everyone, regardless of their level of hearing. As consumers, we are constantly assaulted by the media blitz promoting telecommunications choices. (It's one of those instances where not hearing may be a blessing!) From Internet connections to wireless providers and cell phone options, the deluge of information vying for our attention, allegiance, and device dollars is endless. The one thing we rarely see, beyond the occasional print ad, is information for telecommunications solutions for D/deaf and hard of hearing people. These options are also affected by the current explosion in access options. For once, those of us with hearing loss derive collateral benefit from these research and development dollars. Many solutions for the hearing loss community have arisen as a direct result of advances made in this field for the general population.

> Having literally grown up in the assistive communication industry, I have witnessed the development of hearing assistive technology over the past three decades. These past few years have been quite thrilling as we are bringing digital technology to the world of hearing assistance. For example we can now offer digital TTY service, utilizing advanced intelligent devices such as the PC to deliver digital communication services to the deaf equivalent to those found in advanced voice communications systems. Other products such as amplified phones have been designed with the realization that with the right technology such as wide band frequency management, all levels of hearing loss can be addressed from mild to profound with low frequency loss to high frequency loss. These advances in technology are making a profound difference in the lives of so many people. We are extremely proud of our involvement in this technology as we focus on leaving no one behind.
>
> —*Michele Ahlman,*
> *President, ClearSounds Communications, Inc.*

Additionally, long-awaited legislation concerning equal access to telephone and television services is finally being passed. Legislative issues, including bundling, broadband, and universal service, are addressed extensively on the Internet and will not be addressed in this text. Information for accessing a Consumer's Guide to Using the Telecommunications Relay Service, TTY Etiquette Guidelines, and pertinent laws is included in Additional Resources at the end of this chapter.

Auditory Solutions: Telephone Amplifying Devices

- *Hearing aid-compatible phones* come with an amplifying coil; many, but not all, standard telephone receivers are hearing aid-compatible. This coil is activated when a person whose hearing aid or cochlear implant is in the "T" position picks up the telephone receiver. These phones can be obtained from your telephone company or an appropriate vendor.

- *Amplified phones* are specially designed telephone receivers that amplify sound. Most of these devices have volume control dials. Some are recommended for use in households where all members have hearing loss. Some return to standard sound levels automatically and can be used in homes by people with or without hearing loss.

- *Cell phones* can now be utilized by persons with hearing loss. There are a limited number of cell phones available that meet the needs of persons who are hard of hearing.

It is highly recommended that all phone purchases be thoroughly researched and tested to ensure adequate db gain and compatibility with hearing aids and cochlear implants before purchase.

Visual Solutions: Traditional and New

TTY or TDD?

A TTY is a device similar to a typewriter that has a small readout. It is also called a telecommunication device for the Deaf (TDD), but that name was devised by the hearing community and is not accepted by Deaf people, the actual users of TTY technology, who still prefer the term TTY. A TTY can be used to send text over the phone. A TTY conversation is typed and read, rather than spoken and heard, by each party. If one party does not have a TTY, calls can be placed via the free state relay service.

Some features to look for include direct connect (TTY plugs right into your telephone line), acoustic connect (handset of the phone rests on TTY "ears" and information is transmitted audibly), Baudot (standard transmission) or ASCII (faster and computer-compatible transmission) code, cell phone compatibility, built-in printer, memory, and even pocket-sized and battery-operated versions.

Since TTYs communicate by using sounds that represent characters, they can use any phone, except cell phones. Cell phones use various digital and analog technologies to send their signals, so the tone-equals-character technique is disrupted. However, there are some strategies for integrating the two. Many cell phones can be made TTY-compatible by choosing a setting in the "phone options" menu. If you are interested in a TTY-compatible cell phone, you must be mindful of that option when choosing a phone initially. These all have an adapter plug for your cell phone to minimize interference and background noise (New Jersey Speech and Hearing Association 2005).

VCO

Voice Carry Over (VCO) is an option of the relay service that allows a person who can speak but not hear well to talk on the phone with someone who can hear. With a normal relay call, a relay operator, called a "communication assistant," acting between the two communicating parties, will type what the hearing person says so that the other person can read it on their TTY or computer. There are also VCO phones on which you can read on the phone itself what the communication assistant types.

With a VCO relay call, the person who speaks, but cannot hear, does not have to type their message, but can speak it directly. VCO can make a relay call much more convenient for hard of hearing people or those who may be late deafened, since only one side of the conversation has to be typed, and that is done by the relay operator. A normal relay telephone call requires a single phone line to the relay operator. You can also do VCO calls using IP-Relay on your computer (Assistech Special Needs 2005).

Captioned Phones

Ideal for people with some degree of hearing loss, the captioned telephone works like any other telephone with one important addition—it displays every word the caller says throughout the conversation. Calls are made in the usual manner, by dialing the telephone number directly for the person you are calling. Captioned telephones automatically connect to captioning services, which are part of the relay service. The user never needs to dial the service or speak to the captioner. Users can enjoy natural telephone conversations, listen to the caller, and appreciate the added bonus of reading the written captions in the phone's display window. Captions appear nearly simultaneously with the spoken words. Hearing family members can use the captioned phone by simply turning off the captions feature to use it as a traditional telephone. These phones also include an amplified handset and tone control for clarity. This service is not yet available in all areas, but represents a wonderful innovation in visual telecommunications (Hearing Loss Association of North Carolina 2005).

Wireless Paging Systems

There are about 400 million wireless communication devices used in the world today, and that number grows continually. Wireless systems for persons with hearing loss are completely portable, two-way, handheld devices with multiple capabilities. This device vibrates to alert the user to a message. The user can send and receive e-mail to or from anywhere in the world, send faxes, and send a message to any hearing person to hear; hearing people can send messages to be read. A text message can be received via the regular relay or through a dedicated toll-free number that any hearing person can use to call and send a message and text to any pager. This is a leased service contracted much like a cell phone or other phone contract including option packages.

There are device options available that include increased memory so the user can prepare messages ahead of time, save them, and send them later; an address book with entry capabilities for voice phone numbers, fax numbers, TTY numbers (using this device with a TTY is basically the same), and e-mail addresses; the ability to chat with any TTY number in the United States—two-way near real-time conversation between your wireless system and their TTY; caller ID; and answering machine capabilities (Naturale 2005).

The Near Future

According to the National Association of the Deaf, ideal telecommunications solutions via cell phone for D/deaf and hard of hearing people are just around the corner. It will soon be possible to get much longer, full-motion video that shows about twenty frames per second, good enough for signing to be clear. (To put that speed into context, consider that broadcast and cablecast television displays thirty frames per second.)

HAT AND You

There are many different degrees and types of hearing loss. No one knows exactly what anyone else hears or how it sounds. We can only evaluate that through our own experience. There is much controversy and disillusionment over the quality of sound generated with assistive technology at any level. The user has a responsibility and right to the best sound attainable for him or her and should pursue appropriate technology earnestly. The system is not being "fixed," just remediated. Technology has paved the way for many innovative products designed to improve a broad range of hearing and communications challenges, but results require acceptance, patience, and diligence.

How Do You Make Sense of the Choices?

Given the scarcity of assistive technology funds, the ever-expanding array of options, and the race to implement the best and most recent technology, how do you make sense of your choices? How do you best use your funds to obtain appropriate access solutions for yourself or persons who are D/deaf, hard of hearing, and Deaf Blind?

Hopefully you can now refer to your "1-2-3 plan of action" to begin to resolve your access needs in a newly confident state of awareness and self-advocacy.

Devices You Need to Have to Be Safe!

- Smoke detectors
- Telephone devices
- TTYs
- Amplified phones
- Emergency phones

Devices You Must Have to Meet Your Responsibilities

- Telephone capabilities
- Alerting devices
- Interface enabling devices
- Meeting/conference accommodation

Devices You Should Have to Enhance the Quality of Your Life

- Telephone capabilities
- TTY
- Amplified phones
- Wireless
- Conference accommodation
- Room listening systems
- CART
- CAN
- Personal listening systems

My wife Janet and I were in San Diego one evening conducting a workshop at one of the schools for parents of children who have hearing loss. We were using a public address microphone that was also linked to an FM system so that people in the room who had hearing loss and who were using a receiver could increase their ability to understand what we were saying.

On one side of the room, next to the wall, sat a Philippine woman with her teenage son who has Down syndrome. They had come in late, and he did not have an FM receiver. He remained seated as we were doing the presentation, but his head was turning and his eyes were wandering incessantly around the room. It was obvious that he was paying zero attention to what we were saying. I gave him an FM receiver to couple to his hearing aids, and he immediately locked on to every word we spoke from that moment on. Personally, I had never seen such an immediate and dramatic change in someone's attention and interest levels.

At the end of the session, his mother approached us and expressed amazement, stating that she had never seen him attend so completely to anything anyone ever said prior to that evening. She took information about the FM equipment and where to purchase a personal system, which she subsequently purchased and which he frequently used thereafter. We kept in touch with that family for several years and saw them at other workshops. She told us that, from that night on, he had become a "different person" and was performing at much higher levels in school.

The moral? Using assistive listening systems allows people with hearing loss to receive more auditory information and to function at higher levels here on planet Earth and to attend better to events of interest to them that are happening right here and now in this plane of existence.

—Sam Trychin, Ph.D., Director,
Living with Hearing Loss Program Erie, PA

ADDITIONAL RESOURCES

The Law Is the Law

Beyond our civil right to equal and effective access to all information and services being offered, various laws as well as a number of organizations, offices, and agencies protect the rights of persons with hearing loss. It is helpful to have an awareness of their existence and responsibilities and a broad understanding of their function in order to understand and pursue one's rights and entitlements. Pertinent topics include the Rehabilitation Act, Section 504 of the Rehabilitation Act of 1973, the Federal Communications Commission (FCC), the ADA, Title III of the ADA, and Title IV of the ADA. All can be found at www.usdoj.gov, the official website for the U.S. Department of Justice.

Consumer's Guide to Using the Telecommunications Relay Service

The Telecommunications Relay Service (TRS) enables standard voice telephone users to talk to people who have difficulty hearing or speaking on the telephone. The Consumer's Guide to Using the Telecommunications Relay Service is adapted from the FCC's Consumer and Governmental Affairs Bureau website (www.fcc.gov/cgb/dro/trs/con_trs.html), which was produced with cooperation from the

Maryland Relay System and Gallaudet University's Technology Assessment Program. The guide describes how the TRS works and offers examples of callers that use the relay service.

TTY Etiquette

TTY conversations have their own etiquette. Tips for appropriate usage, as well as a TTY typing abbreviation list can be found at http://www.soundbytes.com/resource_tty.html.

REFERENCES

Assistech Special Needs. 2005. Personal/TV listening systems. http://azhearing.com/listeningsystems.htm (accessed July 2005).

Barr Productions. 2005. Listening devices. http://www.barrproductions.com/listening-devices.html (accessed July 2005).

Christiansen, J. B., and I. W. Leigh. 2002. *Children with cochlear implants: Ethics and choices.* Washington, D.C.: Gallaudet University Press.

Dogs for Deaf and Disabled Americans. 2005. http://www.neads.org (accessed July 2005).

Gilbert, J. 2000. *Clear speech from the start student's book: Basic pronunciation and listening comprehension in North American English.* Cambridge: Cambridge University Press.

Hearing Loss Association of America. 2005. http://www.hearingloss.org (accessed June 2005).

Hearing Loss Association of North Carolina. 2005. TTY. http://www.nchearingloss.org/tty.htm?fromncshhh (accessed July 2005).

National Association of the Deaf. 2005. http://www.nad.org (accessed June 2005).

Naturale, J. 2005. Internet resources—deafness. Rochester Institute of Technology. http://wally.rit.edu/internet/subject/deafness.html#asst (accessed July 2005).

New Jersey Speech and Hearing Association. 2005. Frequently asked questions: Assistive living devices. http://www.njsha.org/faq/assistive.htm (accessed June 2005).

The Signal Source. 2005. http://www.thesignalsource.com (accessed July 2005).

2   A Conversation with Alfred Sonnenstrahl: Focus on Telecommunications

Alfred Sonnenstrahl is the telecommunications access consultant for Sonny Access Consulting. At the time of this interview (May 2007), however, he was special projects director at Communication Service for the Deaf (CSD), a national organization that promotes equal communication access for deaf and hard of hearing people. CSD was the first organization to initiate video relay services (VRSs), discussed in this interview.

His path to this career was long and varied in ways we believe will be of interest to our readers, so we asked him to describe it as the opening part of the interview.

We thank Karen Peltz Strauss for her helpful comments on the content of this interview.

EDITORS: Please tell us a bit about your history, schooling, and training for the work you have done.

AL: My parents were deaf; I grew up in New York City and attended both the Lexington School for the Deaf and Public School 47, also a school for deaf people, and then attended Stuyvesant High School, a school attended only by those who passed a very competitive entrance examination. In those days, there were no interpreter services. For college, I completed my B.S. degree in mechanical engineering at New York University (NYU) and subsequently got a job as a mechanical engineer for the Department of the Navy, again without interpreter services. After ten years, I became bored and decided on a career change; I entered the human services field, where I could work on equal access for deaf people in multiple ways. To prepare for this career change, I went to California State University, Northridge, to get my master's degree in administration and supervision in special education. There I had interpreter services for the first time. After graduating, I got a job as job placement specialist for the Michigan Department of Labor where I advocated for and succeeded in changing the status quo so that deaf applicants were finally allowed to sit for the U.S. Postal Service employment examinations.

EDITORS: Could we interrupt you a moment, Al? What you just told us is huge; your advocacy effected a countrywide change with the potential to touch thousands of lives. Since then, of course, you've been involved in many projects with national scope, but this was your first, right? That must have been very satisfying. Was this the beginning of your desire to move into national advocacy?

AL: Yes, that fed my desire to continue advocating. My position in Michigan had no room for growth. As a result, I moved to Massachusetts to become the state director of deaf services for the Massachusetts Rehabilitation Commission. While in Massachusetts, I helped to found D.E.A.F., Inc., an evaluation and training center for deaf clients. I also worked to establish the Massachusetts State Association of the Deaf as well as the Massachusetts Office of Deafness, the predecessor to the Massachusetts Commission for the Deaf and Hard of Hearing. Subsequently, I moved to Minnesota to direct a residential treatment center for deaf psychiatric clients. After three years, I moved to the greater Washington, D.C., area to direct the Section 504 training program for the National Association of the Deaf. Section 504 of the Rehabilitation Act of 1973 is the regulation which requires that entities which receive monies from the federal government provide appropriate access for persons with disabilities. I then went to Gallaudet University for postgraduate work in administration and supervision, and in 1987 became executive director of Telecommunications for the Deaf, Inc. (TDI), remaining as director until 1996. After that, I moved on to Communication Service for the Deaf (CSD), where I'm presently special projects director.

EDITORS: We can see the development of your interest in advocacy, but how did you become involved in advocacy for telecommunications, in particular?

AL: In 1977, I went to the TDI convention in Rye, NY, to support my father's involvement since he was on their convention committee. TDI was a volunteer not-for-profit organization originally formed in 1968 to handle the acquisition, conversion, maintenance, and distribution of old teletypewriters (TTYs) discarded by AT&T for use by deaf people, thereby enabling them to communicate using telephone lines. There were 300 deaf attendees at that convention who had gathered together to brainstorm ways to expand nationwide. Not one person from the telephone industry was there. And I started to realize that there were approximately 25,000 TTYs nationwide at that time, meaning 25,000 new customers for AT&T. With deaf consumers paying a monthly rate of approximately $50 a month, the revenue for AT&T was in the ball-park of approximately 10 to 15 million dollars. Nonetheless, AT&T did not contribute anything towards convention sponsorship for that convention, nor did AT&T facilitate access to their operator services provided for hearing users. My previous experience of discrimination based on not being able to get a job at first in the federal government due to the fact that regulations did not permit the hiring of a deaf person for an engineering position reinforced my desire to strongly advocate wherever I found discrimination.

EDITORS: Can you tell us a little more about this discrimination incident?

AL: During my senior year at NYU, I applied for a position as a mechanical engineer with various federal agencies in the Washington, D.C., area. They all responded saying that I was ineligible due to "medical reasons." I eventually learned that the U.S. Civil Service Commission (CSC) had a ruling that one must be able to hear conversational voice with at least one ear to become an engineer. I was fortunate enough to have friends with internal contacts who enabled me to obtain temporary status employment to prove my abilities. In one year, my supervisors were able to convince the CSC to revise its ruling to admit deaf engineers. Thus started my passion for advocacy in terms of the rights of deaf people for more equitable access. After some thought, I felt the need to advocate for the rights of deaf people for better phone services from AT&T. I wrote a letter to the AT&T chairperson at the time requesting that since deaf consumers gave them additional significant revenues, AT&T should provide these consumers with services already provided to hearing consumers, for example, operator services, directory assistance, and employment of deaf people.

Additional requests included a discount on long distance calls due to longer use of telephone lines based on slow typing speed in comparison with more rapid spoken language speed, and an office for disability services. Since I lived in Minnesota at the time, the AT&T chairperson forwarded my letter to Northwest Bell, a regional affiliate of AT&T with headquarters in Omaha, Nebraska, which had jurisdiction over Minnesota. Northwest Bell subsequently formed a deaf panel which met on a bimonthly basis to review and make recommendations that would meet the needs of deaf consumers. Eventually, practically all my recommendations were met.

EDITORS: AT&T's responsiveness seems ideal. Did this make you expect other companies to be so accommodating? Did this spur you on?

AL: Encouraged by this success with AT&T, I looked for more opportunities to work in telecommunications by becoming the secretary of TDI's Board of Directors in 1983. In 1987, when the executive director resigned, based on the fact that I was the only board member living near TDI's home office in the greater metropolitan D.C. area, where I was a doctoral student at Gallaudet University, I was asked to become acting director. As soon as I realized that there were efforts to develop Americans with Disabilities Act (ADA) legislation, I abandoned my doctoral ambitions, moved towards full-time advocacy, and became the full-time director of TDI.

EDITORS: Back in 1968, when TDI was established, telecommunications access meant primarily the availability of TTYs. How did that change, and what telecommunications access did TDI promote?

AL: As I mentioned earlier, TDI was established with the intention of training volunteers to collect abandoned teletypewriters from AT&T and Western Union and recondition these discarded machines into TTYs for free distribution to deaf consumers. Its original name was Teletypewriter for the Deaf Distribution Committee, thus reflecting its original mission. The name was later changed to Telecommunications for the Deaf, Inc. TDI also developed a national (later to become international) directory of text phone numbers so that deaf consumers could have their own telephone network. I was more interested in application aspects than in equipment per se during my tenure as TDI director. Specifically, we collected and shared information that led to the creation of several networks of local TTY news centers all over the U.S. to distribute information about current events, because at that time, news telecasts were not captioned. Additionally, in order to establish telephone relationships between deaf and hearing people, TDI collaborated wherever possible to set up volunteer relay services through churches and various agencies throughout the U.S. Typically these services had limited hours, limited length of communication, and limited number of calls per day per person. It was often difficult to get through to the relay service provider due to high demand for services and low number of available volunteers and relay phone lines for deaf callers.

That changed with the passage of the ADA of 1990. Prior to the enactment of ADA, TDI became very involved in lobbying for and developing ADA language requiring that the telephone industry assume responsibility for telecommunications relay services and that all 911 emergency services be accessible through TTYs. Together with other colleagues, particularly Karen Peltz Strauss, a civil rights lawyer, I worked closely with many senators, including Senators Tom Harkin of Iowa, Daniel Inouye of Hawaii, John McCain of Arizona, and Robert Dole of Kansas, as well as Representatives Steny Hoyer of Maryland, Ed Markey of Massachusetts, and David Bonior of Michigan, to draft requirements for relay services, provide testimony at congressional hearings, and contribute language to legislative reports to ensure the appropriateness of the language in the ADA legislation prior to Congress's passing of this law. Subsequently, the requirements of this legislation led to TDI's working with the Federal Communications Commission (FCC) to establish regulations related to how telephone relay services should function and with the Department of Justice (DOJ) on how emergency TTY calls should be handled by all 911 centers. In my capacity as executive director of TDI, I coordinated several national conferences to gather industry, governmental, and consumer experts to assist these agencies as they drafted their rules. As telephone companies entered the relay service provider market after passage of the ADA, TDI also became involved in the training of service providers.

In the early 1990s, as Congress began developing ideas for what eventually became the Telecommunications Act of 1996, local telephone carriers approached TDI to request assistance in removing restrictions implemented by the consent decree that broke up the monolithic AT&T into smaller telephone companies. In response, TDI, together with other disability-related organizations, requested that language be added to the pending legislation to ensure equal telecommunications access for persons with disabilities, such as having all television programs captioned and ensuring that telecommunication equipment and services designed for the mainstream public were accessible and usable by deaf and hard of hearing consumers. Currently, TDI promotes not equipment per se, but rather service delivery in terms of the processes by which products can be best utilized to serve the needs of deaf people, and training of public policy developers, service providers, and those who prepare legislation, regulations, and specifications related to laws and regulations that affect the lives of deaf and hard of hearing consumers.

EDITORS: Part of the mission of TDI currently involves advocating for and educating deaf consumers about their rights to telecommunications and media accessibility. What are these rights? How does TDI go about educating the consumer?

AL: TDI continues to keep consumers informed about telecommunications and media accessibility through newsletters and electronic mail updates. Early on, TDI also developed a network of national consumer-oriented organizations for the purpose of sharing information related to ever-changing technology and policy issues that affect the lives of deaf and hard of hearing consumers. That led to the development of DHHCAN: Deaf and Hard of Hearing Consumer Advocacy Network, created for that very purpose. This organization is currently composed of representatives of various national consumer-oriented organizations of deaf and hard of hearing individuals. TDI also holds biennial conventions to keep deaf and hard of hearing consumers and all telecommunications industry-related entities updated on current and future technology. TDI's primary focus is on national rights in terms of facilitating equal access to whatever new telecommunications-related technology or needs emerge on the scene. To summarize all of the above, first, TDI worked to ensure access to telephone services. Then came the need for access to emergency services, together with the appropriate utilization of new technology to ensure compatibility for deaf consumer use. All of these efforts have required significant involvement with government agencies such as the FCC and the DOJ.

EDITORS: What is the FCC's role in ensuring telecommunications access for deaf people?

AL: The FCC is a United States government agency established by the Communications Act of 1934 with the charge of regulating interstate and international communications by radio, television, wire, satellite, and cable. Before issuing regulations, the FCC provides opportunities for the public, including consumers and industry representatives, to provide input which can be based on legal considerations or life experiences related to the regulations being considered. Such input can assist the FCC, which is charged with acting in the public interest, in making appropriate telecommunications policy decisions and coordinating telecommunications policy efforts with industry and with other governmental agencies.

Deaf organizations did not have significant involvement with the FCC until 1995, when Reed Hundt, the FCC chair at that time, traveled to the TDI convention in Boston to learn about visually oriented telecommunication technology and the needs of deaf consumers. This was a historical first, as prior to this time, the FCC did not typically send representatives to consumer-oriented trade events. Based on increased awareness of the needs of deaf consumers, Reed Hundt initiated the formation of a Disability Issues Task Force to monitor the rights of individuals with disabilities and influence the development of regulations that impact telecommunications access issues for persons with disabilities. Under Chairman William Kennard, who succeeded Hundt, this task force evolved into a full-fledged Disability Rights Office (DRO), staffed with permanent FCC employees. Currently, with the assistance of DRO, TDI and related organizations are able to perform watchdog functions through the public notice process and ensure the provision of telecommunications access for deaf and hard of hearing individuals in a great variety of FCC proceedings. At times, the FCC needs extra input from TDI and allied organizations to understand the rationale of comments provided in the interest of enhancing telecommunications access.

Even after the FCC issues orders related to telecommunications, there may be insufficient provision for quality control issues, thereby necessitating further negotiation with the FCC to minimize potential consumer problems. For example, when new VRS technology emerged, providing the ability for deaf consumers with high-speed Internet access to connect with sign language interpreters on either a computer screen via webcam or a television monitor via videophone when making calls to hearing persons, there were no regulations covering quality of interpreters, average speed answers (meaning that users could be kept waiting for interpreters to appear on the screen sometimes even as long as an hour or more), problematic interoperability of equipment and services (similar in concept to an AT&T phone connecting with the Sprint network system), and issues related to the equitable distribution of video equipment, which have limited the ability of hearing and deaf family members to communicate directly via videophone. Some of these issues have been resolved; others are still in need of corrective action.

The FCC is also charged with developing regulations for TV captioning. There are various current captioning issues, such as the lack of quality control over captioning and the lack of standard procedures for turning on TV captions. For example, you have to go through various menus to figure out how to turn on the captions, since TV manufacturers have created different ways to set up captioning. Also, at times, the captions are not on default, which means that the captions turn off each time the TV is turned off, thereby necessitating a return to going through the complicated menu process. At times, you can do it through remote control, but not for all TVs. Now we are changing from analog to digital technology: Congress recently mandated that all television broadcasts be digital by 2009. Although the FCC already has rules requiring digital TV programming to contain captions, many consumers are reporting extensive problems with getting captions to work on their new digital televisions. Work with the FCC never stops.

EDITORS: What is the role of the DOJ in ensuring access for deaf people?

AL: The DOJ is responsible for overseeing civil rights issues for all Americans and ensuring equal public access for everyone. When the ADA was passed, the FCC was given jurisdiction for access issues pertaining to telephone-related communications, while 911 emergency-access issues, falling under the public-service domain, were assigned to the DOJ for oversight. The DOJ developed training guidelines for all 911 centers to handle emergency TTY calls appropriately and thereby ensure compliance with the ADA. Through TDI, I served as a consultant to DOJ during the guideline development phase. I also served as an expert witness in several 911 litigation efforts when delayed responses impacted the health and life situations of deaf litigants. These lawsuits resulted in decisions mandating appropriate 911 TTY access.

EDITORS: Please describe how VRSs are provided, so we can get a picture of the competitive scene.

AL: The ADA assigns responsibility for relay services to common carriers (telephone companies). Since the FCC has oversight responsibility for relay services, it agreed that telephone companies could assign responsibility to the states for relay calls because it is easy to locate the origins of phone calls through telephone landlines. Each state has its own funding mechanism via statewide contracts with telephone companies which provide relay services, such as surcharges added to telephone bills or tariffs billed to telephone companies. The FCC maintains jurisdiction over interstate relay calls since states do not have jurisdiction for calls that cross state lines. These services are offered by various providers, thereby ensuring a competitive market where success can be based on aspects such as quality of text-based relay operators or VRS sign language interpreters and speed of responses to calls into the relay center. To facilitate payment for interstate relay calls, the FCC contracts with an independent administrator, the National Exchange Carriers Association (NECA), which collects monies from all intrastate, interstate, and international common carriers to cover the costs of interstate relay services. The FCC has mandated that all text and video relay Internet protocol (IP) relay services be funded by NECA because it is not possible to pinpoint the origins of these calls based on Internet protocol addresses. The FCC's decision to allow all IP relay and VRS calls to be compensated through the interstate fund was also intended to encourage competition; it successfully enabled companies to develop VRSs, hire sign language interpreters, and develop the Internet access systems needed to handle these calls.

EDITORS: How much does a VRS cost? Are there ways to defray that cost if a person has low income?

AL: VRS competitors receive compensation for the calls that they handle based on a per-minute rate from NECA. There is no relay cost for the VRS user. The only cost is the use of high-speed Internet lines and either a computer with a webcam or a television monitor with a videophone. Unfortunately no system exists that provides low-cost Internet lines or related equipment for low-income consumers.

Currently, some VRS providers manufacture and control the distribution of videophones which are required for access to VRSs. To maximize the generation of VRS funds, the providers tend to "lease" their videophones to potential VRS users at no cost. Some states have programs to distribute non-committed telecommunications-related equipment to people who have low income. Since videophones tend to be programmed to be compatible with their respective manufacturers, the states are reluctant to get involved since they, as public agencies, must avoid the appearance of preferring specific vendors.

EDITORS: What types of equipment do you promote for home use? Which, if any, are better suited for an office environment?

AL: Technology has definitely enhanced the quality of life for deaf persons. In the home, there can be TTYs or CapTel equipment. (CapTel relay technology includes connection with a call center that permits the deaf person to speak on the phone via voice carry over [VCO] and to read the hearing person's communication via text produced by speech recognition devices.) One can also find videophone equipment so that deaf persons can see each other on video screens for visual communication needs or speak to hearing persons directly via phone (VCO) while watching the VRS sign language interpreter. Other technology options include text pagers, televisions equipped with decoder chips for captioning purposes, electronic mail via access to the Internet and text-based Internet access, and visual alerting systems that involve doorbell lights, phone light systems, burglar/fire/smoke alarm systems, and baby crier or voice alert systems. Essentially, the goal is to convert what hearing people hear into visually accessible equipment such as doorbell lights as opposed to doorbells, and so on.

As for the office, the concept of visually accessible equipment is also important. Additional issues to take into consideration include whether the office phones are connected to multiple telephone lines, for which visual pager signalers are required to let deaf workers know which line to use. At work, deaf people are increasingly requesting videophones or webcams for VRSs, which can enable them to connect to sign language interpreter call centers for communication with hearing persons. The biggest concerns that companies or agencies have are related to firewall issues for protection purposes as well as the need to have high-speed Internet lines for picture clarity. If existing Internet systems are used, there is a need to open specific ports to permit access, which can be problematic because of concerns related to potential hacking. Having a separate high-speed Internet line can become a cost factor that companies may not be willing to consider.

Editors: Not everyone finds technology easy to use. Do you get involved in helping individuals, businesses, and institutions choose the equipment that suits their needs? Do you get involved in teaching any of these consumers how to install and use their equipment?

AL: Many people do not know how to set up wired visual alerting or paging systems at home or the office due to lack of expertise or unavailability of experts in the area, so they become more dependent on visual alerting wireless systems, which tend to be less reliable. I often recommend visual alerting and communications systems in homes and offices. Right now, it is not common to have text and voice information on the same phone line because, if shared, when the phone rings, it is difficult for deaf employees to figure out whether it is a voice or text call. However, having an additional line just for text telephones represents additional cost for the employer. I provide choices, and employers or individuals make decisions themselves. They may want to use direct line TTY, direct line TTY with voice or text answering machine, TTY without a specific designated line (meaning voice calls can be received as well on this line), or videophone equipment for VRSs. In general, we have to provide training on how to use relay services effectively. This is true for deaf people as well as for hearing users.

Editors: What do you see as critical issues in telecommunications for deaf and hard of hearing people?

AL: It is critical to maintain text format in all avenues of telecommunications. At this time, televisions are going digital. But the digital TV industry has not yet developed a way to transmit and display captions as effectively as they do for analog televisions. Also, television programmers and providers overlook captioning requirements or try to circumvent these requirements. We need to ensure that FCC regulations are in place so that captioning can be regulated, monitored, and maintained, especially during the transition to digital TV.

For computers, many Web-based videos are increasingly dependent on audio-based information with no text. The DOJ probably has sufficient authority to require that all websites set up by places of public accommodation be accessible, but has not yet issued regulations specifically requiring such access. Similarly, it is not clear whether the FCC has authority to require that television programming shown over the Web be captioned. Currently, there are efforts to obtain explicit congressional directives to get the DOJ and the FCC to move on these issues.

We need to monitor interoperability and interconnectivity so that different devices and different systems can connect and work together in tandem. Interconnectivity refers to two devices connecting with each other, while interoperability is demonstrated by, for example, Blackberry pagers "communicating" with Sidekick pagers or pager systems interfacing with computer-based systems.

Another critical issue has to do with how to connect with 911 through the Internet. With telephone landlines used by TTYs, 911 centers can identify the source of emergency calls and direct the appropriate 911 center to respond. But with wireless systems and the Internet, 911 emergency centers are unable to identify call locations. The problem is that deaf persons are giving up TTYs in favor of videophones and text pagers without realizing what could happen in emergency situations. Current efforts to include global positioning systems in wireless mobile equipment may solve this problem, but reliance on the Internet will continue to be problematic unless individuals who use IP relay services are given their own telephone numbers. Specifically, if you call 911 through an Internet relay service or VRS, the operator assisting the call cannot locate the source. A system needs to be developed that can connect Internet relay or VRS centers to a central numbering database that will be able to locate the most appropriate 911 center for the caller when time is of the essence.

3 ▊ Cochlear Implants

Robert C. O'Reilly, Amanda J. Mangiardi, and H. Timothy Bunnell

Cochlear implants are quickly changing the landscape of hearing loss. Children with a severe-to-profound hearing loss who do not benefit from conventional hearing aids are now able to receive a cochlear implant. Children who receive an implant quickly after the onset of deafness and who use the implant consistently have the potential to develop spoken language skills that approach those of their normally hearing peers. This chapter is intended to provide a broad overview of cochlear implants and issues related to their use in children. We begin with a description of the anatomy and physiology of the human auditory system and how the electrode array of a device is implanted into the cochlea to restore, in a limited way, the function of the auditory system. In the chapter's second section, we discuss the team approach that is used at the Alfred I. duPont Hospital for Children in Wilmington, DE, to evaluate candidacy for cochlear implantation, to educate parents on the risks, benefits, and realistic expectations for cochlear implantation, and describe the intensive (re)habilitation that is required for children who do receive cochlear implants. In the chapter's third and final section, we review recent research on the factors that are believed to promote success in developing spoken language for pediatric cochlear implant recipients.

AUDITORY ANATOMY AND PHYSIOLOGY

The human ear can detect sound along a wide range of frequencies, from 20 to 20,000 Hz (Campbell 1998). The range of loudness that the auditory system can handle (dynamic range) is enormous, with pressures from the quietest sound detectable to the loudest sound tolerable of 100 to 120 dB (Sanes and Rubel 1988). The ear performs this task through an intricate mechanism in the middle ear that enables sound pressure in air to be transferred to liquid in an efficient fashion ("impedance matching," see later discussion). The resulting sound-pressure waves in the cochlear fluids are converted into an electrical signal that is relayed to the cochlear nerve. The signal then passes along the neural arc of the central auditory pathways and is perceived in the auditory cortex of the temporal lobe as sound.

The ear has three general divisions: the outer ear, consisting of the pinna and cartilaginous and bony external auditory canal; the middle ear, which includes the tympanic membrane and ossicular chain (malleus, incus, and stapes); and the inner ear, consisting of the cochlea and vestibule and the cochlear and vestibular nerves coursing through the internal auditory canal to the brain stem (Fig. 1a).

The pinna is made of skin-covered elastic cartilage folded into a complex, somewhat cone-shaped, structure that tapers to form the external auditory canal. The medial one-third of the external auditory canal is made up of the bone of the tympanic ring, which extends to form the circular groove (sulcus), into which the tympanic membrane is inserted. The membrane itself is an approximately dime-sized condensation of fibrous tissue covered with squamous epithelium (skin cells) on its lateral side and mucosa on its medial side.

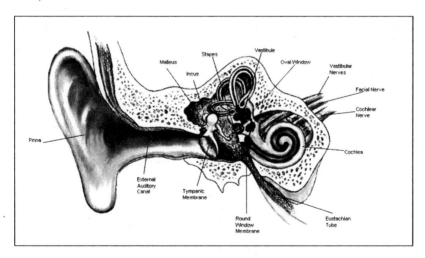

Figure 1a. Anatomical structures of the outer, middle, and inner ear. Courtesy of Susan M. O'Reilly.

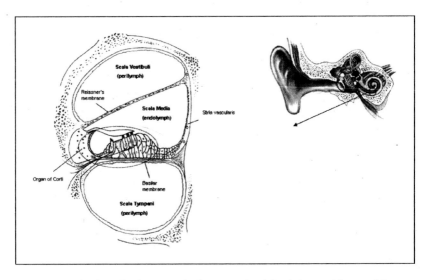

Figure 1b. Detail of anatomical spaces (scala) of the cochlea and its relationship to the organ of corti. Courtesy of Susan M. O'Reilly.

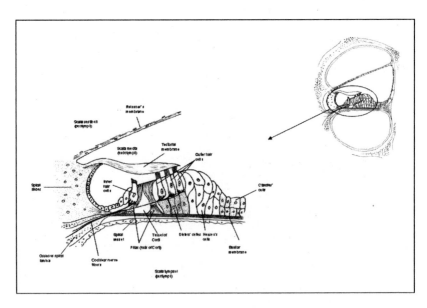

Figure 1c. Organ of corti showing hair cells, position of basilar membrane, and connections to the cochlear nerve. Courtesy of Susan M. O'Reilly.

The middle ear houses the ossicular chain. The most lateral bone (malleus) is firmly attached to the tympanic membrane. The globular body of the malleus attaches to the body of the anvil-shaped incus. The long process of the incus attaches with a synovial joint to the top (capitulum) of the stirrup-shaped stapes bone. The footplate of the stapes is rectangular and fills one of the windows into the cochlea (the "oval window"). The footplate is sealed at its periphery into the oval window by a gasket of fibrous tissue called the annular ligament. This ligament allows for the pumping movement of the stapes during energy transfer while the fluids of the inner ear remain sealed.

The cochlea (and the connected vestibular apparatus) are a series of membranous sacs suspended in liquid (perilymph) inside the very dense bone of the otic capsule. The sacs are filled with a fluid (endolymph), which has a different ionic composition than the perilymph.

The cochlea consists of three separate spaces coiled for two-and-one-half turns around a central axis (modiolus) that encloses the nerve cell bodies and fibers of the cochlear nerve. If the cochlea is unfolded along its length, there is a superior space (scala vestibule) in contact with the footplate of the stapes through the oval window, a central space (scala media) containing the sensory organ of corti, and an inferior space (scala tympani) in contact with a second window (the round window) into the cochlea at its terminal end. The round window is sealed with an elasto-fibrous membrane. Reissner's membrane separates the scala vestibule from the scala media, and the basilar membrane partitions the scala media from the scala tympani (Fig. 1b).

The organ of corti lies on the basilar membrane in the scala media. It is composed partly of three rows of outer hair cells and one row of inner hair cells. The apical surfaces of these hair cells contain numerous stereocilia. For the outer hair cells, the apical surfaces are also in contact with a pivot point called the "tectorial membrane." The bases of the inner hair cells have synaptic connections with the dendrites of the cochlear nerve cell bodies emanating out from the modiolus along a thin bony ridge called the osseous spiral lamina (Fig. 1c).

The axons of the cochlear nerve travel in a bundle through the internal auditory canal along with the vestibular and facial nerves to enter the posterior cranial fossa and synapse with the cochlear nuclei in the brain stem. Pathways from the cochlear nuclei pass through the superior olivary complex, lateral lemniscus, inferior colliculus, and medial geniculate body on their way to the auditory cortex of the temporal lobe (Schuknecht 1993).

Sound pressure waves in air are focused by the pinna and external auditory canal onto the surface of the tympanic membrane. The pressure on the tympanic membrane results in vibrations that are then passed along the ossicular chain. The difference in the surface area of the tympanic membrane (when compared with the smaller area of the footplate of the stapes as well as the lever arm advantage of the geometry of the ossicular chain) imparts an important efficiency to the transfer of sound from a gas (air) to a liquid (perilymph). Without the impedance matching of the sound energy, much of it would be reflected off the surface of the liquid interface. The sound energy then travels very efficiently through the perilymph via the scala vestibule around the apex of the cochlea (helicotrema) to its connection with the scala tympani and, to a certain degree, is released through the round-window membrane. However, some of the sound energy is transferred to the soft membranes of the intervening scala media. Specifically, a traveling wave is set up in the basilar membrane. The stiffness of the basilar membrane varies from the basilar to the apical turns of the cochlea due to several factors, including its width and contractile effects of the three rows of outer hair cells. The maximum amplitude of displacement of the basilar membrane in response to the traveling wave is thus determined by the resonant frequency characteristics of the basilar membrane. For individual pure-tone frequencies, high frequencies cause maximum displacement along the basilar coil of the cochlea and low frequencies along the apical coil. This allows for frequency separation along the length of the cochlea, called "tonotopicity."

When the basilar membrane is set into motion, rapid responsive contractions of the three rows of outer hair cells, which are mechanoreceptors, allow for "fine-tuning" of the point response along the length of the cochlea and spectral separation of the sound. The vibration causes flow of endolymph across the top of the row of inner hair cells deflecting the stereocilia and causes depolarization of the inner hair cells. Neurotransmitters are then released into the synaptic cleft between the inner hair cells and dendrites of the cochlear nerves. The nerve is depolarized, causing a compound action potential and delivery of signal to the respective cochlear nuclei. The cochlear nuclei are also tonotopically arranged, and this is maintained throughout the central auditory pathways. In the normal ear, the mechanical properties of the organ of corti and the neurophysiologic characteristics of the cochlear nerve allow for the capture of three features of sound: loudness, frequency, and timing (intensity, spectral, and temporal information; Santos-Sacchi 1988; Cochlear Corporation 2005).

Hearing loss involving the outer and middle ear causing disruption of the transfer of mechanical sound energy is termed "conductive hearing loss." Disorders of the cochlea, cochlear nerve, or central auditory pathways are termed "sensorineural hearing loss." "Mixed hearing loss" is a combination of these two types. Conductive hearing loss can be addressed by surgical correction of the conductive defect or by amplification of the sound energy to overcome the conductive defect via hearing aids. Sensorineural hearing loss, in most cases, can be addressed with sound amplification via hearing aids. However, in some cases, the degree of sensorineural hearing loss precludes the effective use of sound amplification. Often, in these cases, the cochlea itself, including the inner and outer hair cells, is damaged, causing a loss of the mechanical tuning properties of the outer hair cells and loss of spectral resolution and sound clarity. Loss of inner hair cells diminishes the transfer of signal to the cochlear nerve and raises auditory threshold.

COCHLEAR IMPLANT TECHNOLOGY

Most patients with sensorineural hearing loss have malfunctioning cochlear elements and serviceable neural function in the cochlear nerve. Because of this, direct stimulation of the cochlear nerve with electrical impulses has been studied (Luxford and Brackman 1985). Early attempts at direct electrical stimulation of the cochlear nerve resulted in sound awareness but with little useful auditory information.

In the 1980s, W. House and his group introduced a single-channel, ball-shaped electrode device that enabled stimulation of the cochlear nerve and began to produce useful auditory information (Berliner and House 1982; Eisenberg and House 1982). Clinical trials first included adults, and, because results were promising, were later extended to children. Subsequent technological advances led to the introduction of multichannel intracochlear devices capable of discrete electrical stimulation along the length of the cochlea. These improvements afforded a dramatic increase in the sophistication of delivery of auditory information and predictably improved auditory, speech, and language acquisition in cochlear implant recipients. To date, there are three companies producing seven FDA-approved cochlear implant devices (U.S. Food and Drug Administration 2006). The National Institutes of Health (NIH) convened two Consensus Development Conferences in 1988 and 1995 on cochlear implantation, and as the safety and efficacy of cochlear implants have been confirmed, candidacy guidelines have been expanded (National Institutes of Health 2006). Approximately 100,000 cochlear implantations have been performed worldwide, with approximately one-half in children (University of Michigan News Service 2006).

Cochlear implants are designed to take advantage of the fact that in severe-to-profound cases of sensorineural hearing loss, there is often a significant preservation of cochlear nerve cell bodies and their central connections. This allows for direct electrical stimulation of the nerve cell bodies and axons. The tonotopic arrangement of the cochlea and auditory pathways results in frequency-specific delivery of sound information along an electrode array.

The cochlear implant consists of two separate components: the external sound processor (worn on the ear or attached elsewhere) and the surgically implanted receiver/stimulator (Fig. 2). The sound processor contains a sophisticated directional microphone that detects sound. This acoustic signal must then be converted to electrical impulses for

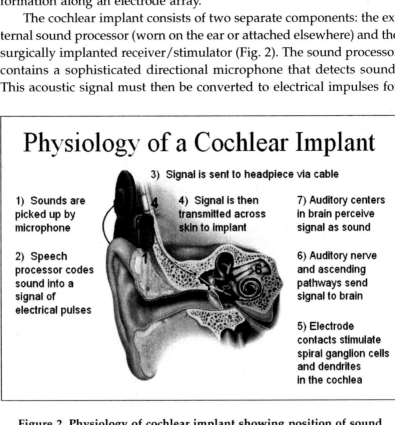

Figure 2. Physiology of cochlear implant showing position of sound processor, receiver/stimulator, and electrode array in cochlea. Courtesy of the Med-El Corporation.

the stimulator. Various strategies have been developed for the sound processor to encode the features of the acoustic signal that are most important for conveying speech information. This is a daunting task, as it is difficult to duplicate the elegance of the natural auditory system, including transmission of spectral, intensity, and timing information. Additionally, the electrical dynamic range of the cochlear nerve is much narrower than the acoustical dynamic range of the ear; therefore, the processed signal must be compressed. The analog signal can be digitized and sent as discrete impulses or transferred as a continuously varying electrical signal.

The processed signal is then sent along a cable connecting the processor to the headpiece. The headpiece is held in place over the scalp via a magnet that adheres to the internal component, the receiver stimulator. The receiver stimulator has an antenna under the headpiece, a "can" containing electrical circuits, and an electrode array with discrete band electrodes (sixteen to twenty-four, depending upon the manufacturer). The signal is sent across the skin via radio-frequency waves to the antenna (telemetry coil) of the internal component. The signal impulses are then sent to their respective electrodes along the electrode array coiled inside the cochlea. Rapid stimulation of individual electrodes, singly or in combination according to the sound-coding "strategy," results in the relay of the signal to the tonotopically arranged cochlear nerve axons and on to the central auditory pathways. Because speech perception involves pattern recognition, a sound-coding strategy that more accurately represents the acoustic patterns of speech over multiple channels or electrodes along the cochlea allows for improved auditory perception.

COCHLEAR IMPLANT SURGERY

The surgical procedure for cochlear implantation is a modification of a standard approach to access the mastoid and middle ear for chronic otitis media. The goals of the surgery are to place the receiver/stimulator in a secure pocket under the scalp, obtain access to the middle ear cleft and the surface of the basal turn of the cochlea, and create an opening into the cochlea in the scala tympani to allow the electrode array to be fully inserted into the cochlea adjacent to the modiolus.

Prior to surgery, all risks and potential benefits are discussed with the patient and family, and informed consent for surgery is obtained. The surgery is done under general anesthesia. An incision is placed behind the pinna, and the mastoid bone is exposed. The mastoid is opened with a surgical drill, and a space is created to enter the middle ear. A small opening is then made into the basal turn of the cochlea. The receiver/stimulator is secured into a small recess created in the skull, and the electrode array is passed into the scala tympani of the cochlea and fully inserted (Fig. 3). The wound is closed, and a pressure dressing is applied overnight.

The patient may be discharged the same day or kept in the hospital overnight depending upon the level of nausea and dizziness. It is not uncommon to have some imbalance and even mild vertigo after the surgery as the vestibular apparatus is necessarily disturbed by the cochleostomy. Incisional pain is mild to moderate and generally lasts for a few days. The superior aspect of the pinna may be numb as the cutaneous nerves supplying sensation to this area are cut by the incision, but sensation returns within several months.

The day after surgery, the pressure dressing is removed, and the wound is inspected for any blood clot formation under the skin (hema-

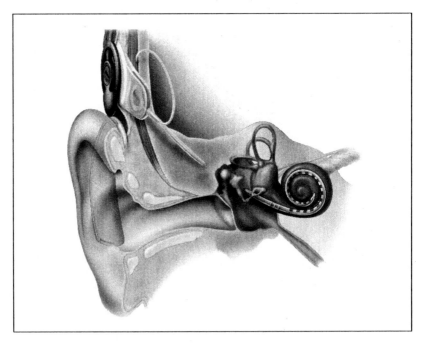

Figure 3. Pathway of electrode array from mastoid into cochleostomy and coiled around modiolus of the cochlea. Courtesy of the Cochlear Corporation.

toma) and integrity of the wound edges. The patient may return to regular activity as tolerated, and the wound can be washed without harm. One month is typically allowed for the swelling (edema) of the skin flap to resolve before the external processor is worn and the head-piece attached to the telemetry coil. The tissue is typically too thick with edema to allow the magnet to attach before this time.

The first audiometry session, or "mapping" session, allows the audiologist to determine the psychoacoustic perception of the patient by varying the stimulation of the electrodes. This is a very technical process that varies in difficulty depending upon whether the patient has preexisting established central auditory pathways ("postlingually deaf"), is congenitally deaf, or lost hearing prior to the age of approximately one year (what is called "prelingually deaf" in the literature, although some of those children may well have had linguistic input, as in the case of a deaf child exposed to sign since birth from Deaf parents, who in all probability is signing before the age of one). Postlingually deaf patients can respond to the electrical stimulation subjectively and provide feedback about which levels of electrical stimulation are at threshold (T-Level), which are most comfortable (M-Level), and which are uncomfortable (C-Level). Thus the electrical dynamic range can be mapped to the acoustical perception. The frequency placement of sound can be confirmed, and the level of clarity of different sound processing strategies can be assessed. However, in the prelingually deaf patient, the first and subsequent sessions as well as rehabilitation are aimed first at recognition of the electrical stimulation as "sound" followed by the gradual pattern recognition that emerges as the auditory pathways develop. As described in the next section, this is a time-intensive habilitation process involving a team of skilled auditory and speech therapists and audiologists.

EVALUATION FOR COCHLEAR IMPLANTATION USING THE TEAM APPROACH AND AUDITORY REHABILITATION FOR CHILDREN AND FAMILIES

Whether to receive a cochlear implant is an important decision for every family whose child has a severe-to-profound hearing loss. A team of specialized professionals in a cochlear implantation program can evaluate the child's candidacy and provide comprehensive services to assist the family in this decision. This team should include professionals who can evaluate the total child, including family and educational settings, to determine candidacy. Team members may include otoneuro-surgeons, audiologists, speech-language pathologists, a research scientist, a social worker, a teacher of deaf children, and a psychologist.

Each member of the team carries a portion of the responsibility in educating and counseling the parents and in evaluating the child and family. A series of audiological tests must be performed to determine if the child is a candidate for cochlear implantation. Newborn hearing screening can determine hearing loss through a procedure called oto-acoustic emission (OAE) testing. This test allows the audiologist to evaluate the function of outer hair cells located within the cochlea. By placing a small ear plug (containing an ultrasensitive microphone and two miniaturized speakers) in a child's ear, it is possible to deliver sounds to the ear and measure the sound (the OAE) generated by the cochlea's outer hair cells in response to the stimuli. These OAEs indicate whether the cochlear outer hair cells are functioning normally.

It has become a more recent practice to screen hearing in newborns using an automated auditory brain stem response (ABR) test in addition to OAE testing. An ABR allows the audiologist to measure the electrical activity of a child's hearing system in response to a sound stimulus (usually a "click-type" sound). For an ABR test, electrodes are secured to a child's skin behind the ear and at the forehead, and a sound is delivered to the child's ear. The electrodes detect the activity within auditory nerve pathways that is triggered by the sound. By measuring this electrical activity, it is possible to determine if the child's ear has responded to the sound at normal or abnormal levels. Occasionally, children will require sedation (e.g., chloral hydrate syrup) to allow the test performance. But, commonly, this noninvasive and non-painful test can be done with the child falling asleep spontaneously. The ABR has been added to newborn hearing screening so that a particular type of hearing loss termed auditory neuropathy/dys-synchrony (AN/AD) or Auditory Neuropathy (AN) Spectrum is not missed. In this type of hearing loss, children can have normal otoacoustic emission readings but abnormal functioning of other parts of the auditory pathway (inner hair cells or cochlear nerve) and an abnormal ABR.

The task of the team audiologist is to accurately determine hearing thresholds and use that information to prescribe appropriate amplification usually in the form of bilateral behind-the-ear (BTE) hearing aids. A three- to six-month trial with appropriate and consistent hearing aid use is required to establish candidacy for a cochlear implant. The absence of appropriate benefit from the hearing aids must be documented with behavioral audiometry in the form of an audiogram. According to federal recommendations, the unaided hearing loss must be documented as a profound or severe-to-profound sensorineural hearing loss with thresholds of 90 dB HL or greater at 1,000 Hz and above. It must also be documented that hearing aids do not provide adequate gain for a child; that is, the aids cannot amplify the speech enough to allow the child to hear speech at normal conversational levels.

During family counseling, one team goal is to educate parents about their child's hearing loss and its implications. For example, parents need to know that a child with a profound sensorineural hearing loss, even with the best amplification, will probably not be able to hear many of the sounds in speech. This will promote realistic expectations about the results from a cochlear implant. A cochlear implant will not "fix" the child's hearing but should be considered a hearing prosthesis. The cochlear implant can excite the auditory nerve in a way that only approximates the excitation delivered by the inner cochlear hair cells of a healthy ear. Whereas a healthy ear has several thousand sensory hair cells to excite the auditory nerve fibers, cochlear implants must attempt to convey the same information with only about twenty-two points of excitation (channels).

Once a child is determined to be an implant candidate using audiological criteria, evaluations are scheduled with other team members. These include an evaluation by the speech-language pathologist, whose task is to document the child's receptive and expressive spoken language skills and establish future goals and objectives for auditory rehabilitation after implantation. The hospital social worker will meet with the family to discuss educational settings and family participation during rehabilitation. The social worker also serves as a resource for the family and as an expert in facilitating specialized services in the family's local educational setting. A genetic counselor from the hospital will administer testing to provide information regarding the cause and progression of the hearing loss as well as possible related syndromes. The physicians will order a computed tomography scan to discover possible pathology related to the cochlea and a magnetic resonance image of the auditory nerve to determine if the child has a viable cochlear nerve. This multidisciplinary evaluation will determine if there are any factors relevant to rehabilitation after surgery or if there are any other needs to be resolved or addressed prior to considering implantation. Ideally, the team's evaluation for the child and family, as well as the hearing aid trial, are accomplished before the child's first birthday.

Research indicates that children who are implanted at an early age show the greatest benefits. For example, in one study (Govaerts et al. 2002), children who had received implants up to the age of six years derived some benefit. Children who were less than two years old when they received implants achieved auditory performance scores that were appropriate for their age almost immediately after implantation and had a 90% probability of entering mainstream education. Children who received implants between two and four years of age required about three years to achieve normal auditory performance scores and had about a 66% probability of entering mainstream education. Children implanted after four years of age rarely achieved normal auditory performance scores, and only 20–30% were integrated into mainstream education by the age of seven years. Increased professional and parental awareness of the importance of the critical period of language acquisition, together with universal hearing screening, should help ensure early referral and ability to achieve maximum potential using cochlear implants. Still, early implantation does not lessen the need for support services when a child is mainstreamed. And, as Marschark, Rhoten, and Fabich (2007) show, the evidence for reading achievement is somewhat mixed. While children with cochlear implants show early gains, especially when implanted young, these gains are not maintained; children with cochlear implants fall behind their hearing peers with increasing age. In other words, cochlear implants do not turn a deaf child into a hearing child. Nevertheless, if implantation is chosen, overall the earlier the better.

It takes time and auditory rehabilitation therapy for the child's brain to learn to interpret the signals sent by the cochlear implant. Early implantation will allow the child optimal results in learning to listen with the implant; the goal of the implant team is to schedule the surgery as close as possible to a child's first birthday. At this time, federal guidelines recommend that a child be at least twelve months of age before implantation. However, in cases with potential for ossification of the cochlea (e.g., with meningitis) the surgery may be done before age twelve months. In general, if a profoundly deaf child is implanted as early as age twelve months, it is highly likely that their learning of language will be the same as a child with normal hearing. Conversely, the longer the wait until implantation, the more time is required to acquire spoken language. Cochlear implants, coupled with intensive post-implantation therapy, can help young children to acquire spoken language skills, cognition based on spoken language, and developmental and social skills. Age eighteen months to two years seems to be the point where the brain stops being plastic and starts to solidify its "hardwiring." So, if implantation can be done at age one year or before eighteen months, spoken language can develop to a significant degree.

Parents must realize that even when a child receives the cochlear implant early, it is only the first step in a long rehabilitation process. The follow-up therapy is when the real work begins for the child and family. For a child to be successful in using the implant, the family must be willing and able to access professional therapy, facilitate spoken language acquisition in the home, and successfully maintain the device. In the beginning, there are multiple appointments to program the device to the child's specific needs. Auditory rehabilitation sessions are usually held twice a week for one hour. The family must make a commitment to ensure the success of the child. They must have the desire to develop the child's auditory skills and be willing to follow through with the required effort. Families are counseled that after implantation, the first year of use is critical, because that is when the child will learn to use the device or learn to ignore it. This is the most important time for rehabilitation, and it is critical that the child wear the device all day and the device be kept in proper working order. Inconsistent use or broken equipment will lead to an intermittent signal being sent to the brain. The brain cannot learn to process sounds when the signal is inconsistent. So, the child begins to rely on other methods to learn about the environment. Even when the implant is on and functioning, he or she will not be able to make use of the signal.

When implanted early, children can learn to use the cochlear implant signal to develop their spoken language skills. Cochlear implants have been shown to have the ability to improve a child's speech detection abilities to a level comparable with that of a child with a mild hearing loss. Through auditory rehabilitation, children's brains learn to perceive the artificial electrical stimulation provided to the cochlea. In the first stages of auditory rehabilitation, the therapist uses his or her voice and couples the vocalizations with particular toys. Since a child of one year is still figuring out where speech comes from, the therapist will usually allow speechreading. Research indicates that normal spoken language comprehension is a product of both hearing and vision. Auditory rehabilitation must serve to link sounds to meaning through the use of motivational activities and systematic auditory exposure to spoken language. Therapy becomes increasingly auditory-only as the child progresses.

Pre-implant auditory rehabilitation therapy may begin even before the child receives a cochlear implant in order to establish a "listening mode" in the child. These sessions should include parent education to help parents realize their prominent and necessary role in their child's auditory development and spoken language acquisition. Parents are taught to be consistent about hearing aid use prior to implantation, thus establishing positive habits regarding monitoring and utilizing amplification. Parents come to realize that through play, children can learn to react to loud low-frequency sounds received through the use of the new hearing aids, and they can teach their child that speech is powerful and can make things happen. They also learn optimal times to talk to their child, such as at feeding time, when the baby is only eighteen inches or so from the parent's face, or during diapering and bath time. Baby talk or "motherese" is also taught as a natural and functional aspect of language acquisition that encourages their child to listen. This type of talking includes lots of syllable repetition; exaggerated head motions; a smiling, happy face; prolongation of vowels; and a higher pitch. While it has been argued that motherese is not relevant to first language acquisition in hearing children, the very fact that it helps children to recognize that they are the targets of the speech act may be beneficial to children with cochlear implants. Parents should be encouraged to talk to their child often, even though he or she cannot hear all that is said before implantation. In everyday life, almost everything is a language opportunity, and parents should take advantage of everyday learning situations. It is critical that parents be taught the importance of such incidental language exposure.

After implantation, auditory rehabilitation serves a dual role in promoting the development of listening and speaking skills. The age of the child is not as important as the "hearing age" that begins upon the initial stimulation of the cochlear implant. A child's overall language levels are determined during the speech and language evaluation, using the modality of the child (whether it is auditory-oral or visual-manual). This establishes whether or not there are cognitive or linguistic delays that must be addressed. An older child, for example, may be functioning at an age-appropriate level using sign language. After these levels are tested, it may be discovered that the child is cognitively at a level commensurate with hearing peers. Since continued growth is desired, therapy sessions can be structured using activities that are appropriate for the child's cognitive level. Since the desire for the child to develop auditory skills has been determined during preimplantation parental counseling, the primary goal of auditory rehabilitation therapy is to move the child's auditory abilities forward. The child must learn to use the implant to identify sounds of speech and develop the ability to control the articulators to produce the sounds of speech. An auditory feedback system must be developed by the child to monitor emerging speech and compare it with an auditory model. In addition, the child must develop an auditory memory in order to retain and reproduce speech sounds in the correct order. The child must progress through all the stages of auditory and spoken language development, regardless of the child's chronological age (Stokes 1999).

To guide the child through these auditory stages, the initial emphasis is on bringing meaning to an auditory signal. By pairing auditory experiences with physical and visual experiences, the rehabilitation therapist encourages the child to form associations between sound and meaning. Once these associations begin, the therapist then stresses acquisition of auditory skills. Therefore, at some point during the sessions, the therapist may begin to prevent the child from speechreading by covering the mouth. This encourages the child to develop the auditory ability to perceive the sound using the "unisensory" approach, more commonly known today as the Auditory-Verbal approach (Beebe 1978). Other therapy techniques combine hand cues or sign language to facilitate linguistic and cognitive growth during a delayed period of spoken language acquisition (Vieu et al. 1998).

The therapist's goal is to help the child comprehend spoken language and acquire expressive language at a level commensurate with hearing peers. Research indicates that this is a realistic goal in children who are implanted early. Therapy typically begins by allowing the young child to speechread, and as therapy progresses, the therapist places more emphasis on auditory-only comprehension. It is thought that in everyday life, successful comprehension of speech is a combination of the auditory sense of what is heard and the visual perception of the lips and body of the speaker. The brain of a child with normal hearing has learned that in conversation, the lips and face make certain gestures that always occur together with certain sounds. Knudsen and Sewall studied whether children with cochlear implants were able to meld their newly acquired hearing capability with their ability to speechread (Stanford School of Medicine Office of Communication and Public Affairs 2005). They found that children implanted early did develop this ability. "The brain is always combining what it sees with what it hears and making the best guess at what was said," states

Knudsen. In most situations, hearing speech alone is adequate. That is why people can use telephones. But in noisy situations when hearing is poor, brains rely heavily on lip and facial movements to identify what someone is saying. If a listener is presented with an audio recording of a single syllable while watching a synchronized video of a speaker's face mouthing a different syllable, in some cases, a third syllable is heard due to the brain's fusing of nonmatching audio and visual information. This is called the McGurk effect (McGurk and Macdonald 1976). It is an unnatural situation that is not normally encountered, but it simply and powerfully reveals that speech perception is a product of both sound and sight. With that in mind, a therapist encourages the young child to both listen and look to help make that link. Later, in order to emphasize the auditory signal, the therapist may begin to cover the mouth or sit alongside, rather than across from, the child while drawing attention to the toys on the therapy table. This research indicates that the children who fully merged the visual and auditory effects of speech were those who were implanted before they were age thirty months old and had received appropriate auditory rehabilitation therapy. It also indicates that the earlier the implantation, the better the chances for fully integrated speech perception in the brain. Children who received implants later in life showed little evidence of integrating both lips and face into their attempts to interpret speech. Instead, they relied solely on what the lips were doing when they were presented with the conflicting auditory and visual information (Stanford School of Medicine Office of Communication and Public Affairs 2005). As a result, they did not display the McGurk effect. This research illustrates the importance of early implantation and appropriate auditory rehabilitation, as well as the ability and necessity of the child to link auditory perception, visual perception, and experiences to meaningful language.

For the child to successfully integrate auditory development with spoken language acquisition, auditory rehabilitation must create motivational and meaningful activities to encourage the important connection between sound and meaning and engage interest and imagination. In effect, the auditory rehabilitation therapist must create a teachable moment during therapy and then continue to teach, being always aware of the child's auditory level and potential.

Auditory rehabilitation therapy must address a child's specific needs and ability levels. In the very beginning, regardless of the child's age, he or she must learn to determine whether or not sound is present in the environment. The therapist teaches the child a conditioning task so that there is a conditioned response to the presence of sound. Many therapists use the "six sounds test" developed by Daniel Ling (1976). These are six phonemic productions that cover the speech spectrum. The theory is that if the child can detect these six sounds, he can hear all the sounds of speech. The child is taught to signal that he or she has detected these sounds by completing a conditioned response (e.g., dropping blocks into a bucket). Eventually, the child can perceive these six sounds at long distances and can successfully imitate them.

The therapist labels toys with arbitrarily associated sounds to help the child attach meaning to the sounds. The sound used may be paired with an action with the toy. Children who focus on the toy and its movement tend to rely less on speechreading. The therapist, child, and parent all have joint attention as the toy moves, and they take turns making the sound. For example, a set of zoo animals may each have their own sound and movement, which is repeated over and over during the therapy session. Cars can go "beep-beep" as they travel on the table, and cows can go "moo-oo-oo." Vocalization models must include long and short utterances, varying vowels, and consonants. The therapist introduces sounds that a child with normal hearing would initially learn to identify and produce.

This order of presentation is nicely described in several texts by Daniel Ling, for example, *Speech and the Hearing Impaired Child: Theory and Practice* (1976). For many years, his texts have served therapists who provide auditory rehabilitation to deaf children. Ling teaches that in the beginning, the emphasis is on auditory stimulation and helping the child learn to attach meaning to sounds. This ability facilitates the acquisition of receptive language skills. The child must be "bathed" in language and sounds. Parents are taught to use full sentences rather than single words with their child in order to facilitate development of natural-sounding phrases when the child begins to speak. At some point, the child will begin to imitate the sounds using the suprasegmentals of language (the intonation, timing, and intensity) and begin to produce them spontaneously at appropriate times. This is the beginning of expressive language. The development of cognition and age-level vocabulary is also considered as language is introduced. Therapy sessions must include both receptive and expressive activities, allowing the child time to process sounds and create sounds at his or her ability level.

The ultimate goal of auditory rehabilitation is to guide the child through the language stages in an auditory manner in order to facilitate maximum success when listening with the cochlear implant. The therapist must always continue teaching the parent how to facilitate spoken language development in the home. Therefore, the parent should attend and participate in the therapy sessions. Parents are encouraged to create an "experience book" in which they paste or draw an event that happened to the child in daily life. This experience book is brought to therapy to share with the therapist. The child relays the experience to the therapist, and through discussion, is exposed to a set of vocabulary words that accompany the experience.

When the child becomes ready for preschool, the cochlear implant team continues its support. Helping to find an appropriate school and training the teachers is one of the team's tasks. It is important that the school meet criteria to facilitate the continued development of the implanted child's auditory skills. Ideally, the school will be small with a favorable teacher-to-student ratio. The room should be acoustically appropriate, meaning small in size with rugs and objects on the wall to prevent reverberation of sound. There will be spoken language models for the child to imitate. The speech therapist is trained in the delivery of cochlear implant therapy, and the team may be able to offer that training. The team can also help the parents advocate for their child by teaching them how to develop an appropriate educational program for their child.

With regular and appropriate programming of the cochlear implant, successful and regular therapy sessions, consistent language stimulation at home, and an appropriate educational environment, a child can become adept at using the implant to navigate the auditory world. The eventual goal is to close the language gap between the implanted child and his typically hearing peers. Children who are implanted early and receive consistent and constant auditory rehabilitation have an excellent chance to learn to use spoken language successfully. They often develop beautiful speech that is melodic and intelligible. They enjoy music and learn to use the telephone. They are often successfully mainstreamed in their neighborhood schools with parents who know how to advocate for them. These children go on to become adults who function successfully in the hearing world, professionally and personally, maintaining connections to family and friends. They are not limited in their career choices or in their interactions with nonsigning hearing people because they have successfully learned to listen with their cochlear implant. In the words of Daniel Ling, "If we are going to put limits on these (deaf) children, let the sky be the limit" (1976).

SPOKEN LANGUAGE DEVELOPMENT AND COCHLEAR IMPLANTATION

In a recent survey (Li, Bain, and Steinberg 2004), about one-third of the parents of children who were eligible to receive a cochlear implant decided against that option, primarily because they placed relatively lower priority on educational mainstreaming and higher priority on bilingual education and signing. Conversely, the majority of the parents of eligible children in the Li et al. (2004) survey considered use of cochlear implants because they placed emphasis on factors like speaking and educational mainstreaming. Thus, a majority of parents of children who are eligible for cochlear implants consider them, and if they choose to proceed with implantation, do so with the expectation that the implant will permit their child to develop spoken language.

Despite this parental expectation and a constantly improving success rate for cochlear implants in achieving the goal of supporting oral communication, there is considerable variability in how well implanted children acquire spoken language. This section examines spoken language development in children who have received cochlear implants, with an emphasis on investigating the factors that might account for this variability in development of spoken language.

There are two broad areas to consider. First, which conditions obtained prior to implantation may predict successful development of spoken language? In this category, one must consider intrinsic factors, such as the cause of deafness, the child's cognitive capabilities, and the age at which the child lost his or her hearing, as well as extrinsic factors, such as family structure and demographics, the age at implantation, the child's educational setting prior to implantation, and the type of cochlear implant chosen.

The second broad area to consider is the nature of the child's experience following implantation. That is, what can be done after a child has received a cochlear implant to best promote spoken language development? Discussion of this topic centers on what type of educational setting most likely promotes spoken language development, but it is extremely difficult to identify the many confounding factors that make problematic a simple comparison of children in different educational settings. Table 1 presents a selection of twenty-seven articles from recent research literature on spoken language and cochlear implants. This is a small, but representative, sample of the research that addresses the broad question of what factors determine successful outcomes for cochlear implants.

Table 1. Summary of 27 studies that examined the effects of device characteristics, Age at Implantation (AAI), educational setting (OC or TC), or some combination of these for children with cochlear implants. For Device effects, MC+ indicates that the study demonstrated that new multi-channel systems were better than older (e.g., single channel) systems and ALG+ indicates that the study found improvements associated with changes in the device processing algorithms. For AAI, 'Y >' indicates studies that found younger age at implant led to better performance on the study measures and NS indicates AAI was examined but did not have a significant effect. For Education, OC > TC indicates that children in an OC program performed better than children in a TC program. NS indicates non-significant differences for Educational setting and OC ≈ TC indicates that on most measures no significant difference was found, but on some measures there were significant effects of educational setting (see comments for specifics).

Study	N	Device	AAI	Measure	Education	Comments
(Berliner, Tonokawa, Dye, & House, 1989)	51	—	Y >	Sp. Perc.	OC > TC	shorter dur deaf better; single channel device
(Chin, 2003)	12	—	—	Sp. Prod.	OC > TC	More Eng segs in OC; More non-Eng segs in TC
(Connor, Hieber, Arts, & Zwolan, 2000)	147	MC+	Y >	Sp. Prod. & Voc.	OC ≈ TC	HLM analysis to separate effects
(C. Dillon, Pisoni, Cleary, & Carter, 2004)	88	—	—	Nonword rep.	OC > TC	
(Geers, 2002)	136	MC+	—	Lang & Sp.	OC > TC	IQ
(Geers, 2004)	133	ALG+	NS	Lang & Sp.	—	Shorter time deaf better & <2 better
(Geers, Nicholas, & Sedey, 2003)	181	—	NS	Lang & Sp.	OC > TC	
(Govaerts et al., 2002)	70	—	Y >	Sp. Perc.		
(Hodges, Dolan-Ash, Balkany, Schloffman, & Butts, 1999)	40	—	—	Sp. Perc.	OC > TC	
(Kirk et al., 2002)	73	—	Y >	Lang & Sp.	OC > TC	
(Lachs, Pisoni, & Kirk, 2001)	27	—	—	A-V integration	OC > TC	

Study	N			Domain	Result	Notes
(Manrique, Cervera-Paz, Huarte, & Molina, 2004)	182	—	Y >	Sp Prod. & Perc.	—	infant implanted at 6 mo.
(Miyamoto, Houston, Kirk, Perdew, & Svirsky, 2003)	1	—	Y >	Lang.	—	
(Miyamoto, Osberger, Robbins, Myres, & Kessler, 1993)	19	—	—	Sp Perc.	OC ≈ TC	2 of 13 tests OC > TC
(Osberger et al., 1991)	28	—	—	Sp Perc.	OC ≈ TC	open response set OC > TC
(Osberger, Zimmerman-Phillips, Barker, & Geier, 1999)	58	MC+	—	Sp Perc.	OC > TC	
(Peng, Spencer, & Tomblin, 2004)	24	ALG+	Y >	Sp Prod.	—	
(Richter, Eissele, Laszig, & Lohle, 2002)	106	—	Y >	Lang & Sp.	—	
(Robbins, Bollard, & Green, 1999)	23	—	—	Lang & Sp.	NS	Rate lang ^ > normal
(Sehgal, Kirk, Svirsky, & Miyamoto, 1998)	11	ALG+	—	Sp Perc.	—	
(Somers, 1991)	68	—	—	Sp Perc.	OC > TC	mixed HA and CI group
(Stallings, Kirk, Chin, & Gao, 2002)	32	—	—	Sp Perc. & Voc.	—	Home language environment important
(Svirsky, Chute, Green, Bollard, & Miyamoto, 2002)	44	ALG+	—	Lang.	—	lang dev parallel normal + delay
(Svirsky, Teoh, & Neuburger, 2004)	75	—	Y >	Lang. & Sp Perc.	—	developmental trajectory analysis
(Tobey, Geers, Brenner, Altuna, & Gabbert, 2003)	181	ALG+	NS	Sp Prod.	—	insertion, electrodes, dynamic range IQ SEX
(Tobey, Rekart, Buckley, & Geers, 2004)	131	—	—	Sp Prod.	OC > TC	mainstream+
(Tomblin, Barker, Spencer, Zhang, & Gantz, 2005)	29	—	Y >	Expr. Lang.	—	
(Uchanski & Geers, 2003)	181	—	—	Sp Prod (acoust)	OC > TC	

Before the factors that may account for variance in acquiring spoken language are discussed, it may be useful to briefly consider the question of how one should assess progress in spoken language. Perhaps the two most obvious measures are speech perception (i.e., how accurately can children perceive the speech they hear) and speech production (i.e., how intelligible is the speech of a child to others with normal hearing). However, even these seemingly obvious measures have been operationally defined in a variety of ways. For example, to measure speech perception, one may choose tasks that emphasize the ability of a child to recognize whole familiar words in the context of a short meaningful sentence, or words in isolation. The latter task, because it does not allow the child to guess what a word is based on its context, may be a more sensitive measure of speech perception, but it is less like real-world communication and therefore might be less useful as a measure of the child's ability to communicate orally. Another measure of speech perception, the modified rhymes test (House, Williams, Hecker, and Kryter 1965), requires children to listen to a word spoken in isolation and select it from a small set of rhyming alternatives (e.g., *bought, pot, dot, tot, got, cot*). From the child's responses, it is possible to assess his or her ability to process the specific sound features that account for the acoustically minimal differences among the alternative words.

These are only a few of the many ways that researchers have measured speech perception ability in children with cochlear implants. Obviously, these measures of speech perception can provide very different results depending on the nature of the task (e.g., meaningful sentence, isolated word, rhyme test) and whether they are presented in an auditory-only or auditory-visual mode. This can make comparisons between different studies difficult.

There is similar variability in the methods that have been used to assess the intelligibility of speech produced by children with cochlear implants. At one extreme are studies where one or more experienced judges listen to utterances produced by children and rate them for "intelligibility" (e.g., on a 7-point rating scale where 1 is completely intelligible and 7 is completely unintelligible). At the other extreme, there are studies in which a panel of listeners (generally unfamiliar with speech produced by people who are deaf or hard of hearing) are presented with children's utterances and are directed to write down what they hear. The written words are then marked correct (i.e., the word intended by the child) or incorrect, and each original utterance is given a score that is proportional to the number of listeners who correctly identified it. It is even possible in the latter case to analyze the nature of the errors listeners tended to make in transcribing utterances to identify the type of production errors made. In most studies that have compared these two methods of estimating utterance intelligibility, the two are reasonably well correlated. Nonetheless, it is clear that simply rating intelligibility is more subjective and depends crucially on the training of the rater, while using a panel of naïve listeners is a more objective, but much more time-consuming, way to obtain intelligibility measures.

One particularly interesting and sensitive measure of spoken language development, non-word repetition, combines aspects of both perception and production (Dillon, Burkholder, Cleary, and Pisoni 2004; Gathercole, Willis, Baddeley, and Emslie 1994). In a non-word repetition task for English-speaking children, the child hears an utterance that could be, but is not, an English word, such as *ballop*, *skiticult*, or *fennerizer*, and must immediately repeat it. The child's utterance is then scored as correct or incorrect, and the percentage of correct responses over a list of non-words is taken as the child's score on the overall task. In the original CNRep task described by Gathercole et al. (1994), the list contained forty words of varying length from two to five syllables. Dillon, Burkholder, Cleary, and Pisoni (2004) used a twenty-word subset of the words from the CNRep in a study of children with cochlear implants. Thus, the task assesses the child's ability to process unfamiliar speech (obviously a crucial skill for acquiring new words), the child's ability to hold the unfamiliar item in working phonological memory long enough to repeat it, and the child's ability to construct and execute an articulatory plan for the unfamiliar item (Dillon, Burkholder, Cleary, and Pisoni 2004).

In addition to tests that explicitly examine production and perception of spoken language, many studies have used other instruments designed to measure general language development (i.e., not necessarily spoken language) such as the Reynell Language Development Scales. In some of the studies discussed below, these tests have been used to ensure that measurements of speech production and perception do not miss important general language skills that may be developing independent of perceptual and articulatory skills.

For children who are born with severe-to-profound hearing loss, many studies show a strong relationship between age at time of implantation and success in the subsequent development of spoken language. During the postnatal period (approximately the first six months), infants have a well-developed peripheral auditory nervous system, up to and including the brain stem, but cortical structures are relatively undeveloped (Moore 2002). In this period, infants with normal hearing demonstrate a variety of innate speech discrimination abilities, including the ability to discriminate phonetic distinctions in any language, the ability to associate speech with speakers, and recognition of individual's voices (e.g., Aslin, Jusczyk, and Pisoni 1998; Eimas, Siqueland, Jusczyk, and Vigorito 1971; Kuhl 1979). Interestingly, sometime around age six months, infants start to specialize perceptually in their native language, showing a tendency to attend differentially to elements of the native language they are learning and to disregard elements that are non-native. For example, in the first six months, infants developing in a Japanese language environment discriminate r-sounds from l-sounds just like infants developing in an English language environment. However, around age six months, children in a Japanese environment will begin to lose this discrimination as they learn that their language places both these sound segments within a single phonemic category.

These developmental changes appear to be related to neurophysiological changes in infants that occur as a response to auditory (speech) stimulation. Normal sensory input is essential for normal brain development. Children who are deaf from birth go for a variable length of time with little or no auditory input to the brain. This sensory deprivation delays development of the parts of the brain responsible for processing spoken language. Since infancy is a period of extremely rapid development of the brain and nervous system, the longer that auditory pathways and the brain structures to which they connect are deprived of sensory input, the more profound the consequences. Thus, it would be expected that the sooner a child receives a cochlear implant, the less the delay in the child's spoken language skills, and that is precisely what most reports show (Govaerts et al. 2002; Manrique, Cervera-Paz, Huarte, and Molina 2004; Miyamoto, Houston, Kirk, Perdew, and Svirsky 2003; Miyamoto, Kirk, Svirsky, and Sehgal 1999; Osberger, Zimmerman-Phillips, and Koch 2002; Peng, Spencer, and Tomblin 2004; Richter, Eissele, Laszig, and Lohle 2002; Svirsky, Teoh, and Neuburger 2004; Tomblin, Barker, Spencer, Zhangand, and Gantz 2005).

These studies also support the notion that there is a critical period of neurological development up to about age five years. After this, development is permanently altered by the absence of auditory input. If children do not begin to receive effective auditory stimulation, either through appropriate amplification or through a cochlear implant, before the end of this critical period (and the sooner the better), they are extremely unlikely to develop strong spoken language skills.

Of course, some children are born with measurable hearing and a progressive hearing loss that results in their deafness after some months or years. For these children (assuming that they are fitted with adequate amplification while they are able to make use of it), it is the length of time after loss of measurable hearing rather than absolute age that is probably the most important factor. For example, Geers (2004) found normal speech and language skills in 80% of children who lost hearing after birth if they underwent implantation within a year of onset of deafness. Even more dramatically, as described previously, Govaerts et al. (2002) found that all children in their study who were implanted before age two years achieved normal auditory performance scores immediately and had a 90% probability of being mainstreamed in school.

With progressive losses, an important consideration is when to replace hearing aids with one or more implants. Federal guidelines recommend demonstrating that children are unable to benefit from hearing aids before they are considered eligible for a cochlear implant. However, at least one study (Zwolan, Zimmerman-Phillips, Ashbaugh, Hieber, Kileny, and Telian 1997) has shown that children who still receive borderline benefit from hearing aids perform better after implantation than children who are not implanted until they reach the level of hearing loss where they receive no benefit from the hearing aids. This raises the possibility that current guidelines are too restrictive and that children with progressive hearing loss might benefit from receiving implants sooner.

One extensive study, progressively developed over years by Geers and colleagues (e.g., Geers 2002, 2004; Geers and Brenner 2003), examined 181 children with cochlear implants over a four-year period to identify the many factors that contribute to the success of children with cochlear implants in developing spoken language. Geers (2002) examined the characteristics of the child, the family, and the implant itself as factors influencing spoken language development. The design of their study allowed the authors to estimate the amount of variability in their outcome measures accounted for by these factors as well as the amount of variability associated with educational setting. The authors reported that nonverbal IQ and factors related to the family accounted for roughly 20% of the variance in outcomes for implanted children. The fact that nonverbal IQ is important in predicting outcomes may reflect the general importance of cognitive factors in language development. This is consistent with the observation that children with genetic deafness that affects only the cochlea (and not broader cognitive functioning) have better outcomes from cochlear implantation than children with deafness related to other factors (Bauer, Geers, Brenner, Moog, and Smith 2003). However, apparent IQ effects may also reflect more general family and environment factors. Children with higher nonverbal IQs may have parents with higher IQs who are generally well educated and actively involved in the early diagnosis and treatment of their deaf children. Additionally, the overall "linguistic environment" that parents establish in how they talk to their children impacts spoken language development in children with cochlear implants (e.g., Stallings, Kirk, Chin, and Gao 2002).

In addition to the characteristics of the child and family, about 24% of the variance in the Geers (2002) study was associated with the properties of the implanted device itself. The best multichannel implants using the latest speech processing algorithms consistently supported better spoken language development. Similar conclusions regarding the advantages of better processing algorithms with multichannel implants have been reported by others as well (e.g., Osberger, Zimmerman-Phillips, Barker, and Geier 1999; Peng et al. 2004; Sehgal, Kirk, Svirsky, and Miyamoto 1998; Svirsky, Chute, Green, Bollard, and Miyamoto 2002; Zimmerman-Phillips, Osberger, Geier, and Barker 1997). Additionally, other important device-related factors are the degree of insertion of the electrode array and measures of the electrical integrity of the electrode array (Tobey, Geers, Brenner, Altuna, and Gabbert 2003).

In summary, the best outcomes for spoken language development in children with cochlear implants are associated with 1) receipt of the implant within about one year of birth or within a year of becoming deaf, if their hearing loss is progressive, 2) higher nonverbal IQ scores and more favorable family environment, and 3) use of fully inserted and functioning multichannel implants with the best acoustic processing algorithms (e.g., SPEAK algorithm). What does this mean for the parents of a deaf child? Of course, parents cannot choose the nonverbal IQ of their children, but if they opt for an implant, they can decide to have their infant or child receive a cochlear implant as early as possible, they can choose an implant that supports the latest processing algorithms, and they can talk to their child.

As described in the previous section of this chapter, all children who receive cochlear implants must also receive appropriate (re)habilitation similar to auditory verbal therapy. In addition, aspects of the educational setting are apparently crucial for developing spoken language. Children who are deaf or hard of hearing are often enrolled in special educational programs, of which two types are most prevalent: oral communication (OC) programs, which emphasize communication in an oral/auditory mode where sign language is not used, and total communication (TC) programs, which utilize oral communication coupled with simultaneous sign, typically using Signed English (SE) or Pidgin Signed English (PSE). Both SE and PSE share lexical items (i.e., the word signs) with American Sign Language (ASL) but differ from ASL in grammatical structure. ASL is completely distinct from English in many ways, notably word order (see DeLuca and Napoli, 2008); however, SE and PSE are essentially variants of English cast in sign and thus use the same word order as English. Signed English and PSE differ in that SE requires signers to adhere strictly to English structure—every word, even articles and verb modifiers in a spoken sentence, is signed—whereas PSE allows signers to skip the "little words" while preserving enough of the English structure to convey the sentence meaning. Of course, the importance of using SE or PSE for TC education is to permit instructors to speak while signing and maintain a clear correspondence between spoken words and signs. Note that we are reporting here on the most common programs rather than promoting them. Indeed, the value of SE and PSE for enhancing language development in general and for enhancing literacy, in particular, is questionable (see Wilbur, 2008, among many others).

In addition to the TC and OC educational approaches, there are also programs referred to as "bilingual." These programs teach ASL and spoken English separately as two different languages. There are few reports of children with cochlear implants in bilingual programs.

A general review of the literature on educational factors affecting spoken language development for children with cochlear implants would appear to show that OC programs are more appropriate than TC programs (the literature survey did not uncover evaluations of bilingual programs for children with cochlear implants). Of sixteen reports identified in the recent literature (see Table 1) that evaluated the effects of educational setting on speech and language development with cochlear implants, twelve reported significantly better overall outcomes for OC programs (Berliner, Tonokawa, Dye, and House 1989; Chin 2003; Dillon, Pisoni, Cleary, and Carter 2004; Geers 2002; Geers, Nicholas, and Sedey 2003; Hodges, Dolan-Ash, Balkany, Schloffman, and Butts 1999; Kirk, Miyamoto, Lento, Ying, O'Neill, and Fears 2002; Lachs, Pisoni, and Kirk 2001; Osberger et al. 1999; Somers 1991; Tobey, Rekart, Buckley, and Geers 2004; Uchanski and Geers 2003). Of the remaining four studies, two reported a significant advantage for OC programs (Miyamoto, Osberger, Robbins, Myres, and Kessler 1993; Osberger, Miyamoto, Zimmerman-Phillips, Kemink, Stroer, Firszt et al. 1991), but only on a small subset of their outcome measures; one study failed to find a significant difference (Robbins, Bollard, and Green 1999), and one study reported a mixture of different programs having more favorable outcomes for different outcome measures (Connor, Hieber, Arts, and Zwolan 2000). Thus, no study has reported significantly better overall outcomes for TC programs, although some reports suggest better performance on selected outcome measures for children in TC programs (Connor et al. 2000).

The studies cited above used a variety of outcome measures, including speech perception, speech production, and general language skills. Moreover, in studies that measured general language skills (as opposed to strictly spoken language skills), investigators used each child's preferred mode of communications (speech or sign; e.g., Connor et al. 2000; Geers 2002). This allowed investigators to guard against the possibility that children in TC programs do advance in linguistic and cognitive skills but do not show those advances on tests that are biased toward speech perception and production.

While most studies appear to favor the conclusion that OC programs are much better than TC programs for children with cochlear implants, it is also important to keep in mind some serious limitations of these studies. First, and most importantly, children in these studies have not been assigned randomly to one educational program or another. Instead, children are enrolled in educational programs for a variety of reasons that may include highly confounding factors such as the child's demonstrated success with one mode of communication or another, or the extent to which parents want their child to learn to sign as well as speak. Furthermore, while it is highly probable that children will receive ample exposure to spoken language in an OC program, there may be wide variability in the amount of spoken language a child is exposed to in a TC program. Thus, children in some TC programs may receive ample exposure to spoken language, but children in other TC programs may not. If there is, on average, less exposure to spoken language in TC programs, this may reduce the rate of development for these children.

A large majority of the studies that compare OC versus TC programs for children with cochlear implants suggest that children in OC programs develop superior spoken language skills. However, it is not clear that this represents a fundamental deficiency in the concept of a TC approach for cochlear implants. Alternatively, these results could be due to factors like a deficiency in the implementation of existing TC programs, a tendency for placement of children who are inherently more proficient in spoken language (for other reasons as discussed earlier) in OC programs, or other factors that are not specific to TC. Research is still needed to better understand the educational requirements of children who have received cochlear implants. Although recent results with early implantation and multichannel implants are impressive, it is crucial to remember that children with cochlear implants have severely impaired auditory sensory capabilities when compared with normally hearing children. Almost certainly, children with cochlear implants have special educational requirements, and because of their specific auditory deficits, it seems reasonable that these children would benefit from additional linguistic support, perhaps in the form of signing. However, from available evidence, it is equally certain that additional linguistic support cannot come at the expense of auditory stimulation.

This chapter has provided a comprehensive overview of cochlear implants. From the surgeon's perspective, the anatomy and physiology of the human auditory system and how implants are inserted to restore, in a limited way, the function of the auditory system have been described. From the auditory-verbal therapist's perspective, the intensive (re)habilitation that is required for children who receive cochlear implants and the factors that motivate this effective therapeutic approach have been detailed. Finally, from the view of the researcher, the factors that are presently believed to best promote success in developing spoken language for pediatric cochlear implant recipients have been addressed.

REFERENCES

Aslin, R. N., P. Jusczyk, and D. B. Pisoni. 1998. Speech and auditory processing during infancy. In *Cognition, perception, and language*, ed. D. Kuhn and R. Siegler, 147–98. New York: Wiley.

Bauer, P. W., A. E. Geers, C. Brenner, J. S. Moog, and R. J. H. Smith. 2003. The effect of GJB2 allele variants on performance after cochlear implantation. *Laryngoscope* 113(12): 2135–40.

Beebe, H. 1978. Deaf children can learn to hear. *Journal of Communication Disorders* 11: 193–200.

Berliner, K. I., and W. F. House. 1982. The cochlear implant program: An overview. *Ann Otol Rhinol Laryngol Suppl* 91(2Pt3): 11–14.

Berliner, K. I., L. L. Tonokawa, L. M. Dye, and W. F. House. 1989. Open-set speech recognition in children with a single-channel cochlear implant. *Ear and Hearing* 10(4): 237–42.

Campbell, K. 1998. The basic audiologic assessment. In *Essential audiology for physicians*, ed. K. Campbell, 1–11. San Diego: Singular Publishing Group.

Chin, S. B. 2003. Children's consonant inventories after extended cochlear implant use. *J Speech Lang Hear Res* 46(4): 849–62.

Cochlear Corporation. 2005. Technology update.

Connor, C. M., S. Hieber, H. A. Arts, and T. A. Zwolan. 2000. Speech, vocabulary, and the education of children using cochlear implants: Oral or total communication? *J Speech Lang Hear Res* 43(5): 1185–1204.

DeLuca, D. and D. J. Napoli. 2008. A bilingual approach to reading. In *Signs and voices: Deaf culture, identity, language, and arts*, ed. K. A. Lindren, D. DeLuca, D. J. Napoli, 150–62. Washington, D.C.: Gallaudet University Press.

Dillon, C. M., R. A. Burkholder, M. Cleary, and D. B. Pisoni. 2004. Nonword repetition by children with cochlear implants: Accuracy ratings from normal-hearing listeners. *J Speech Lang Hear Res* 47(5): 1103–16.

Dillon, C., D. B. Pisoni, M. Cleary, and A. K. Carter. 2004. Nonword imitation by children with cochlear implants: Consonant analyses. *Arch Otolaryngol Head Neck Surg* 130(5): 587–91.

Eimas, P. D., E. R. Siqueland, P. Jusczyk, and J. Vigorito. 1971. Speech perception in infants. *Science* 171(968): 303–06.

Eisenberg, L. S., and W. F. House. 1982. Initial experience with the cochlear implant in children. *Ann Otol Rhinol Laryngol Suppl* 91(2Pt3): 67–73.

Gathercole, S. E., C. S. Willis, A. D. Baddeley, and H. Emslie. 1994. The children's test of nonword repetition: A test of phonological working memory. *Memory* 2(2): 103–27.

Geers, A. E. 2002. Factors affecting the development of speech, language, and literacy in children with early cochlear implantation. *Language speech and hearing services in schools* 33: 172–83.

Geers, A. E. 2004. Speech, language, and reading skills after early cochlear implantation. *Arch Otolaryngo Head Neck Surg* 130(5): 634–38.

Geers, A. E., and C. Brenner. 2003. Background and educational characteristics of prelingually deaf children implanted by five years of age. *Ear and Hearing* 24(1): 2S–14S.

Geers, A. E., J. G. Nicholas, and A. L. Sedey. 2003. Language skills of children with early cochlear implantation. *Ear and Hearing* 24(1): 46S–58S.

Govaerts, P. J., C. De Beukelaer, K. Daemers, G. De Ceulaer, M. Yperman, T. Somers et al. 2002. Outcome of cochlear implantation at different ages from 0 to 6 years. *Otology and Neurotology* 23(6): 885–90.

Hodges, A. V., M. Dolan-Ash, T. J. Balkany, J. J. Schloffman, and S. L. Butts. 1999. Speech perception results in children with cochlear implants: Contributing factors. *Arch Otolaryngol Head Neck Surg* 121(1): 31–34.

House, A. S., K. E. Williams, M. H. Hecker, and K. D. Kryter. 1965. Articulation testing methods: Consonantal differentiation with a closed response set. *J Acoust Soc Am* 37: 158–66.

Kirk, K. I., R. T. Miyamoto, C. L. Lento, E. Ying, T. O'Neill, and B. Fears. 2002. Effects of age at implantation in young children. *Ann Otol Rhinol Laryngol Suppl* 189: 69–73.

Kuhl, P. K. 1979. Speech perception in early infancy: Perceptual constancy for spectrally dissimilar vowel categories. *J Acoust Soc Am* 66(6): 1668–79.

Lachs, L., D. B. Pisoni, and K. I. Kirk. 2001. Use of audiovisual information in speech perception by prelingually deaf children with cochlear implants: A first report. *Ear and Hearing* 22(3): 236–51.

Li, Y. L., L. Bain, and A. G. Steinberg. 2004. Parental decision-making in considering cochlear implant technology for a deaf child. *Int J of Ped Otorhinol* 68(8): 1027–38.

Ling, D. 1976. *Speech and the hearing impaired child: Theory and practice.* Washington, D.C.: Alexander Graham Bell Association for the Deaf, Inc.

Luxford, W. M., and D. E. Brackman. 1985. The history of cochlear implants. In *Cochlear implants,* ed. R. F. Gray, 1–26. London: Croom Helm.

Manrique, M. M., F. J. Cervera-Paz, A. Huarte, and M. Molina. 2004. Prospective long-term auditory results of cochlear implantation in prelinguistically deafened children: The importance of early implantation. *Acta Otolaryngol Suppl* 552: 55–63.

Marschark, M., C. Rhoten, and M. Fabich. 2007. Effects of cochlear implants on children's reading and academic achievement. *Journal of Deaf Studies and Deaf Education* 12(3): 269–82.

McGurk, H., and J. Macdonald. 1976. Hearing lips and seeing voices. *Nature* 264(5588): 746–48.

Miyamoto, R. T., D. M. Houston, K. I. Kirk, A. E. Perdew, and M. A. Svirsky. 2003. Language development in deaf infants following cochlear implantation. *Acta Otolaryngol* 123(2): 241–44.

Miyamoto, R. T., K. I. Kirk, M. A. Svirsky, and S. T. Sehgal. 1999. Communication skills in pediatric cochlear implant recipients. *Acta Otolaryngol* 119(2): 219–24.

Miyamoto, R. T., M. J. Osberger, A. M. Robbins, W. A. Myres, and K. Kessler. 1993. Prelingually deafened children's performance with the nucleus multichannel cochlear implant. *Am J Otology* 14(5): 437–45.

Moore, J. K. 2002. Maturation of human auditory cortex: Implications for speech perception. *Ann Otol Rhinol Laryngol Suppl* 189: 7–10.

National Institutes of Health. 1995. Consensus Development Conference. http://concensus.nih.gov/1995/1995CochlearImplants100html.htm.

Osberger, M. J., R. T. Miyamoto, S. Zimmerman-Phillips, J. L. Kemink, B. S. Stroer, J. B. Firszt, et al. 1991. Independent evaluation of the speech perception abilities of children with the Nucleus 22-channel cochlear implant system. *Ear and Hearing* 12(4 Suppl): 66S–80S.

Osberger, M. J., S. Zimmerman-Phillips, M. Barker, and L. Geier. 1999. Clinical trial of the CLARION cochlear implant in children. *Ann Otol Rhinol Laryngol Suppl* 177: 88–92.

Osberger, M. J., S. Zimmerman-Phillips, and D. B. Koch. 2002. Cochlear implant candidacy and performance trends in children. *Ann Otol Rhinol Laryngol Suppl* 189: 62–65.

Peng, S., L. J. Spencer, and J. B. Tomblin. 2004. Speech intelligibility of pediatric cochlear implant recipients with 7 years of device experience. *J Speech Lang Hear Res* 47(6): 1227–36.

Richter, B., S. Eissele, R. Laszig, and E. Lohle. 2002. Receptive and expressive language skills of 106 children with a minimum of 2 years' experience in hearing with a cochlear implant. *Int J of Ped Otorhinol* 64(2): 111–25.

Robbins, A. M., P. M. Bollard, and J. Green. 1999. Language development in children implanted with the CLARION cochlear implant. *Ann Otol Rhinol Laryngol Suppl* 177: 113–18.

Sanes, D. H., and E. W. Rubel. 1988. The development of stimulus coding in the auditory system. In *Physiology of the ear*, ed. A. F. Jahn and J. Santos-Sacchi, 438–39. New York: Raven.

Santos-Sacchi, J. 1988. Cochlear physiology. In *Physiology of the ear*, ed. A. F. Jahn and J. Santos-Sacchi, 271–93. New York: Raven.

Schuknecht, H. F. 1993. *Pathology of the ear*. Philadelphia: Lea and Febiger.

Sehgal, S. T., K. I. Kirk, M. Svirsky, and R. T. Miyamoto. 1998. The effects of processor strategy on the speech perception performance of pediatric nucleus multichannel cochlear implant users. *Ear and Hearing* 19(2): 149–61.

Somers, M. N. 1991. Speech perception abilities in children with cochlear implants or hearing aids. *Am J Otology* 12 Suppl: 174–78.

Stallings, L. M., K. I. Kirk, S. B. Chin, and S. J. Gao. 2002. Parent word familiarity and the language development of pediatric cochlear implant users. *Volta Review* 102(4): 237–58.

Stanford School of Medicine Office of Communication and Public Affairs. 2005. Sooner Is Better with Cochlear Implants, Stanford Scientist Shows. December 5 press release. http://mednews.stanford.edu/releases/2005/december/cochlear.html.

Stokes, J. 1999. Auditory development: A checklist of auditory objectives. In *Hearing impaired infants: Support in the first 18 months*, ed. J. Stokes. London: Whurr Publishers, Ltd.

Svirsky, M. A., P. M. Chute, J. Green, P. Bollard, and R. T. Miyamoto. 2002. Language development in children who are prelingually deaf who have used the SPEAK or CIS stimulation strategies since initial stimulation. *Volta Review* 102(4): 199–213.

Svirsky, M. A., S. W. Teoh, and H. Neuburger. 2004. Development of language and speech perception in congenitally, profoundly deaf children as a function of age at cochlear implantation. *Audiology and Neuro-otology* 9(4): 224–33.

Tobey, E. A., A. E. Geers, C. Brenner, D. Altuna, and G. Gabbert. 2003. Factors associated with development of speech production skills in children implanted by age five. *Ear and Hearing* 24(1): 36S–45S.

Tobey, E. A., D. Rekart, K. Buckley, and A. E. Geers. 2004. Mode of communication and classroom placement impact on speech intelligibility. *Arch Otolaryngol Head Neck Surg* 130(5): 639–43.

Tomblin, J. B., B. Barker, L. J. Spencer, X. Y. Zhangand, and B. J. Gantz. 2005. The effect of age at cochlear implant initial stimulation on expressive language growth in infants and toddlers. *J Speech Lang Hear Res* 48(4): 853–67.

Uchanski, R. M., and A. E. Geers. 2003. Acoustic characteristics of the speech of young cochlear implant users: A comparison with normal-hearing agemates. *Ear and Hearing* 24(1 Suppl): 90S–105S.

University of Michigan News Service. 2006. New cochlear implant could improve hearing. http://www.umich.edu/news/index.html?Releases/2006/Feb06/r020606a (accessed February 2006).

U.S Food and Drug Administration. 2006. Devices@FDA: A catalog of cleared and approved medical devices. http://www.accessdata.fda.gov/scripts/cdrh/devicesatfda/index.cfm.

Vieu, A., M. Mondain, K. Blanchard, M. Sillon, F. Reuillard-Artieres, E. Tobey et al. 1998. Influence of communication mode on speech intelligibility and syntatic structure of sentences in profoundly hearing impaired French children implanted between 5 and 9 years of age. *Int J of Ped Otorhinol* 44: 15–22.

Wilbur, R. 2008. Success with deaf children: How to prevent educational failure. In *Signs and voices: Deaf culture, identity, language, and arts,* ed. K. A. Lindgren, D. DeLuca, and D. J. Napoli, 117–38. Washington, D.C.: Gallaudet University Press.

Zimmerman-Phillips, S., M. J. Osberger, L. Geier, and M. Barker. 1997. Speech recognition performance of pediatric Clarion patients. *Am J Otology* 18(6 Suppl): S153–54.

Zwolan, T. A., S. Zimmerman-Phillips, C. J. Ashbaugh, S. J. Hieber, P. R. Kileny, and S. A. Telian, S. A. 1997. Cochlear implantation of children with minimal open-set speech recognition skills. *Ear and Hearing* 18(3): 240–51.

Part Two
Education and Literacy

4 | Civil Rights in Deaf
Education: Working
Toward Empowering
Deaf Students and
Their Parents

Jami N. Fisher and Philip J. Mattiacci

Several laws have been enacted in the past thirty plus years to benefit
persons with disabilities. The Rehabilitation Act of 1973 banned discrimination against persons with disabilities; PL-94 142, the Education
for All Handicapped Children (now known as IDEA) was passed in
1975 and has been revised twice since then, most recently in 2004; and
the Americans with Disabilities Act (Public Law 101-336) was passed
by Congress in 1990, thus acting to further extend the laws against discrimination of disabled people set forth in 1973. In each of these laws,
deaf people have received benefits because legally they are considered
to be disabled. Those people who consider themselves to be culturally
Deaf, however, do not feel they fit in the disabled category, yet they
need legal recognition and support to offset the discrimination they
face as individuals who are different from the majority of American
society and to meet the needs they have as a linguistic minority.[1]

1. We label the culturally Deaf with a capital D. Anything referring to audiological status only uses the lowercase d—deaf. In addition, we assume that all
culturally Deaf students also use and espouse American Sign Language as
their preferred and natural mode of communication.

There has been an ongoing battle to reconcile the effects of being considered "disabled" and having "different" needs than the hearing majority. This battle plays out in very particular and peculiar ways in education, as one of the aforementioned laws—IDEA—actually seems to work against the needs of the Deaf children whom it intends to protect. It is the purpose of this chapter to explain the legal and cultural factors that cause this conflict. First, we review the current laws that shape educational choices for d/Deaf children. Second, we offer a brief historical overview of the American Deaf community in order to show how educational choices affect a child's ability to participate fully in this community. Third, we explore specific instances of flaws and injustices in current educational plans for Deaf children, using Lawrence Siegel's work on behalf of the National Deaf Educational Project (NDEP) as a framework.[2] We cite specific accounts of these injustices, demonstrating that IDEA is not, in practice, meeting the needs of most Deaf children in education today. Last, we present our thoughts on how to empower Deaf children and their parents to ensure that their rights are considered and safeguarded under the current laws of the land.

Current Law and Its Impact on Deaf Education

In the 1970s, the U.S. Congress enacted laws intended to abolish the unjust and discriminatory practices against individuals with disabilities. This landmark legislation includes the Rehabilitation Act of 1973 and the Education for All Handicapped Children (Public Law 94-142), passed in 1975, later known as the Individuals with Disabilities Education Act (IDEA). IDEA mandates that students who are identified via evaluations as having a disability have the opportunity to enroll in a special education program. Should the proposed educational program be accepted by the child's parents or legal guardians, a team of educational professionals, the parent(s), and sometimes the student convenes a meeting in which they discuss evaluations of the child, current academic and social-emotional levels (and other relevant developmental milestones and evaluations), performance in school, and any other specific needs that are indicated by the student's disability. In turn, this team develops an Individualized Education Plan (IEP).

---

2. Siegel (2000) argues that IDEA's provisions for students with disabilities neglect the cultural and linguistic needs of the Deaf child. As such, he suggests ways in which the law should be amended to serve Deaf children best.

During the IEP process, the IEP team will consider all the student's needs and come to a decision as to where the services will be implemented. By law, the team must consider the "least restrictive environment" (LRE), which is defined as follows:

> To the maximum extent appropriate, children with disabilities . . . should be educated with children who are not disabled, and . . . special classes, separate schooling, or other removal of children with disabilities from the regular educational environment should occur only when the nature or severity of the disability is such that education in regular classes with the use of supplementary aids and services cannot be achieved satisfactorily. (20 U.S.C. 1412(a)(5)(B))

In practical terms, this law mandates that children be placed in educational programs closest to their neighborhood school or closest to the educational path that they would have followed had they not been identified as having a disability. This mandate of "inclusion" is a triumph and a great leap toward equality for most children identified as disabled because it requires that they be included in the "mainstream" of education rather than segregated and hidden away. However, this mandate has wreaked havoc on the appropriate education of the Deaf child. The Deaf child has different linguistic needs than other children who are identified as disabled. Indeed, the Deaf community does not view deafness as a disability. Instead, Deaf people view themselves as a language minority group who are fully capable of functioning normally unless removed from a milieu that employs sign (American Sign Language [ASL]) for communication.

Legal Conflict for the Deaf Child: FAPE vs. LRE

In addition to promoting education in the LRE, schools are also mandated by Section 504 to provide a "free and appropriate public education" (FAPE) to all students who are identified as disabled. Initially, Section 504's concern was ensuring that students with disabilities were not discriminated against (29 U.S.C. 794). When IDEA was enacted, the federal government became the body that defined what was "appropriate." As cited above, the LRE requires that students be placed "to the maximum extent appropriate with their non-disabled peers" and states that "removal of children with disabilities occurs only when the nature or severity of the disability of a child is such that education classes with the use of supplementary aids and services cannot be achieved satisfactorily." (20 U.S.C. 1412(5)(B))

Although IDEA should be applauded for its effort to remedy the inequities between students "with disabilities" and students in "regular" education, its effects on the education of Deaf children have been disastrous. The Deaf child's linguistic and social needs are superseded by the notion of what is "least restrictive" and "appropriate." Because Deaf children have been labeled disabled under IDEA, the LRE, by default (according to the law) is inclusion with "non-disabled," or hearing, peers. However, culturally Deaf children would insist that they are not disabled; were they to be placed in an environment in which all linguistic needs are met—in which all could use and understand ASL— no disability would exist.

Meeting the linguistic and social needs of the Deaf child is crucial to his or her educational success; without access to ASL and Deaf peers, the Deaf child is relegated to a *de facto* "most" restrictive environment even though *de jure*, he is in the "least" restrictive environment. Lane, Hoffmeister, and Bahan (1996) explain that

> The LRE principles as interpreted by OSERS [Office of Special Education and Rehabilitative Services], the residential schools for the Deaf, which are a core element in the very identity of many members of the Deaf-World, and where the Deaf children of hearing parents may encounter peers and adults fluent in ASL for the first time, are referred to as institutions, and hence positioned at the bottom of the placement hierarchy. Second, most Deaf children require the use of a unique, visual language, which is the language neither of instruction nor of conversation in the preferred setting for the education of most children with disabilities, that is, regular public schools. (231)

Indeed, as we will detail below, the notions of LRE and FAPE, as determined by IDEA, are in direct conflict with the historical foundations and values of Deaf culture and the communities that support it.

HISTORY OF THE DEAF AND DEAF CULTURE

In the above section, we have articulated that those who identify themselves as culturally Deaf do not consider themselves to be disabled. However, to those who may not be well-versed in the cultural values and norms of American Deaf culture and the Deaf communities on which it thrives, the idea that deafness is not disabling may be puzzling (for details on Deaf cultures and communities, see Padden 1980). Thus, it is important to give some background and information on the history of the American Deaf community. We will suggest that the ideas and practices put forth by IDEA and LRE are inimical to Deaf culture because the law, as written, discourages the accumulation of a critical mass of Deaf students in any one educational setting. This critical mass is essential to meeting the social and linguistic needs of the individual Deaf students. Yet, because Deaf people have been misplaced under the disability umbrella of IDEA (instead of being seen as a linguistic and cultural minority), Deaf students in K–12 education in the United States are now scattered throughout programs on the LRE continuum instead of in classrooms composed of their true peers—other non-disabled Deaf students.

Deaf communities across the country comprise and feed into a collective sense of community into which Deaf people can travel with relative ease because they share common cultural values of deafness. Those who are considered to be part of Deaf culture "behave as Deaf people do, use the language of Deaf people, and share the beliefs of Deaf people toward themselves and other people who are not Deaf" (Padden 1980, 5). In essence, culturally Deaf people embrace two important things: their language—ASL—and the ability to use and express their language in social and educational settings that foster the use of this language.

Prior to the establishment of the American School for the Deaf in Hartford, Connecticut, in 1817, deaf people in the United States were scattered and had no specific and universally applied mechanism for education. Indeed, most deaf people lived in relative isolation from one another. Some families who had the means could send their deaf children abroad for education (Jankowski 1997, 20). Otherwise, with the exception of the Martha's Vineyard community, where there was a large deaf population (Groce 1985), there was no one way or place where deaf children would be educated or congregate.

The inception of the Deaf community occurred within a historical context that saw many improvements in the lives of the American people. Between 1815 and 1845 in the United States, "institutions displaced the traditional role of the family and transcended familiar, local authorities" for deaf people (Mattingly 1987a, 46). Based on the efforts of multiple benefactors, including Thomas Gallaudet, the first deaf school was established (now known as the American School for the Deaf in Hartford, CT). This school was a "locus for the energies of many disparate individuals, of resources from many locales," a factor that strongly influenced the formation and future of Deaf culture (Mattingly 1987b, 47).

Historically, the dominant group in society has had the rhetorical power to construct and label those who are "abnormal" as compared to those who are the norm, or "normal." The group that assumes the normal role then has rhetorical power to label and dominate the abnormal for its own benefit and to promote its own agenda (Foucault 1970). This kind of oppressor/oppressed dynamic also applies to the historical interactions among deaf and hearing individuals in caring for and educating deaf people. Deaf people were sent to residential schools (then known as asylums) as a means of keeping deaf people in the periphery of American society. In their isolation, deaf people were also given their own sort of autonomy in residential schools. Within the school community, deaf people were able to create a new "normal" that enabled them to be autonomous and empowered.

In these schools, deaf people relied on sign language for communication. The Deaf community revered the sign language (now known as ASL) that hearing people proclaimed to be abnormal communication. Indeed, sign language became the common bond among Deaf people, and the Deaf school was the locus for academic and cultural instruction. Jankowski (1997) explains that

> . . . while for most people school is primarily a place to secure an education, for Deaf people, school means much more. For many Deaf people, school is where they meet other Deaf people, often for the first time; at school they develop socialization patterns and friendships that frequently last throughout their lifetimes; there they meet spouses, acquire a language that accommodates their visual orientation, and become a part of a culture that extends beyond the school years. (19)

Jankowski (1997) summarizes how fundamental the Deaf school is to the Deaf community and Deaf culture as a whole by stating, "The educational system [for Deaf people] in its early years, offered an opportunity for Deaf people to build a community, and eventually became the mechanism through which the Deaf social movement would thrive" (19).

Historically, deaf individuals within the Deaf community were thrust together due to assumptions that deaf people need to be taken care of and/or kept out of sight. Although today, this kind of educational isolation is viewed as paternalistic and hegemonic, this means of educating deaf people is the historical cornerstone on which the Deaf community is founded, and it provides many rich memories of social and linguistic opportunities for Deaf individuals. Members of the Deaf community value the opportunity to socialize with one another and to communicate readily and directly—not through an interpreter—with their Deaf peers. As such, the essence of the Deaf community, a close-knit group that shares the same language, values, and beliefs on how to educate "their" deaf children, is inherently at odds with IDEA, a law that looks at deaf children as disabled individuals who have needs based not on social or linguistic factors but only on their audiological status. Furthermore, by looking only at audiological status, IDEA neglects the historical and social foundation of Deaf culture—the Deaf sense of community defined as having a critical mass of individuals with the same linguistic and communication needs. Until the needs of Deaf people as a linguistic minority are included in IDEA, Deaf students' individual needs will not be met, and their rights as a linguistic minority will be violated.

IDEIA, LRE, AND THE DEAF CHILD

In 2004, IDEA was scrutinized, supplemented, and then reauthorized by Congress and signed into law by President Bush. Henceforth, it became known as the Individuals with Disabilities Education Improvement Act (IDEIA). While there were amendments to and improvements in IDEIA that benefit districts, teachers, and students alike, the linguistic and social needs of the Deaf child were still not being met.

Members of the Deaf community, linguistic experts, and professionals with extensive knowledge of Deaf culture have long recognized that FAPE and LRE conflict with the needs of the Deaf child (e.g., see Lane et al. 1996, and Siegel 2000, 32). Lawrence Siegel (2000) documents such problems in the following accounts:

> In 1989, Dr. Larry Stewart testified before the U.S. House of Representatives, Sub-Committee on Select Education, that IDEA is "not being implemented properly—many deaf children have been neglected, sometimes to the point of mental and emotional abuse." A parent testified after Dr. Stewart that a regular classroom was a "nightmare" for her child; he was a "victim" of IDEA and the damage to him "irreparable." (32–33)

There are many problems that Deaf and hard of hearing children face on a daily basis at regular schools where they are "included" with "normal," hearing children. The authors have witnessed and document below some instances of what Siegel (2000, 18) calls "unacceptable" features of the current state of deaf education. We include only the features with which we have had direct experience. Although some of these failures exist throughout the LRE continuum, most occur in settings where there is an intermediary or barrier to direct instruction. This may be a result of inclusion and education via interpreter, or it may occur when another sign method (Signing Exact English [SEE], for example) is used instead of ASL. The fact that these anecdotes exist and are not unique to a particular city or region of the country is testimony to the fact that Deaf education, as we know it, is not working.

> 1. There are significant variations in age, cognitive skills, and language among children in existing classes for deaf and hard of hearing children. (Siegel 2000, 18)

In the multi-age, self-contained classes that the authors have observed, the age range can vary up to three to four years (depending on whether the child is an elementary or secondary student). If the children are grouped based on ability level, there is a potential for social stigma for the individual who is oldest, yet academically behind. He may be a nine-year-old in a classroom with some six-year-olds. While this kind of grouping might help the child catch up academically, socially and emotionally it leaves him embarrassed, which can lead to a disinterest and lack of motivation in school.

However, the lack of equal access to the target lesson and language is evident not just in an all-deaf class. Siegel (2000) documents Dr. Steven Nover's ethnographic study in which hearing children are exposed to exponentially more English than their deaf counterparts. He writes, "in classrooms in which there are hearing and deaf students and sign language interpreters, the hearing students were exposed to 15 times more English words than were the deaf students" (Siegel 2000, 18).

Many teachers, administrators, interpreters, psychologists, and other support staff are not adequately trained in, or knowledgeable about, deafness and the educational and communications needs of deaf and hard of hearing children. Many are not proficient in the child's communication mode/language. In addition, there is an insufficient number of professionals available to serve deaf and hard of hearing children (Siegel 2000, 19).

The authors have observed several teachers, mostly in mainstream settings, who have taught students in a self-contained (all-deaf) environment for years. In that time, many teachers have not made improvements or updated their ASL and Deaf culture awareness through workshops or social interactions. While professional development in "how to teach" deaf people (and topics related to deaf education) is mandated, the requirement that teachers meet a standard acceptable level of sign mastery is not.[3] For example, some school districts provide training to hearing teachers who want to understand how to properly utilize interpreters, how to better work with Deaf students, how to design their classroom to properly accommodate their Deaf students, and how to have a better understanding of Deaf culture. The fact that teachers may be signing a "language" that is not standard and is not the language used by their students is a non-issue to several district administrators with whom the authors have worked in the past.

Until recently, there have not been laws in place that regulate the quality of interpreters for Deaf people. This includes interpreters in public schools where Deaf students might be included in the regular education curriculum and roster. As a high school student in the early 1990s, the second author was fully mainstreamed with an interpreter in academic classes along with three Deaf classmates. The following is one of his experiences.

> Because the high school program at a local school for deaf people was disbanded, my Deaf classmates and I had to enroll in a public high school that offered deaf/hard of hearing classes and interpreters for students who wanted to be mainstreamed into "hearing" classrooms. At the time, there were about seventy-five Deaf and hard of hearing students, many of whom had been mainstreamed since they were in kindergarten. We were either enrolled in a deaf/hard of hearing classroom with a teacher who used sign language or mainstreamed partly or fully in regular academic classes. Four of us attended full-time regular academic classes along with other hearing students. Unfortunately, we experienced several incidents with unqualified interpreters.

---

3. Some schools (usually all-Deaf day or residential) require that their teachers meet the requirements of an ASL Proficiency Interview (ASLPI). They are required to have their abilities scored and documented and are monitored for progress in their language skills.

One time, in history class, the interpreter was unable to understand our signs well enough to translate them into spoken English. This interpreter could not fully or accurately interpret most of what the hearing students said during class, and most importantly what the history teacher lectured during the class. This resulted in the four of us understanding very little of what occurred in the classroom—vital exchanges of information between peers and educational lectures, comments, as well as anecdotes from the teacher were totally lost to us. We knew we had to have this interpreter removed. However, the administrators in the high school had never encountered a situation where Deaf students demanded a change in the interpreters because their needs were not being met. Ultimately, our families had to get involved and ensure that their request was heeded and met. Eventually, that interpreter was replaced with a more acceptable interpreter for the rest of the year. However, the former interpreter remained on the staff of the school.

This interpreter was not new to the school; there were students before us who endured weeks, maybe years, of misunderstanding and miscommunication. The students who preceded us probably did not know of their right to request a change of interpreters if they felt they did not understand the interpreters, or vice versa. Parents cannot be found at fault for not informing their Deaf children, because they may not have been told by school districts about their right to remove interpreters that have poor signing skills.

Almost ten years later, I returned to my high school on a work-related visit and was astonished to see this very same interpreter still on staff and working as an interpreter for students in mainstreamed classes. Through my conversation with this interpreter, it became clear that this person had not updated and enhanced her signing (either receptive or expressive skills) through ASL workshops or even attended any Registry of Interpreters for the Deaf (a national organization for registered and qualified ASL interpreters) trainings for professional development.

School districts frequently hire educational interpreters who are not certified or are unqualified to interpret for Deaf children in schools because of fiscal concerns. For example, a mother of a deaf child mentioned that she was upset to learn that her child's interpreter had inadequate training; this interpreter had taken only two basic ASL courses prior to interpreting for this child full-time in school. This lack of training is obviously unacceptable; not only did the interpreter not get the extensive training in the countless academic signs that she needed to master for effective classroom interpretation, she also did not have the courses in the interpretation major that would have trained her in the ethics of interpreting. The mother did not discover this atrocity until about three months into the school year. Even worse, this interpreter had never encountered a Deaf child prior to this assignment; in other words, this interpreter had never spoken to or practiced signing with a Deaf child prior to starting this very important job.

It takes an interpreter about seven years to be fully proficient in ASL and to complete her or his knowledge and understanding of Deaf culture in a satisfactory manner. Unfortunately, noncertified and underqualified interpreters are much cheaper to hire than fully certified and qualified interpreters. Fortunately, though, there are now laws throughout the country that require interpreters for Deaf people to register with the state before they can become paid interpreters. As a prerequisite for registry in Pennsylvania, for example, an interpreter must be certified by one of the national organizations for interpreters for Deaf people (Sign Language Interpreter and Transliterator State Registration Act 2004). This certification requirement precludes any interpreter from getting a paid position without the proper credentials, thus eliminating most situations like the ones above.

The authors have also seen teachers who were not certified to teach deaf children be hired and placed in charge of educating deaf students. One teacher explained that when he was hired to teach Deaf children in a public school (in an intermediate unit/magnet setting), he was certified, but not in Deaf education. He taught for many years under this setup. Another teacher we encountered openly admitted that when he was hired to teach deaf children in the 1970s, he had not one word of sign to his credit. He also said that the students taught him sign. How can learning happen when the "teacher" cannot understand or convey a simple concept to the students whom he is supposed to educate? Granted, these scenarios are relatively old and will no longer be a possibility now that No Child Left Behind is law. However, unfortunately, these stories are more prevalent than we would like to know. Imagine all the students who have experienced classrooms like this; the detrimental impact that these unqualified teachers have had on our Deaf children is incalculable.

2. There is inadequate parent support and training. (Siegel 2000, 19)

The inclusion programs with which the authors are familiar offer parents no training in understanding the cultural or linguistic needs of their Deaf child. In addition, there is no support for enabling their Deaf child to thrive as a culturally Deaf individual. Schools are focused on pathological perspectives and thus create IEP goals that focus on speech therapy and audiological status; however, with such a focus, educators and families of Deaf children forget there are other needs— linguistic and social—that feed into one's ability to access and thrive in an educational program. Training parents to meet all of the child's needs in an educational setting is crucial; provision of parent training must start when the Deaf child is identified and must continue throughout his educational career.

Deaf residential and day schools have traditionally had much stronger parental support and training opportunities than inclusion programs at neighborhood schools. One school for deaf people with which the authors are familiar is equipped with an array of counselors, psychologists, teachers, and Deaf mentors who specialize in working with Deaf children. These specialists are trained in outreach skills needed to educate and work with hearing parents of Deaf children. This school realizes that parent involvement in their children's education and lives is critical; they provide every mechanism to ensure parent involvement, including transportation and short-term incentives for involvement (i.e., food, a safe place to meet and learn new ideas, follow-up, and an opportunity to discuss how to continue positive, Deaf child-centered activities at home).

Many Deaf schools have their own early intervention programs, which often include free seminars in ASL and Deaf awareness to parents of Deaf children. Early intervention programs also dispatch teachers on home visits to households that have Deaf children, where they work on cognitive, social-emotional, and other developmental skills with those children. They also involve parents in those activities, provide emotional support for parents, and answer any questions they may have. Early intervention programs provide classes during school hours that both parents and children can attend, allowing for opportunities to learn from the early intervention specialists and early childhood educators at the school.

3. There is a lack of cultural/linguistic awareness and a failure to provide deaf and hard of hearing adult role models. (Siegel 2000, 19)

This factor applies mostly to the authors' observations and encounters in a mainstream or magnet school setting. The all-Deaf day and residential schools we have encountered encourage ASL in the classroom, in leisurely conversation, and in extracurricular activities. Indeed, with so many students and staff who sign—essentially, in the Deaf schools, everyone can sign—there are constant opportunities for students to be exposed to and access all "environmental" information—that is, information that is all around them, including both purposeful instruction and incidental learning, whereas, in the mainstream school, our personal contact with individually mainstreamed Deaf students tells us they may not have any exposure or access to sign, signing peers, or information about Deaf cultural experiences (see Oliva 2004).

The Deaf schools with which we are familiar require that all staff members undergo an American Sign Language Proficiency Interview (ASLPI) evaluation and have their scores recorded (for details on the ASLPI scale and the evaluation, see Gallaudet University n.d.). Staff that do not meet the intermediate level are provided an ASL mentor with whom they can practice and improve their ASL skills. They are also expected to take ASL classes to improve their abilities. Should a staff member not improve and meet the intermediate level within one to three years (depending on how long he or she has already worked there), he or she will not be rehired for the next school year.

While all-Deaf (student) day and residential schools tend to do a much better job at focusing on the cultural and linguistic needs of their Deaf students, they still contain a significant minority of Deaf role models in a leadership (teacher/administrator) role. Although having few deaf role models in leadership positions does not send as overt a message of "Deaf cannot succeed or make it in higher levels of management" as having no role models at all, it is still a factor that needs to be remedied and rectified in order to improve the self-worth and ambitions of Deaf children in this country.

Providing Deaf leadership and teachers/role models to boost Deaf student self-esteem is, in itself, a worthwhile goal, but Deaf students also need at least a contingent of Deaf teachers to facilitate academic learning. One person whom we interviewed said he and his friends always took advantage of the hearing teachers.

We could never take advantage of the Deaf teachers because they knew what we were thinking; they understood the Deaf-

World and Deaf tendencies. We had a lot of respect for Deaf teachers. Hearing teachers didn't understand us. They often pitied us and we knew it. They were thus more flexible and we took advantage of it easily. We could never get away with that with Deaf teachers. (Matthew Fisher, Deaf of Deaf parents, personal communication, March 15, 2006)

Of course, not all hearing teachers "pity" and are "flexible" with all Deaf students. However, many hearing teachers of Deaf people "go easy" on their students because they think they cannot reach a higher academic potential. Deaf teachers, on the other hand, feel no pity for their Deaf students; they were once in those students' positions and feel an obligation to educate their students to the highest potential possible.

4. There is insufficient access to extra-curricular and other non-classroom activities. (Siegel 2000, 19)

While academics are certainly the main component of K–12 education, extracurricular and nonclassroom activities also contribute significantly to a child's learning and social education. In her book *Alone in the Mainstream*, Gina Oliva (2004) emphasizes just how important extracurricular activities can be for the Deaf child. She writes, "The ostensible purpose of extracurricular activities is to provide an avenue for the development of friendships, skills, and self-esteem. They are opportunities to prove one's value to the group, a factor especially important to a deaf or hard of hearing child" (78). A student who may struggle—for various individual reasons—during the school day might, when given the opportunity, excel in after-school activities, thus providing what sometimes is the only school-related time that is positive for that child.

Not being able to participate in extracurricular activities is therefore probably the biggest missed opportunity for the Deaf child to prove himself successful to his peers and, perhaps, to himself as well. In one district, the authors have encountered egregious violations of Deaf children's civil rights regarding equal access to extracurricular and other nonclassroom activities. The violations seem to center on two issues: lack of provision of after-school transportation and lack of provision for interpreters to stay after school.

Deaf students are bussed in from across the county to attend the Deaf and hard of hearing programs of the district's magnet schools. Transportation is provided to and from school (often from dozens of miles away), but not after school. Very few students live near the school, and thus very few can get home should they wish to stay after school. This has resulted in an overarching inability of Deaf students to access such programs as extended day enrichment, sports, or summer school unless the children find transportation to and from school on their own. Indeed, those who could use the most help, those who are failing or otherwise behind, cannot get this much-needed assistance and tutoring because they live so far from the school where the Deaf and hard of hearing program is housed. As for the mandatory summer school attendance policy for students who are failing or not meeting the proficient level in standardized tests mandated by No Child Left Behind (for more information on the law, see No Child Left Behind Act of 2001), the district "remedies" the students' subsequent failures in subjects and possible nonpromotion to the next grade by waiving the summer school requirement for those students. Of course, these students fall further and further behind their peers; the lack of education and remediation compounds each time the student is pushed ahead a grade. These students are at risk of dropping out of school, where "at-risk" is defined as those who are experiencing failure, behaving poorly, or falling short of achieving their educational potential (Hallahan and Kauffman 1997). The most disheartening and disturbing part of this situation is that these students are at risk for failure and dropping out of school not because they do not wish to get help but rather because they have to choose between getting help and getting home.

Suppose a Deaf student manages to find a way to both stay after school and get home. His battle to access equal extracurricular support and leisure is not over yet; many students who rely on interpreters for communication with their teachers and peers do not have access to them after school. Interpreters in the district must have a contract with the school district for school hours, not after-school hours. If they are to stay after school to interpret for sports or any extracurricular activities, many will need to be paid overtime. Sometimes the district is not willing to pay the overtime, and sometimes they are unable to find an interpreter who is willing to stay past her contracted school day.

At a school for Deaf students, however, interpreters are unnecessary. The staff that run after-school and sports programs use ASL as their primary mode of communication, thus eliminating the need for interpreters. Students at the day school for Deaf people in our area are not required to find their own transportation should they want to participate in after-school activities; they are given access to transportation to and from school, including after school, should they choose to (or be required to) stay.

These failures to meet the educational needs of Deaf students constitute what the authors consider an offense to Deaf children's civil rights; if all of the Deaf child's needs—including linguistic, social, and cultural—were addressed by every IEP team, Deaf children would be placed overwhelmingly in settings that are more conducive to the support and growth of the aforementioned needs. In turn, the quality of their education and their educational lives would improve exponentially.

RECOMMENDATIONS: EMPOWERING DEAF CHILDREN'S RIGHTS

In *The Mask of Benevolence*, Harlan Lane (1992) suggests a need to "return to a Deaf-centered education" (165). He points out the merits of a maintenance bilingual educational system for Deaf people in which they would be educated in and learn the rules of their natural language, ASL, while building up and eventually mastering their second language, English. Lane highlights the need to restructure deaf education by "centering [it] on the deaf child rather than on the hearing teacher" (184). Ironically, the very essence of IDEA, the Individuals (and we emphasize the word) with Disabilities Education Act, attempts to shift the focus back to the student, creating an Individualized (and, again, we emphasize this word) Education Plan on which the student's educational future hinges. Yet, this individualized plan—developed by a team of school representatives, the parent(s), and the student himself—generally does not consider the social needs of the deaf child as per his place in what historically has been the foundation of the Deaf community, the Deaf school. Lane states, "the decision to construe and shape [the Deaf student's] fate in psychometric terms [or audiological ones] rather than historic ones is the most powerful determinant of that future it claims to predict" (82). The IEP in such a context might be student-centered, but not Deaf-centered. However, as we have argued above, the IEP for the Deaf child cannot benefit the Deaf student unless it is also Deaf-centered. A Deaf-centered IEP would look at the student's individual needs and recognize that he is a student from a linguistic minority who has a rich history and community that can support his educational development and success. No specially trained educator can take the place of the wealth of knowledge that comes from those who have mastered and use daily the Deaf child's language—ASL—and are fully immersed in the Deaf community.

How, then, can we reconcile the inherent flaws of IDEA and LRE for the Deaf child? Indeed, as we have shown above, in the current educational system, the Deaf child's civil rights are being violated as he is forced into an educational environment that is in no way linguistically or socially "least restrictive." Although we are advocates for the changes proposed by the NDEP, we do not feel that we can wait for the lawmakers and educators of the United States to make the aforementioned and recommended changes to meet the needs of the Deaf student. As such, we propose the following be considered when discussing the education of the Deaf child.

1. For children who are identified as needing ASL to communicate, it is essential that the students have ASL standards that they are expected to master (through IEP goals) and ASL standards that their teachers (those specializing in Deaf education) should meet in order to be considered "qualified" in their content area.

Should ASL be determined necessary for meeting the child's communication needs, that child should not only have the opportunity to use ASL in the educational setting, he should have the opportunity and requirement to master it. Overwhelmingly, Deaf children are not formally taught their native language, ASL. Schools for Deaf people have only recently begun to teach ASL formally to their students. IEPs and their goals are based on the identified needs of an individual child. If ASL is determined to be a need of that child, then why is it not included as a goal? Some schools do not include it because they do not have the resources—qualified teachers and funding—to teach ASL to a handful of students. However, should this be a true need of the child, they must, by law, find a way to provide the service to meet the child's needs. In our experience, children who need an ASL setting are referred to an all-Deaf day or residential school. However, students who use ASL and are in a magnet or total inclusion program should not miss out on the opportunity to learn their language formally. To ensure the formal instruction of ASL, it should be written into the IEP as a goal for the individual Deaf student.

Time and again, the authors have heard about and observed Deaf students who are, in theory, in an all-signing (full-/part-time Deaf/hard of hearing) educational setting but are not exposed to or taught in ASL. No Child Left Behind requires that educators be "highly qualified" in their field. The chances are extraordinarily high that any educator who specializes in teaching Deaf/hard of hearing students will teach at least one child who uses ASL. As such, for that teacher to be considered highly qualified, she should have proficiency in ASL, as determined by a sign language proficiency exam such as ASLPI or Sign Communication Proficiency Interview (SCPI). Having this qualification would significantly improve the educational prospects for Deaf children in education today.

2. Deaf students who do not use ASL as a primary means of communication should be exposed to ASL and culturally Deaf experiences as a part of their education.

Many deaf and hard of hearing children either themselves choose not to sign and be involved in the Deaf world, or their parents have decided that they do not need to be exposed to, or included in, the Deaf world. Whatever the reason, they do not use ASL or consider themselves to be part of the Deaf community, so exposure to ASL and Deaf cultural values will at least give the deaf children the tools needed to cope in whatever educational setting they find themselves. Indeed, knowledge of all possibilities, opportunities, and experiences will empower d/Deaf children so that they can make decisions rather than have decisions made for them. Gina Oliva (2004) captures the power that this d/Deaf child would have in the following interview with a mainstreamed deaf student. The student/informant says,

> I can envision an ideal life: Parents know sign language and are educated about Deaf culture. . . . They expose the deaf child to EVERYTHING: speech therapy, interpreters in school, a deaf school, hearing aids. They take the child to special deaf social events. . . . Just so that the deaf child will not be deprived of meeting others who are exactly like herself. I wish I had this ideal life. I'd be getting a perfect balance of deaf and hearing culture. And I can guarantee that . . . trying all these choices would definitely help me later in life to find what's comfortable for me. I would be choosing what works for me and what doesn't. And I'd be well rounded and happy. (86)

3. Deaf individuals should be schooled in settings in which they are part of a "critical mass" of Deaf students.

Although some may argue that social and cultural components of schooling are secondary to the direct instruction that a child receives, for the Deaf child, the social and cultural benefits of being a part of a Deaf community have a significant impact on academic success. When Deaf children have others with the same linguistic and cultural needs available to them within the school setting, they are less likely to be and feel isolated and are more likely to learn and use the language with which they are most comfortable—ASL. Of course, the more students who share the same Deaf cultural values and language, the better access and opportunity there is for all.

When Deaf children are schooled with other Deaf children, they have more opportunities to collaborate on projects and learn from peers. Students take in others' opinions and thus shape and form their own perspectives. One person whom we interviewed said that he very much valued the opportunity to interact and collaborate with other Deaf students for formal assignments and group projects. When in a self-contained class, he was able to access 100 percent of the information all the time. However, because there were very few mainstreamed classes that he shared with one or more of his Deaf peers, the opportunity to collaborate was very limited. He stated that there was no interaction on projects and very little communication or socialization with his hearing peers in his mainstreamed classes.

This same person had gone through almost the entire LRE continuum in his K–12 educational career. He started in an all-Deaf day school and then moved to a residential school in another state. He stayed there for eight years and then spent two of his high school years in another residential school. In his sophomore year, he decided he had had "enough" of being away from home and enrolled in the magnet school for Deaf students in his county. Interestingly, he came from a Deaf family; his parents sent him to the residential schools because they felt it would be the best educational option for him. The following is his opinion on what he would choose if he had the opportunity to redo his educational experience:

> For me, I would choose the mainstream [magnet program] experience. But, that is because I have a Deaf family and have had ample opportunity to interact with and learn the language and culture of the Deaf-World. I feel mainstreaming is for Deaf kids with Deaf families who already have Deaf culture and ASL exposure. For Deaf kids with hearing families, I feel they should go to all-Deaf day schools. They need that exposure to and knowledge of being Deaf that they don't get at home. (name withheld, personal communication, March 10, 2006)

One large magnet program for Deaf people in Orange County, California, has enjoyed the luxury of having the critical mass to provide its Deaf students with an exceptional academic and social experience. University High School's program has had at least 125 Deaf students for a number of years. Their numbers peaked at 150 students in 1993. Their Web site boasts of their strong sports teams, their Deaf-centered clubs, and their West region second-place finish in Gallaudet's Academic Bowl, a competition to promote the academic excellence of Deaf and hard of hearing students across the United States (University High School n.d.). Indeed, this school is evidence that with large numbers, Deaf students do thrive academically and socially in a mainstream setting.

Unfortunately, though, University High School is an exception, not the norm. Most magnet mainstream programs require the use of interpreters for most, if not all, of the school day. In theory, interpreters could capture a good portion of what is said during class. The reality, though, is that even the best interpreter cannot capture everything that is said; there are always side-conversations and simultaneous conversations that cannot be captured by one person. Unfortunately, not all interpreters in schools are qualified or certified. One of the men interviewed above made the following comments about his mainstream experience:

> The communication was a bit different than I usually got when I grew up in residential schools for the deaf. When I had to communicate through sign language interpreters, many were not able to interpret me most of the time. All of them were not certified interpreters, which is probably the reason why they couldn't understand my fluent and high-speed American Sign Language. I had to sign at below normal speed and frequently repeated the spelling or sign to be sure that the sign language interpreter understood what I wanted to say. (Matthew Fisher, personal communication, March 15, 2006)

4. All schools/districts that house programs for Deaf and hard of hearing people or districts that have at least one d/Deaf child enrolled in their schools should have parent and student training available that caters to the needs of educating and empowering d/Deaf students.

Because over 90 percent of parents with a Deaf child are hearing, there must be a significant effort to provide them with education about the cultural, linguistic, and social needs of their Deaf child. Exposure to the abilities of Deaf people and the benefits of Deaf-centered educational programs will endow parents with a clearer understanding of their child's unique needs. Parents of Deaf children and the Deaf students themselves must also be made aware of their rights. Receiving a copy of the *Procedural Safeguards* is not enough. This document, which contains twenty-plus pages listing advocacy groups and offering advice on how to proceed should one disagree with program recommendations, contains enough legal jargon to confuse any parent or student. For a Deaf student and his family whose first language is not English, it is virtually inaccessible. Deaf advocacy groups should be called on to elucidate these rights.

It is essential that there be training to ensure that parents feel they can learn about, feel welcome in, and be included in the Deaf community. Too often, hearing parents refer to Deaf people as "they" and view "them" (Deaf people) as a foreign group of which they have little knowledge or understanding. Many parents fear their Deaf child will be "lost" into the Deaf world and thus prevent children from learning ASL and socializing with their Deaf peers. Hearing parents must be made to feel that they are welcome to join the Deaf community along with their child. The mechanisms to implement such training are included in IDEA; parent training is mandated by the law. However, this training must be organized by a person or a group that has a Deaf focus. Deaf community outreach and education groups are the best resources for this training.

Parents are, in theory, the most powerful decision-makers on the IEP team; a program can be proposed, but they have the power to decide whether they agree or disagree with it. When parents have a more balanced view that includes knowledge of all the educational options available to their child, they will be able to advocate for a Deaf-centered program—one that has a critical mass of Deaf students with whom their child can interact, learn, and be Deaf.

Lastly, Deaf children should have opportunities to learn about themselves to ensure they are acknowledged and empowered within any school setting. Most of this knowledge comes from being exposed to the ways of culturally Deaf people. However, opportunities to learn about themselves and their rights as students protected under IDEA should be incorporated into their educational programs. Deaf students can be exposed to cultural and political activities such as Deaf Awareness Week and Junior NAD, but unless they have an understanding of what their needs and rights are, they cannot take full control of their education. While it is true that most teenagers, deaf or hearing, do not take full advantage of all educational opportunities they are afforded, unless Deaf children are made aware of these rights, they are not fully equipped to analyze and advocate for their own needs. As such, the authors feel that workshops should be instituted specifically for Deaf students that inform and remind them of a key component of IDEA: that the child's placement and program are determined by his or her individual needs. These needs are based not only on psychometric or audiological assessments, but also on social, linguistic, and cultural requirements for accessing the child's education. These needs are not static; they evolve as the child grows and goes through the educational program. If at any time children feel their needs are not being met, they, too, have a right to call an IEP meeting to discuss their progress or lack thereof. They and their parents have a right to disagree with the school or the local educational agency about their proposed or current educational program. Should they disagree, there are specific legal steps that the family can take to remedy or rectify this conflict. In essence, these workshops will empower students and allow them to take control of their educational destiny, a power that very few Deaf or disabled students currently experience.

5. At the request of the Deaf student or his parents, Deaf advocates should be available for consultation on any decision that would potentially impact his education. These Deaf advocates should be available to consult on various levels in the educational process, from individual IEP decisions to state and federal policy initiatives.

There have been a few particular and egregious instances where the education and lives of Deaf children were uprooted because of a lack of Deaf cultural representation and advocacy.[4] In these instances, the individual and collective needs of the Deaf children were not considered; instead, external audist agendas were foisted on the children's educational trajectory, potentially throwing them off course educationally (and cultur-

---

4. Two particular instances come to mind: First, the removal of a Deaf child from his Deaf parents' custody almost resulted in cochlear implantation at the request of a judge and against the biological parents' wishes; second, the Nebraska School for the Deaf was closed by the State Department of Education with little to no consultation and input from the Deaf community. See McClellan (2002) and National Association of the Deaf (1998).

ally) for life. This cannot and should not happen. Should a Deaf child be removed from a Deaf family, especially if this removal is temporary, there should be a Deaf advocate present to support and maintain the child's cultural and linguistic needs as per his or her current IEP and Deaf family's wishes. Furthermore, any policy considerations that would impact the options for educating Deaf students should include input that is representative of the Deaf community's perspective.

CONCLUSION

The current law responsible for ensuring the proper education of Deaf students—IDEA—is inherently in conflict with the educational needs of the Deaf child. The premise of LRE, by law, gives preference to and advocates for an educational placement that is the equivalent of isolation for the Deaf child—in a neighborhood school with his "non-disabled peers." In the neighborhood school, and even, to some extent, in a magnet school with other Deaf children, the Deaf child experiences restricted access to the use of his natural language, ASL. In addition, she or he becomes schooled in a socially restricted environment, one that is counter to the historical tendencies of the Deaf community and the basic human need to interact with people with whom one can identify and relate, not to mention communicate, without restrictions.

Indeed, the authors have seen first-hand the negative effects of educational placement outside of the all-Deaf educational setting as a "first resort" and not a "last resort." We have reported to you such effects and the impacts they have had on Deaf individuals and on the Deaf community as a whole. We are not saying that all deaf people belong in one place. Instead, we ask that the IEP teams truly consider all needs of the d/Deaf child, including linguistic, social, and cultural needs. Only in this way can they make an appropriate and fitting placement.

Although we feel that Deaf people do not fit under the category of "disabled," as defined by the law, we do recognize that Deaf people need accommodations and support to prevent discrimination and to ensure appropriate educational placement. In addition, we recognize that our country and the lawmakers that represent us have a long way to go before they change current legislation so that the disability label is removed from Deaf people and our needs are still met. Therefore, we have proposed several specific mechanisms that consider the linguistic, social, and cultural needs of d/Deaf people and serve to empower individual students to decide how best to meet these needs.

REFERENCES

Foucalt, M. 1970. *The order of things: An archaeology of human sciences*. New York: Vintage.

Gallaudet University. n.d. Center for ASL Literacy. http://gradschool.gallaudet .edu/casll/gu-aslpi.html (accessed April 3, 2006).

Groce, N. E. 1985. *Everyone here spoke sign language: Hereditary deafness on Martha's Vineyard*. Cambridge, Mass.: Harvard University Press.

Hallahan, D. P., and J. M. Kauffman. 1997. *Exceptional learners*, 7th ed. Needham Heights, Mass.: Allyn and Bacon.

Individuals with Disabilities Education Act of 1975 (originally *Education of All Handicapped Children Act*). Public Law 94-142.

Jankowski, K. A. 1997. *Deaf empowerment: Emergence, struggle, and rhetoric*. Washington, D.C.: Gallaudet University Press.

Lane, H. 1992. *The mask of benevolence: Disabling the Deaf community*. New York: Knopf.

Lane, H., R. Hoffmeister, and B. Bahan. 1996. *Journey into the DEAF–WORLD*. San Diego: Dawn Sign Press.

Mattingly, P. H. 1987a. History: Reform in provincial America. In *The Gallaudet encyclopedia*, ed. J. Van Cleve, 46. Washington, D.C.: Gallaudet University Press.

———. 1987b. History: Evangelical origins of reform. In *The Gallaudet encyclopedia*, ed. J. Van Cleve, 47. Washington, D.C.: Gallaudet University Press.

McClellan, T. D. 2002. Deaf mom fights to keep kids from ear implants. *Grand Rapids Press*. September 6. http://www.bridges4kids.org/articles /9-02/GRPress9-6-02.html.

National Association of the Deaf. June 1998. Historic rally held on Nebraska school for the deaf graduation day. http://www.nad.org/site/pp.asp? c=foINKQMBF&b=178020 (accessed April 5, 2006).

No Child Left Behind Act of 2001. Public Law 107-110. http://www.ed.gov /policy/elsec/leg/esea02/beginning.html#sec2 (accessed April 5, 2006).

Oliva, G. 2004. *Alone in the mainstream*. Washington, D.C.: Gallaudet University Press.

Padden, C. 1980. The Deaf community and the culture of Deaf people. In *Sign language and the Deaf community: Essays in honor of William C. Stokoe*, ed. C. Baker and R. Battison, 89–104. Silver Spring, Md.: National Association of the Deaf.

Siegel, L. 2000. The educational and communication needs of Deaf and hard of hearing children: A statement of principle regarding fundamental systemic educational changes. In *American Annals of the Deaf* 145(2): 64–77.

Sign Language Interpreter and Transliterator State Registration Act of 2004. Public Law 492, No. 57 Cl. 63.

University High School: Deaf and Hard of Hearing. n.d. http://www .uhstrojans.net. (accessed April 3, 2006).

5 Inclusion and the Development of Deaf Identity

MICHAEL STINSON

One controversial issue in the education of deaf and hard of hearing children is whether these children should be educated in public schools as opposed to specialized residential or day schools. Another controversy involves whether an inclusive approach should be used with these children placed in public schools as opposed to a mainstream approach. With respect to the first question, the mainstreaming of deaf and hard of hearing students in public schools was given an impetus in the 1970s by the language in Public Law 94-142 (Education of All Handicapped Children Act). The law calls for a free appropriate public education (FAPE) for all children with disabilities. The removal of students with disabilities from public schools would be justified only when satisfactory educational results for those students could not be achieved otherwise. The law placed educational environments on a continuum with respect to restrictiveness, where home school and residential programs were rated most restrictive and placement in regular classrooms was rated least restrictive. The preference was to educate students in the least restrictive environment. In practice, mainstreaming resulted in a large percentage of deaf and hard of hearing students being educated in separate resource or self-contained classrooms in public schools—not necessarily in regular classrooms with hearing peers (Antia, Stinson, and Gaustad 2002).

Traditionally, residential schools have effectively socialized students to become comfortable with Deaf culture. Deaf adults serve as role models and may help children to identify positively with Deaf people. The residential school is the setting where deaf children and youths acquire the values of and come to identify with the Deaf community, in good part through the introduction of a common way of communicating—American Sign Language (ASL). For deaf children, especially those with hearing parents, contacts with other deaf children and with deaf adults may contribute significantly to their acquisition of Deaf culture and a positive view of deafness (Foster 1996; Leigh and Stinson 1991; Stinson and Foster 2000). Members of the Deaf community (including this author) have repeatedly stated that specialized schools are often the more desirable option for a deaf child (National Association of the Deaf 1994; Stinson and Lang 1994; Stone 1994).

This chapter, however, does not focus on these students in specialized schools, but on the large group of deaf and hard of hearing students who are being educated in their local public schools. Data from the Annual Survey of Deaf and Hard of Hearing Children and Youth (Gallaudet Research Institute 2005; Karchmer and Mitchell 2003) show that during the 2000–2001 school year, 75% of all deaf or hard of hearing students were reported to attend public schools, and in the 2004–2005 school year, 63% spent some portion of the school day in classrooms in which most of the students were hearing. Since 1977, there has been a steady increase in the numbers of students attending mainstream classrooms (Holden-Pitt and Diaz 1998).

This chapter addresses three specific issues regarding these deaf students' education in public schools: (a) The first issue is the difference between the practice of inclusion and the theory of inclusion; (b) the second issue is the patterns of social identity of deaf people; and (c) the third issue is the relationship between inclusion and the development of personal identity.

Conceptions of Inclusion

Inclusion and mainstreaming are educational practices in public schools that may be examined from two perspectives: philosophy and placement.

Philosophically, the difference between mainstreaming and inclusion is that mainstreaming implies that the child will adapt to the regular classroom, whereas inclusion implies that the regular classroom will adapt to the child. To successfully mainstream a child, it is necessary to evaluate the child's readiness to function within the hearing classroom. In a mainstream setting, the classroom teacher is a gatekeeper, turning away children who are unable to function within the existing classroom structure and curriculum. In contrast, in an inclusive setting, the classroom practices are expected to change to accommodate individual children. Another philosophical division between the two concepts is classroom membership. Mainstreaming implies that deaf and hard of hearing students are visitors in the regular classroom, whereas inclusion implies that these children are members of the regular classroom (Stinson and Foster 2000).

In programs that promote membership, school personnel act under the assumption that the deaf or hard of hearing student is a full member of the classroom with rights and responsibilities identical to those of the other students; thus, the practices of the classroom must accommodate him, as well as other students in the class (Bassett et al., 1996). The deaf or hard of hearing student's instructional needs are seen as being different from those of some students and similar to others. She may be different from other students because she is the only one who must have a sign language interpreter, but she is similar to other students in that she benefits from clear and frequent visual presentations of curricular material (Antia et al. 2002).

Membership generally implies full-time rather than part-time participation in the classroom, but the perspective here, in contrast to some (Tucker 1989), is that full-time placement is not synonymous with inclusion, nor is full-time placement in the regular classroom a sufficient condition for membership. A school culture that strongly promotes inclusion, and that has a shared vision of inclusion of all students, can promote perceptions of membership despite part-time placement in general education classrooms. On the other hand, the attitudes of, and relationships among, educational professionals and among students themselves can be such that membership is elusive no matter how much time the deaf student spends in the general education classroom (Antia et al. 2002; Lieber et al. 2000).

In the 1980s, the Regular Education Initiative, discussed in Jenkins, Pious, and Jewell (1990), provided the impetus to inclusion. Policy makers expressed concern that having two separate systems of education (special education and general education) was not effectively serving students with disabilities, and calls were made to develop a single system of education that would serve all students (Antia et al. 2002;

Reynolds, Wang, and Walberg 1987). Reformers suggested that all students be educated in regular classrooms in their neighborhood schools with appropriate special education services being provided within the classroom (Antia et al. 2002; Biklen, Lehr, Searl, and Taylor 1987; Wang and Walberg 1988).

Shifting now to the perspective of placement in examining inclusion and mainstreaming, the key issue is the physical setting in which children receive their education. From this perspective, inclusion implies that students who are deaf or hard of hearing receive all or most of their education in the regular classroom. Mainstreaming implies that these students receive their education in the regular public school, but not necessarily within the regular classroom. Thus, children can be mainstreamed into the regular classroom for math or art or recess but may attend a resource room or a self-contained classroom for the remainder of the school day. The term *mainstreaming* can refer to a broader range of placement options than does *inclusion* (Stinson and Antia 1999).

Inclusion in Theory and in Practice

The mere belief that inclusion involves membership is not, of course, sufficient to promote membership of deaf children in an inclusive classroom. For true membership to occur, teachers need to interact with the students in a manner that makes the students genuine members of the class. For this to occur with deaf children, there needs to be use of two languages, ASL and English, as well as an appropriate balance of deaf and hearing children, regular opportunities to interact with deaf adults, and continuous exposure to Deaf culture (Antia et al. 2002). In recent years, a few exceptional situations that promote membership of deaf children have occurred, but typical situations in which deaf students are educated in classes with hearing students for all or almost all of the school day do not promote membership in this manner (Kirchner 1994; Kreimeyer, Crooke, Drye, Egbert, and Klein 2000). An additional concern is that there be sufficient numbers of deaf children for students to have choices in social relationships with deaf peers and opportunities to explore various options in relationships (Stinson and Foster 2000).

Deaf students have much in common with their hearing peers. They share basic human needs for education, for friendship, for identity and self-esteem, and for membership in a community (Gaustad 1999). Studies have shown that negative attitudes exist toward deaf students both before and after hearing students have had contact with them (Cappelli, Daniels, Durieux-Smith, McGrath, and Neuss 1995; Weisel 1988). Misconceptions and stereotypical beliefs among hearing students are common (Blood and Blood 1983; Gaustad 1999). For example, hearing students may interpret a deaf student's failure to respond to them because she did not hear them, as an indication that the deaf student is lazy or stupid (Stinson and Liu 1999). If deaf students are to become full members of the regular classroom, more than ordinary efforts must be made by teachers and by other professionals to improve and facilitate the instructional interaction that occurs in classrooms. This involves removing stereotypes about deafness by providing knowledge about deafness, hearing loss, and Deaf culture; arranging within the instructional setting purposeful and cooperative activities that provide realistic and productive roles for both hearing and deaf participants; and, finally, providing both hearing and deaf students with strategies for interacting with one another (Antia 1985; Antia et al. 2002; Foster and Walter 1992; Gaustad 1999; Kluwin and Stinson 1993). Stinson and Liu (1999) suggest strategies that can facilitate successful interaction between deaf and hearing students. Often deaf or hard of hearing students who are viewed by educators as having an inclusive experience are those who are placed in regular classrooms in a local neighborhood public school. In actuality, these students usually do not have an inclusive experience in which true membership occurs. Usually in this type of program, students are enrolled in their local neighborhood school, attend classes with hearing students, and are often visited by an itinerant teacher who provides special instruction. These students, however, often do not experience full access to communication, especially informal communication, with hearing students in activities such as recess, or the same level of acceptance by hearing peers that hearing peers show toward each other (Stinson and Foster 2000). Typically, there are a small number of students in these programs, often only one.

For students who are educated in classes with hearing students, the most common form of communication in the classroom is spoken English. To follow the classroom discourse, these students rely on speechreading, aided by residual hearing with hearing aids, or, increasingly, a cochlear implant. Many students use frequency modulated (FM) systems in which the teacher wears a wireless microphone that sends a direct signal to the child's hearing aid (Johnson 1998).

Support services in mainstream classes, such as interpreters, notetakers, and speech-to-text services, increase access to formal, in-class communication (Antia, Sabers, and Stinson 2007). Interpreters sign and mouth the words as the teacher or other students speak them so that they are more understandable. Speech-to-text services are growing in popularity, but are used considerably less than interpreters (Bervinchek and Bolesky 1998; Elliot, Foster, and Stinson 2002). With this system, the in-class service provider produces a real-time display of the classroom dialogue in printed English, which the student typically sees on a computer screen at his or her desk. The issues of whether these services are appropriate and whether interpreters are certified or adequately qualified are continuing concerns.

Even when support services are good, students may still have difficulty communicating, participating, and learning in the mainstream classroom (Stinson and Antia 1999; Stinson and Kluwin 2003). The lag time of two to six seconds between the teacher's spoken word and the corresponding signing of that information contributes to difficulty in class participation, because hearing students may have already responded in the interim (Stewart and Kluwin 1996). Interviews with students and observations in classrooms indicate that barriers to classroom participation include the rapid rate of discussion, rapid turn taking, rapid change of topics, the high number of people involved in the discussion, and more than one student talking at a time (Saur, Layne, Hurley, and Opton 1986; Stinson, Liu, Saur, and Long 1996).

The quality of communication experiences in school depends upon both program and individual characteristics. The lone deaf student in the mainstream setting may be more exposed to these difficult experiences than those who are in specialized schools or regional mainstream programs that enroll a good number of deaf students. Also, a child with a moderate hearing loss may be able to adjust to the situation of being the only child with a hearing impairment in a school better than one with a profound hearing loss. Nonetheless, students with moderate hearing impairment often have academic and social difficulties in mainstream settings (Kreever 2002).

With respect to peer interactions of deaf students in programs in which all or most of their education is in classes with hearing students, concern has been expressed that a frequent consequence of this placement is social isolation, rather than integration, primarily because of communication difficulties. Students may experience feelings of loneliness because they cannot easily participate in social activities with hearing peers due to the lack of a common language both hearing and deaf feel comfortable with (Foster 1989). Informal social conversations are most difficult for deaf students to access and the most resistant to intervention by professionals and support service personnel (Ramsey 1997). Once students are in the hallway, in the lunchroom, or on the bus, they are usually on their own regarding communication with peers. An interpreter might be acceptable during a biology lab but would not be welcome when students gather at the back of the school to sneak a cigarette and share weekend plans. As a result, deaf children educated in a hearing classroom often report only limited or superficial conversations with peers (Foster 1989; Mertens 1989). Research on students educated in public schools suggests that students with a range of hearing loss experience an absence of close friendships (Antia and Kreimeyer 2003; Stinson and Antia 1999; Stinson, Whitmire, and Kluwin 1996; Tvingsted 1993).

To summarize, inclusion in theory focuses on how the classroom can be changed to accommodate an individual student so that the student is able to participate fully as a member of the class. In practice, many students, including those who are deaf, and who are viewed by educators as having an inclusive experience, do not have one that is truly inclusive. Students in such a setting often have limited communication access, variable levels of difficulty interacting with hearing peers, and limited or no contact with deaf peers and adults. These experiences may hinder development of identification with deaf students, and also with hearing ones.

DEVELOPMENT OF IDENTITY IN DEAF INDIVIDUALS

Identity development is largely concerned with the establishment of a personal definition of one's self. Part of this consolidation of self involves the definition, integration, and evaluation of various attributes that one has. It also involves defining the various roles and identities that one will take on within social groups and within society at large. This narrowing down and specification of self-definition and the assumption of specific roles that will be continued into adulthood is a major psychological task of adolescence (Harter 1999); some researchers, such as Erikson (1980), argue that this process of identity development is the most significant task of adolescence.

Social and Personal Identity

An important distinction exists between *social identity*, or identity with respect to a reference group, and *personal identity* (Cross 1987). The social or reference component of identity has to do with the question of "Where do I belong?" One's cultural and/or ethnic experiences are clearly important to identity formation. For individuals who are deaf or hard of hearing, attitudes toward other deaf people and toward hearing people, preference for social interaction with deaf and hearing people, and extent of identification with deaf and hearing people pertain to reference group identity (Maxwell-McCaw, Leigh, and Marcus 2000). The other dimension of identity, personal identity, centers around the individual's uniqueness. This component answers the question "Who am I?" Personal identity is concerned with defining one's own special nature. It is the particular ideas, beliefs, and feelings that make each individual's personal identity unique. Personal identity is also concerned with establishing one's direction in life. The pertinent questions are "What do I want to do in my life?" and "What kind of person do I want to be?" These questions are answered, in part, by observing the role models available through one's reference or social group.

The distinction between social and personal identity may be important in helping deaf individuals and other minority groups in establishing connections with various social groups. Research has demonstrated that the distinction helps minority group members maintain high self-esteem in the face of negative attitudes toward that group from society at large (Harter 1999), and the distinction may help deaf individuals similarly.

Cultural Identity of Deaf and Hard of Hearing Individuals

There has recently been some discussion of the extent to which deaf and hard of hearing individuals identify with Deaf and hearing cultures. This discussion falls within recent work on classification of persons according to different acculturation categories that have been used with different ethnic groups (Aponte and Barnes 1995; Leigh, Marcus, Dobosh, and Allen 1998; Maxwell-McCaw 2001). Two approaches to social identity are the racial identity model and the acculturation/bicultural model. The racial identity model proposes that there is a series of stages in the development of identity; furthermore, the healthiest stage of identity development is that in which the individual achieves primary identification with others in the same cultural group (e.g., Deaf), but is able to establish relationships with the dominant culture and have an objective perspective on that culture (Maxwell-McCaw

2001). On the way to achieving this stage, an individual progresses through a stage in which he or she affirms identity with one's ethnic or cultural group (e.g., Deaf) and rejects identification with the dominant culture (e.g., hearing; Glickman 1996). In contrast, the acculturation/bicultural model views the development of two (and possibly more) cultural identities as independent of each other. This model focuses primarily upon the extent to which the individual acquires behavioral participation, cultural competence, and attitudes of a culture. This model is not concerned with the intra-psychic healthiness of levels of acquisition of a culture (Maxwell-McCaw 2001).

Both models describe identification with a cultural subgroup and with a dominant culture (e.g., with Deaf culture and with hearing society, which can be regarded as a culture although it is not usually called one; Glickman 1996; Maxwell-McCaw 2001). Either the racial identification or acculturation/bicultural model may be used to classify deaf individuals into four cultural groups: (a) culturally hearing, (b) culturally marginal, (c) culturally Deaf, and (d) bicultural (Glickman 1996; Maxwell-McCaw 2001). While Glickman (1996) views the four categories as stages in development of identity, Maxwell-McCaw (2001) views them as the result of arbitrary cutoffs in the continuums of the dimensions of Deaf and hearing acculturation.

Culturally hearing. These individuals score relatively high on the Culturally Hearing subscale of the Deaf Identity Development Scale (DIDS; Glickman 1996) or relatively high on the Hearing Acculturation subscale of the Deaf Acculturation Scale (DAS; Maxwell-McCaw 2001) and relatively low on the Deaf Acculturation subscale of the DAS that measures identification with Deaf culture. These individuals may show little interest in associating with deaf peers, have developed limited or no proficiency in ASL, and may not be involved in or have knowledge of the cultural activities of the Deaf community. They may value oral means of communication and may be relatively successful with it. They may not emphasize the significance of deafness as part of one's identity.

Culturally marginal. These individuals score relatively high on the Marginal subscale of the DIDS or low on the Hearing and Deaf Acculturation subscales of the DAS. These individuals may not be comfortable or feel at home with either deaf or hearing groups. These individuals may lack communication and social skills for functioning in a reasonable way with either group (Leigh and Stinson 1991).

Culturally Deaf. These individuals have relatively high scores on the Immersion subscale of the DIDS or high scores on the Deaf Acculturation subscale and low scores on the Hearing Acculturation subscale of the DAS. These individuals have positive views of Deaf culture and deaf peers and may have little interest in interactions with hearing peers. These individuals may show considerable interest in participating in the cultural activities of the Deaf community. They are proficient in using ASL and are likely to have learned it at an early age; furthermore, they may show little interest or proficiency in development of oral skills (Glickman 1996).

Bicultural identity. Bicultural individuals have relatively high scores on the Bicultural subscale of the DIDS or high scores on both the Deaf and Hearing Acculturation subscales of the DAS. These individuals have some degree of social comfort with both d/Deaf and hearing peer groups. Individuals in this group may be committed to sign language and embrace Deaf culture, but they may also value and feel comfortable with hearing people who are seen as supportive. The concept of biculturalism implies that it is possible for one to simultaneously know and understand groups that are associated with different cultures. This concept assumes that an individual can alter his or her behavior to fit the social context (LaFromboise, Coleman, and Gerton 1993).

Foster and Kinuthia (2004) conducted a qualitative study of deaf persons with Asian American, Hispanic American, and African American backgrounds and concluded that patterns of identity of deaf people are more complex than a two-dimensional deaf-hearing orientation model. They emphasized the need to incorporate ethnic minority considerations into conceptions of deaf people's identity and also the importance of recognizing the fluidity of identity. Identity is a function of the individual's response to a given situation as well as the personal characteristics that the person brings to that situation.

Factors Related to Patterns of Identity

Research has identified respondents' hearing status, parental hearing status, communication background, and educational experience as factors that are associated with particular patterns of identity development. With respect to respondents' and parents' hearing status, Leigh et al. (1998) administered a version of the DIDS to 244 adults who were deaf, hard of hearing, and hearing, and whose parents were either hearing or deaf/hard of hearing. They found that identity, as indicated by scale scores, depended on whether the person was hearing, hard of hearing, or deaf, and also on whether the individual's parents were deaf or hearing. Individuals who were hearing or hard of hearing had higher scores on the Hearing identity scale than did those who were deaf. Individuals who were deaf had higher scores on the Immersion subscale than did those who were hearing or hard of hearing. Leigh et al. (1998) also found an interaction between the effects of individuals' own hearing status and that of their parents on ratings on the Culturally Hearing, Marginal, and Immersion identity scales. For example, individuals who were deaf or hard of hearing, and who had deaf parents, had different mean ratings on the Culturally Hearing, Marginal, and Immersion identity scales, but individuals who were deaf or hard of hearing who had hearing parents had mean ratings on these scales that were not significantly different from each other. The results of the Leigh et al. (1998) study show that different groups with different family backgrounds and different affiliations on a deaf-hearing continuum have different patterns of cultural identity.

Maxwell-McCaw (2001) obtained findings consistent with those of Leigh et al. (1998) in that the hearing status of parents influenced a deaf child's identity. For example, if parents were deaf, most respondents were classified as having Deaf or bicultural acculturation.

In regard to communication characteristics, Maxwell-McCaw (2001) reported that age of learning sign was related to acculturation patterns. Participants who learned sign at an early age had a higher level of Deaf acculturation that those who learned sign after age 21.

Stinson and Kluwin (1996) also obtained findings that support a relationship between communication skills and identity in a study of social orientation of deaf and hard of hearing adolescents in public schools. This study focused on orientation toward socializing with deaf peers, hearing peers, both deaf and hearing peers, or neither deaf nor hearing peers. The social orientation measure used by Stinson and Kluwin (1996) appears to assess a relationship dimension, which is one of a number of dimensions that are included in the DAS (Maxwell-McCaw 2001). The DAS has Deaf and Hearing Acculturation scales. Each of these scales has five subscales: cultural identification, cultural participation, cultural attitudes, cultural knowledge, and language competence. The cultural attitudes subscale includes several items that ask about relationships. Stinson and Kluwin (1996) conducted statistical analyses to identify factors that differentiated among students in the four social orientation groups. They found that degree of hearing loss and perceived signing skill differentiated among three groups: the deaf-oriented, the hearing-oriented, and those oriented to both or to neither group. On average, hearing-oriented students rated themselves as least skilled in signing and had the least severe hearing losses. Deaf-oriented students rated themselves as most skilled in signing and had the most severe hearing losses. Students who were socially oriented to both groups and those who were oriented to neither group rated their signing proficiency at a level between the two extremes; the severity of hearing loss for this group was also between the extremes.

Educational experience also relates to identity. This connection will be discussed in the third section of this chapter, which deals with the relationship between placement and development of identity.

Psychological Health and Identity

What is the relationship between the psychological health of deaf people and patterns of identity? Writers have suggested that a marginal identity pattern, in particular, may not be psychologically adaptive (Maxwell-McCaw 2001; Phinney 1992). Maxwell-McCaw (2001) found that respondents with Deaf or bicultural acculturation had the highest mean scores on self-esteem and satisfaction-with-life measures in her study of deaf adults and youths. The mean scores on these measures for the two groups were not significantly different from each other. Respondents classified in the hearing acculturation group had mean self-esteem and quality-of-life scores that were somewhat lower, at statistically significant levels, than those for the Deaf and bicultural groups. Respondents in the marginal group had mean self-esteem and quality-of-life scores that were dramatically lower, at statistically significant levels, than those for the other three groups.

Bat-Chava (2000) conducted a study of 267 deaf adults and classified them as culturally hearing, culturally Deaf, or bicultural. The study did not include a culturally marginal group. She grouped participants on the basis of responses regarding the importance of sign, the importance of speech, group identification, and attitude toward deaf people. She also included a measure of self-esteem. She found that mean self-ratings of self-esteem were lower for those in the culturally hearing group than for those who were culturally Deaf or bicultural, but that the differences between groups were not statistically significant.

Jambor and Elliot (2005) administered a survey to seventy-eight deaf students at California State University, Northridge. The survey included a measure of group identification with Deaf individuals as an independent variable and a measure of self-esteem as a dependent variable. They found that identification with culturally Deaf people was associated with higher self-esteem at a statistically significant level.

Although there were some differences in the results for these three studies, the overall findings indicate that development of a d/Deaf identity is associated with positive self-esteem. Differences in results may be due to variation in assessment approaches, differences in the characteristics of the participants, or a combination of the above.

INCLUSION AND DEAF INDIVIDUALS' IDENTITY

Educational experience plays an important role in the development of one's identity. Social connection to peers at school, whether in informal cliques or membership in formal extracurricular activities, is essential to the development of the students' social identity. The pattern of social identity that one adapts is likely to depend partly on the extent to which relationships with various social groups have been rewarding or discouraging. For example, individuals who are comfortable with sign language may feel a closer bond to people who are Deaf as a social group because shared ways of communication are basic to social relationships and social identity. By joining school activities such as sports and clubs, students become engaged in their school communities and develop a sense of civic responsibility. Positive peer experiences help to develop self-esteem and a feeling of connection to a larger social group (Stinson and Foster 2000; Stinson and Whitmire 2000). These experiences are likely to occur more easily with deaf peers and, as a result, social bonds with these peers may be more likely to develop. In addition, exposure to Deaf adults may contribute to development of a d/Deaf identity.

Enrollment in Local Neighborhood Schools and Development of Identity

Although, in theory, a student in a program with an inclusive philosophy may be able to develop a positive d/Deaf identity, in practice, placement of a deaf student full-time or nearly full-time in the regular classroom rarely provides good opportunities for this development.

The frequent consequence of educational placement of a deaf student based upon an inclusive approach is that the student ends up in the local neighborhood school as the only deaf student or with a few similar peers. Usually, the local neighborhood school does not provide interaction with deaf peers and adults or opportunities to learn about Deaf culture and community. Placement in the neighborhood school may also fail to provide good opportunities for the student to develop strong bonds with hearing peers even though the deaf student is constantly surrounded by these individuals.

Writers have commented on the difficulty that deaf students in local schools have in developing a d/Deaf identity. Oliva (2004) notes how deaf individuals educated in local schools miss contact with other deaf peers who use signs; furthermore, parents of these students often encourage their child to participate in activities with hearing, as opposed to deaf, individuals. Writing about his counseling experiences with deaf children and youths, Glickman (1996) suggests that the establishment of identity with deaf and hearing social groups is often a complex task for deaf adolescents who have been mainstreamed. On the one hand, contact with the family, neighborhood, and school is predominantly with hearing individuals. On the other, it is generally easier for deaf individuals to communicate and establish friendships with each other. They may struggle in their efforts to clarify their affiliation with Deaf and hearing cultures. This struggle includes difficulty in developing a conception of themselves as a d/Deaf person, in defining the nature of the relationships they have with other deaf persons, and also in their relationships with hearing individuals (Stinson and Foster 2000).

Students in local public schools may be unlikely to develop a cultural perspective that views deafness positively and may regard ASL, in part, simply as a mode of communicating that relies on visual input for getting information rather than auditory input (although this can be provided to some extent with hearing aids or cochlear implants; Leigh and Stinson 1991). The following quotation from Charlson, Strong, and Gold (1992) illustrates some of the difficulty an adolescent may have in establishing an identity as either a deaf or a hearing person:

> I don't like the fact that I have trouble talking to people. It seems like people look at me as a hearing person, but in reality, I'm really not. But I think I act like a hearing person, but I

think I can call myself hard of hearing in some ways because I think I'm in between deaf and hearing, I'm in between them. (264)

It can be argued that local neighborhood schools provide the same exposure to the culture at large as hearing students and, thus, provide the best opportunity to develop the skills and personal resources in the larger (hearing) society. However, difficulty with communication access, especially in informal social situations, may make formation of close friendships with hearing peers difficult (Stinson and Foster 2000).

Research Pertaining to Education in Local Public Schools and Development of Identity

Maxwell-McCaw (2001) investigation. The limited research supports the connection between educational experience and development of d/ Deaf identity. In investigating Deaf and hearing acculturation, Maxwell-McCaw (2001) examined the relationship between education placement and patterns of identity. She asked students to report their educational backgrounds with respect to the following categories: (a) hearing school without support, (b) mainstreamed with support (e.g., interpreter), (c) self-contained classroom, (d) oral school for the deaf, (e) day school for the deaf, and (f) residential school. Thus, the first category (a) provided the most extensive experience with hearing peers and adults, and the last (f) provided the most extensive experience with deaf peers and adults. She found that, in general, the more the respondents' exposure to hearing individuals, the higher their score on the Hearing Acculturation subscale, and the more the respondents' exposure to deaf individuals, the higher their score on the Deaf Acculturation subscale.

Of particular relevance here, Maxwell-McCaw (2001) examined the educational backgrounds of individuals who were classified into the four acculturation groups. In regard to placement in local schools, the two groups in the study who had this experience were those who attended hearing schools without support and those who were mainstreamed with support services. The majority of respondents that she classified as hearing acculturated attended hearing schools without support; in addition, the majority of individuals that she classified as marginal attended either hearing schools or an oral deaf school at the elementary level and a residential deaf school at the high school level.

That is, both the hearing and marginal acculturated groups did not develop strong identification with deaf peers.

In contrast, individuals who attended a mainstream program (which meant that they received support services, such as interpreting) com- prised the largest group of respondents with bicultural acculturation and the second largest group with hearing acculturation. Thus, when some components of the school experience, such as a support service or teacher of the deaf, explicitly incorporated the fact that the students were deaf, even if the students attended a local public school, these students were more likely to include Deaf acculturation in their identity.

Stinson and colleagues investigations. Stinson and his colleagues conducted a series of studies on the social relationships of adolescents who are deaf or hard of hearing in mainstream settings (Kluwin and Stinson 1993; Stinson and Whitmire 1991, 1992; Stinson et al. 1996), including programs in the United States, Canada, and England. Their findings suggest that the quality of the relationships that these stu- dents establish depends on the extent of mainstreaming, specific char- acteristics of the setting, and personal characteristics of the student. In particular, students who were most often placed in classes with hear- ing peers had greater difficulty establishing relationships with deaf peers. Although these studies did not focus specifically on develop- ment of deaf and hearing identity, they provide insight regarding stu- dents' desires for contact with deaf peers and perceived limitations in opportunities to do so. These desires for social connections appear as- sociated with the cultural-attitudes component of identity suggested by Maxwell-McCaw et al. (2000).

These studies used self-reports of perceptions of social relation- ships that included the dimensions of participation, emotional security, and need for closer relationships. Participation was measured by self- reports of frequency of involvement in various social interaction activi- ties in school (e.g., helping other students in class) and out of school (e.g., visiting a friend's home). Emotional security was measured as a perception of positive stability in relationships, such as reporting that one feels "happy" and "relaxed" in relationships with peers (Connell 1990; Stinson and Whitmire 1992). The need for closer relationships was an attitude expressed in statements such as "I wish I had more friends who were hearing (or deaf/hard of hearing)."

Across these studies, deaf and hard of hearing adolescents rated themselves as interacting more frequently with deaf and hard of hearing peers overall than with hearing peers (Stinson et al. 1996). However, ratings changed with the extent to which students were mainstreamed. A large number of students were primarily in self-contained placements but went out for a single academic class, such as math, or for a nonacademic class, such as gym or art. Fewer, but still a substantial number, were mainstreamed for two or more academic classes. Ratings of participation with deaf peers decreased from the least frequent level of mainstreaming to the most frequent one. The changes in participation may have partly reflected opportunities for interaction, since the most frequently mainstreamed students had greater interaction with hearing peers and less interaction with deaf peers.

As with the ratings for participation, hard of hearing students assigned higher overall ratings for emotional relatedness with deaf or hard of hearing peers than with hearing peers. That is, both the ratings for participation and relatedness indicated a more favorable response to deaf peers than to hearing peers. The pattern of ratings as a function of mainstreaming, however, was different. Ratings of relatedness with deaf peers increased with greater mainstreaming, in contrast to the ratings of relatedness with hearing peers, which did not change as a function of mainstreaming. These results, in conjunction with those for participation, suggested that these frequently mainstreamed students were more comfortable in their relationships with deaf peers, but that they interacted significantly less with these peers, compared to their less frequently mainstreamed schoolmates.

This pattern of results suggests that many mainstreamed students have unmet needs for close relationships, a sense of belonging in a peer group, and having "real" in-depth extended conversations (Foster 1989). Although they report being more comfortable in relationships with deaf classmates, they are often placed in an environment in which the only social relationships available are with hearing peers, with whom they may experience rejection and neglect (Gresham 1986). These unsatisfactory experiences may take a toll in terms of low self-esteem and decreased satisfaction with social interactions.

The need for closer relationships with deaf peers increased significantly with age. Older students expressed a high need for closer relationships with deaf classmates, suggesting a developmental change in identification with and commitment to the deaf social group. Thus, with age, deaf adolescents may have stronger needs for contact with one another and for opportunities to learn about Deaf culture.

CONCLUSION

Placement of a deaf student full time in the regular classroom with hearing peers in a neighborhood school rarely provides good experiences for development of a d/Deaf identity because the setting does not provide interactions with deaf peers and adults and opportunities to learn about Deaf culture and the ways of d/Deaf people. Research evidence supports this proposition. The more deaf students interact with deaf peers and adults, the more likely they are to develop a d/Deaf identity (Maxwell-McCaw 2001). Furthermore, research has found that deaf students who were placed primarily in regular classes with hearing peers wanted relationships with deaf peers even though they did not have the opportunity to have them (Stinson et al. 1996). Because experience in relationships with members of a social group is important in developing a bond with that social group, this lack of opportunity may hinder development of d/Deaf identity.

Suggestions for Practice

If an inclusive program is to foster positive d/Deaf identity, it is important that the program include opportunities for contact with deaf adults and many deaf peers. Local programs will not include desirable opportunities for interaction with other deaf individuals except in the unusual situation in which the local public school includes a regional mainstream program for deaf students. Regional educational or centralized programs for deaf students usually are not inclusive in the sense of placing most of their students in classes with hearing peers for most of the time, but they may provide a better option for development of a positive d/Deaf identity. These programs are also likely to have other positive features, including sufficient numbers of deaf and hard of hearing peers to permit choice in friendship; various Deaf culture activities, such as a junior National Association of the Deaf and Deaf theater; and activities for both deaf and hearing students, such as sign language classes and clubs (Banks 1994; Kluwin and Stinson 1993).

Educators and parents can take several steps, in addition to provision of support services, to promote the development of a d/Deaf identity by students who are enrolled in local neighborhood schools. One option is to arrange for the student to move between two placements on a regular basis—that is, attend a specialized school for part of the day and join a mainstream class for the other part of the day. If neither a regional mainstream program nor sharing of time between two programs is an option, it is important to provide the deaf student contact with deaf peers and adults outside the regular school environment. Options include attending special activities, which may range from sports festivals to tutoring at a specialized school; participating in deaf sports clubs; attending summer camps for deaf students; and joining online chat groups with deaf peers. When individuals have opportunities such as these, they may more comfortably develop a deaf identity, instead of struggling to do so.

REFERENCES

Antia, S. D. 1985. Social integration of hearing impaired children: Fact or fiction? *Volta Review* 87(6): 279–89.

Antia, S. D., and K. H. Kriemeyer. 2003. In *Oxford handbook in deaf studies, language and education,* ed. M. Marschark and P. Spencer, 164–76. New York: Oxford University Press.

Antia, S., D. Sabers, and M. S. Stinson. 2007. Reliability and validity of the classroom communication questionnaire. *Journal of Deaf Studies and Deaf Education* 12(2): 158–71.

Antia, S. D., M. S. Stinson, and M. G. Gaustad. 2002. Developing membership in the education of Deaf and hard of hearing students in inclusive settings. *Journal of Deaf Studies and Deaf Education* 7(3): 214–29.

Aponte, J. F., and J. M. Barnes. 1995. Impact of acculturation and moderator variables on the intervention and treatment of ethnic groups. In *Psychological treatments and cultural diversity,* ed. J. F. Aponte, R. Y. Rivers, and J. Wohl, 19–39. Boston: Allyn & Bacon.

Banks, J. 1994. *All of us together: The story of inclusion of the Kinzie school.* Washington, D.C.: Gallaudet University Press.

Basset, D. S., L. Jackson, K. A. Ferrell, J. L. Luckner, P. J. Hagerty, T. D. Bunsen et al. 1996. Multiple perspectives on inclusive education: Reflection of a university faculty. *Teacher Education and Special Education* 19(4): 355–86.

Bat-Chava, Y. 2000. Diversity of Deaf identities. *American Annals of the Deaf* 145(5): 420–28.

Bervinchak, D., and C. Bolesky. 1998. *Real-time captioning: Equal access for deaf students.* Unpublished manuscript.

Biklen, D., S. Lehr, S. J. Searl, and S. J. Taylor. 1987. *Purposeful integration . . . inherently equal.* Syracuse, N.Y.: Center on Human Policy, Syracuse University.

Blood, L., and G. Blood. 1983. School-age children's reactions to deaf and hearing-impaired children. *Perceptual and motor skills* 57: 373–74.

Cappelli, M., T. Daniels, A. Durieux-Smith, P. J. McGrath, and D. Neuss. 1995. Social development of children with hearing impairments who are integrated into general education classrooms. *Volta Review* 97(3): 197–208.

Charlson, E., M. Strong, and R. Gold. 1992. How successful deaf teenagers experience and cope with isolation. *American Annals of the Deaf* 137(3): 261–70.

Connell, J. 1990. Contexts, self and action: A motivational analysis of self-system processes across the life-span. In *The self in transition: Infancy to childhood*, ed. D. Cicchetti, 61–97. Chicago: University of Chicago Press.

Cross, W. 1987. A two-factor theory of black identity: Implications for the study of identity development in minority students. In *Children's ethnic socialization*, ed. J. Phinney and M. J. Rotheram, 117–22. Newberry Park, Mass.: Sage Publications.

Elliot, L. B., S. B. Foster, and M. S. Stinson. 2002. Using notes from a speech-to-text system for studying: Research on deaf and hard of hearing high school and college students. *Exceptional Children* 69(1): 25–40.

Erikson, E. 1980. *Identity and the life cycle*. New York: W. W. Norton Press.

Foster, S. 1989. Educational programs for deaf students: An insider perspective on policy and practice. In *Integration: Myth or reality?* ed. L. Barton, 57–82. London: The Falmer Press.

Foster, S. 1996. Communication experience of deaf people: An ethnographic account. In *Cultural and language diversity: Reflections on the deaf experience*, ed. I. Parasnis, 117–35. New York: Cambridge University Press.

Foster, S., and W. Kinuthia. 2004. Deaf persons of Asian American, Hispanic American, and African American backgrounds: A study of intra-individual diversity and identity. *Journal of Deaf Studies and Deaf Education* 8(3): 271–90.

Foster, S., and G. Walter. 1992. *Deaf students in post-secondary education*. London, England: Routledge.

Gallaudet Research Institute. December 2005. *Regional and national summary report of data from the 2004–2005 Annual Survey of Deaf and Hard of Hearing Children and Youth*. Washington, D.C.: GRI, Gallaudet University.

Gaustad, M. G. 1999. Including the kids across the hall: Collaborative instruction of hearing, deaf and hard of hearing students. *Journal of Deaf Studies and Deaf Education* 4(3): 176–90.

Glickman, N. S. 1996. The development of culturally Deaf identities. In *Culturally affirmative psychotherapy with Deaf persons*, ed. N. S. Glickman and M. A. Harvey, 115–53. Mahwah, N.J.: Lawrence Erlbaum Associates.

Gresham, F. 1986. Strategies for enhancing the social outcomes of mainstreaming: A necessary ingredient for success. In *Mainstreaming handicapped children: Outcomes, controversies, and new directions*, ed. C. J. Meisel, 141–73. Hillsdale, N.J.: Lawrence Erlbaum.

Harter, S. 1999. *The construction of the self: A developmental perspective*. New York: Guilford.

Holden-Pitt, L., and J. A. Diaz. 1998. Thirty years of the annual survey of deaf and hard-of-hearing children and youths: A glance over the decades. *American Annals of the Deaf* 142(2): 72–6.

Jambor, E., and M. Elliott. 2005. Self-esteem and coping strategies among deaf students. *Journal of Deaf Studies and Deaf Education* 10(1): 63–81.

Jenkins, J. R., C. G. Pious, and M. Jewell. 1990. Special education and the regular education initiative: Basic assumptions. *Exceptional Children* 56(6): 479–91.

Johnson, C. 1998. *Amplification in inclusive classrooms*. Unpublished manuscript.

Karchmer, M., and R. E. Mitchell. 2003. Demographic and achievement characteristics of deaf and hard-of-hearing students. In *Oxford handbook of deaf studies, language, and education,* ed. M. Marschark and P. E. Spencer, 21–37. New York: Oxford University Press.

Kirchner, C. J. 1994. Co-enrollment as an inclusion model. *American Annals of the Deaf* 139(2): 163–64.

Kluwin, T. N., and M. S. Stinson. 1993. *Deaf students in local public high schools: Backgrounds, experiences, and outcomes.* Springfield, Ill.: Charles C. Thomas.

Kreever, E. M. 2002. *Peer relations of hearing-impaired adolescents.* Unpublished doctoral dissertation. University of Toronto, Toronto, Canada.

Kreimeyer, K. H., P. Crooke, C. Drye, V. Egbert, and B. Klein. 2000. Academic and social benefits of co-enrollment model of inclusive education for deaf and hard-of-hearing children. *Journal of Deaf Studies and Deaf Education* 5(2): 174–85.

LaFromboise, T., H. L. K. Coleman, and J. Gerton. 1993. Psychological impact of biculturalism: Evidence and theory. *Psychological Bulletin* 114(3): 395–412.

Leigh, I. W., A. Marcus, P. Dobosh, and T. Allan. 1998. Deaf/hearing cultural identity paradigms: Modification of the Deaf Identity Development Scale. *Journal of Deaf Studies and Deaf Education* 3: 327–38.

Leigh, I. W., and M. S. Stinson. 1991. Social environment, self-perceptions, and identity of hearing-impaired students. *Volta Review* 93: 7–22.

Lieber, J., M. J. Hanson, S. L. Odom, S. R. Sandall, I. S. Schwartz, E. Horn et al. 2000. Key influences on the initiation and implementation of inclusive preschool programs. *Exceptional Children* 67(1): 83–98.

Maxwell-McCaw, D. L. 2001. *Acculturation and psychological well-being in deaf and hard of hearing people.* Unpublished doctoral dissertation. George Washington University, Washington, D.C.

Maxwell-McCaw, D., I. Leigh, and A. Marcus. 2000. Social identity in Deaf culture: A comparison of ideologies. *JADARA* 33: 14–27.

Mertens, D. 1989. Social experiences of hearing-impaired high school youth. *American Annals of the Deaf* 134: 15–19.

National Association of the Deaf. 1994. Statement on full inclusion. In *Implications and complications for deaf students of the full inclusion movement,* ed. R. C. Johnson and O. P. Cohen, 78–79. Washington, D.C.: Gallaudet Research Institute.

Oliva, G. A. 2004. *Alone in the mainstream: A deaf woman remembers public school.* Washington, D.C.: Gallaudet University Press.

Phinney, J. 1992. The multiethnic identity measure: A new scale for use with diverse groups. *Journal of Adolescent Research* 7(2): 156–76.

Ramsey, C. L. 1997. *Deaf children in public schools: Placement, context, and consequences.* Washington, D.C.: Gallaudet University Press.

Reynolds, M. C., M. C. Wang, and H. J. Walberg. 1987. The necessary restructuring of special and regular education. *Exceptional Children* 53: 391–98.

Saur, R. E., C. A. Layne, E. A. Hurley, and K. Opton. 1986. Dimensions of mainstreaming. *American Annals of the Deaf* 131(5): 325–30.

Stewart, D., and T. N. Kluwin. 1996. The gap between guidelines, practices, and knowledge in interpreting services for deaf students. *Journal of Deaf Studies and Deaf Education* 1(1): 29–39.

Stinson, M. S., and S. Antia. 1999. Issues in educating deaf and hard of hearing students in inclusive settings. *Journal of Deaf Studies and Deaf Education* 4(3): 163–75.

Stinson, M. S., and S. Foster. 2000. Socialization of deaf children and youths in school. In *The deaf child in the family and at school*, ed. P. Spencer, C. Erting, and M. Marschark, 151–74. Mahwah, N.J.: Lawrence Erlbaum Associates.

Stinson, M. S., and T. N. Kluwin. 1996. Social orientations towards deaf and hearing peers among deaf adolescents in local public high schools. In *Understanding deafness socially* (2nd ed.), ed. P. Higgins and J. Nash, 113–34. Springfield, Ill.: C. C. Thomas.

Stinson, M. S., and T. N. Kluwin. 2003. Educational consequences of alternative school placements. In *Oxford handbook in deaf studies, language and education*, ed. M. Marschark and P. Spencer, 52–64. New York: Oxford University Press.

Stinson, M. S., and H. G. Lang. 1994. Full inclusion: A path for integration or isolation? *American Annals of the Deaf* 139(2): 156–59.

Stinson, M. S., and Y. Liu. 1999. Participation of deaf and hard of hearing students in classes with hearing students. *Journal of Deaf Studies and Deaf Education* 4(3): 191–203.

Stinson, M. S., Y. Liu, R. Saur, and G. Long. 1996. Deaf college students' perceptions of communication in mainstreamed classes. *Journal of Deaf Studies and Deaf Education* 1(1): 40–51.

Stinson, M. S., and K. Whitmire. 1991. Self-perceptions of social relationships among hearing-impaired adolescents in England. *Journal of the British Association of Teachers of the Deaf* 15(8): 104–14.

Stinson, M. S., and K. Whitmire. 1992. Students' views of their social relationships. In *Towards effective public school programs for deaf students: Context process and outcomes*, ed. T. N. Kluwin, D. F. Moores, and M. G. Gaustad, 149–74. New York: Teachers College Press.

Stinson, M. S., and K. Whitmire. 2000. Adolescents who are deaf or hard of hearing: A social psychological perspective on communication and educational placement. *Topics in Language Disorders* 20: 58–73.

Stinson, M. S., K. Whitmire, and T. N. Kluwin. 1996. Self-perceptions of social relationships in hearing-impaired adolescents. *Journal of Educational Psychology* 88: 132–43.

Stone, R. 1994. Mainstreaming and inclusion: A deaf perspective. In *Implications and complications for deaf students of the full inclusion movement*, ed. R. C. Johnson and O. P. Cohen, 66–72. Washington, D.C.: Gallaudet Research Institute.

Tucker, J. A. 1989. Less required energy: A response to Danielson and Bellamy. *Exceptional Children* 55(3): 456–58.

Tvingsted, A. 1993. *Social conditions of hearing-impaired pupils in regular classrooms* (monograph no. 773). Malmo, Sweden: University of Lund, Department of Education and Psychological Research.

Wang, M. C., and H. J. Walberg. 1988. Four fallacies of segregationism. *Exceptional Children* 55(2): 128–37.

Weisel, A. 1988. Contact with mainstreamed disabled children and attitudes towards disability: A multidimensional analysis. *Educational Psychology* 8(3): 161–68.

6 | Deaf, Signing, and Oral: A Journey

Lisa Herbert

This chapter will cover many of the people, places, and situations that have shaped me into who I am today as a Deaf, signing, oral, and self-sufficient individual. I am very proud of the journey I have taken this far, and I am still a work in progress.

My life began in Montreal, Quebec, Canada, in 1980. I was born hearing into a family consisting of my mother, father, and older sister, as well as our extended family members. My father is from Trinidad, West Indies, and my mother was born and raised in Montreal. We moved to Miami, Florida, when I was three years old. I was walking, talking, doing all the things a three-year-old does. My favorite movie was *Annie*, which I watched all the time. I enrolled in the nursery school program at the Heritage School of Kendall, a suburb of Miami. About a week after my fourth birthday, which was a grand affair with a piñata and a visit from my grandparents, I became ill with a high fever and was taken to the hospital. I was diagnosed with bacterial meningitis and treated with intravenous antibiotics. Shortly after, my mother pointed out to the doctors that I was not responding to sound, and although I was communicating, it was not in direct response to questions or conversation. She convinced them to conduct hearing tests, and I was diagnosed with a profound hearing loss. The cause was not determined: Was is it the antibiotics, the ear infection, or the destruction of the auditory nerve from bacteria? After a two-week stay, I was still weak, but well enough to go home.

Upon arriving home, I immediately went to my record player to listen to my *Annie* album. I suppose I knew for certain that this was something that produced music and would tell me what exactly was going on, since I was not hearing anything else. I said to myself as well as to my mother, "I know I will hear this," but I did not. My parents scheduled a complete assessment with a diagnostic center in Miami where two days of evaluation confirmed a profound hearing loss. Bilateral hearing aids were ordered. The audiologists, psychologists, and speech therapists assured my parents that because I was very smart, I could return to school and continue as usual after being fitted with the hearing aids. Fortunately, my parents recognized that with no hearing, a regular classroom setting would place serious constraints on my ability to continue learning. They began the search for a deaf education program and were disappointed with what was available in Miami. The closest school for deaf students was a good five hours away in St. Augustine, Florida. They then asked my aunt, one of many family members living in Montreal, to investigate options there. The two options presented were the MacKay Center for Deaf and Crippled Children (a signing program) and the Montreal Oral School for the Deaf (MOSD). The latter was considered a better option, because I already had developed speech and auditory skills, and they wanted to continue me on this path.

I enrolled in MOSD in the summer of 1984, starting in the nursery summer camp. I can still remember the warm faces there and feeling connected to my peers. My memories of MOSD, where I stayed through kindergarten, are mostly positive. I remember plays, field trips, and picnic lunches; but at the same time, I recall feeling detached from those around me in terms of communicating. I have a few memories of crying or feeling sad when I did not do something that was expected of me, such as answering a direct question. Did I not understand, or was I too shy? I cannot remember. I do recall that I enjoyed speech therapy and pleasing the teacher. This does not mean that I was talkative in school; my kindergarten teacher, Jane Kelly, once believed that I was not able to talk at all. My mother had to tape-record me being a "chatterbox" at home and present the tape as evidence. Ms. Kelly even came to my house and could not believe that it was I yapping with my sister, Stacey, upstairs in my room.

However, it got to the point where my speech became so unintelligible that only my mother could understand me. Although I had hearing aids, my hearing loss was so profound that I received no benefit from them. This was particularly evident during my kindergarten year, when I was mainstreamed in the morning at a private school, The Study, with hearing peers, and transported in the afternoon to MOSD for an afternoon program. This is often the case with oral schools where the purpose is early intervention and the development of speech and listening skills, as well as advocacy skills, to prepare a child for the subsequent mainstream setting. My oral deaf kindergarten classmates attended mainstream schools in the morning as well, in their school districts. I do not have many memories of this year, other than having a close friend named Chloe, our green uniforms, and walking up a steep hill to school. At the end of this year, my parents and staff at MOSD began to discuss the next most appropriate step, most likely learning a visual language such as Quebec Sign Language (known as Langue des signes québécoise [LSQ]), or American Sign Language [ASL], at the MacKay Center for Deaf and Crippled Children. The principal of MOSD at the time, Dr. Agnes Phillips, had another idea; she suggested that my parents look into the possibility of me getting a cochlear implant. At this time, cochlear implants were still experimental on children, and I would be among the first 200 children to be implanted at the House Ear Institute in Los Angeles, California, by Dr. Howard P. House. My parents decided to go with this option, and we began the process of getting me a single-channel cochlear implant, with no guarantee of success. I had been considered a good candidate for the cochlear implant because I had a profound hearing loss and was postlingually deaf with a strong language foundation before I lost my hearing. Rehabilitation would not be as difficult for me as for someone born deaf or deafened as a baby.

My parents, sister Stacey, and I traveled to Los Angeles in the summer of 1985. There was a boy my age at the House Ear Institute who was also getting a cochlear implant, and we became friends. To celebrate, my family took a trip to Disneyland days after the surgery. My only memories are before the surgery, when I refused to drink something orange (antibiotics?) unless Stacey drank it too. To help me feel better, the nurses gave her orange Kool-Aid; I noticed that hers tasted better than mine!

With the cochlear implant, I then returned to MOSD and was integrated into a first-grade class at my local elementary school, St. Francis of Assisi, where I was the only deaf child. An itinerant teacher from MOSD, Cheryl Ruediger, visited me there several days per week to work with me outside of class on speech, self-advocacy, reading, and writing. My grandfather drove by the school during the day to see if I was okay when on the playground. In a few short months, my speech skills had improved, as well as my speechreading skills, no doubt due to the auditory information that I received from the implant, and possibly my auditory memory from the early years of hearing. As it was explained to my parents, the electrodes in the implant stimulated my auditory memory and also gave me feedback so that I regained some of my speech and language skills. Follow-up visits were made to the House Ear Institute every six months for two years because I was part of a Food and Drug Administration (FDA) study.

The cochlear implant was very beneficial to me, because the speech information I did receive (i.e., consonants, vowel sounds, syllabic stresses, intonation, volume, etc.), together with speechreading, assisted me in developing my receptive skills. In addition, I could hear my name being called, a doorbell ringing, horns honking, and the beat of music. However, with this single-channel model; I could only hear limited frequencies and could not hear any high-frequency sounds at all, making it impossible to comprehend without speechreading. As my speech improved dramatically, to the point where I could again be understood by strangers, I would say that it was worth it.

My teacher in my first-grade class at St. Francis had a deaf relative, and so was actually quite sensitive to my needs. She used the FM system in the classroom, which amplified her speech through my implant microphone. In spite of this, I was not as comfortable as I had been at MOSD and asked if I could return there for the second grade. My parents agreed immediately and arranged for my enrollment at Westmount Park School (WPS) for grade two, where MOSD housed a number of programs. There were sufficient students at my grade level (about six or seven) at MOSD to make up a discreet self-contained class at WPS, which was integrated with other students in the school for various activities (e.g., choir). It was not that I was not advancing properly at St. Francis, falling behind, or a showing lack of progress; I transferred to WPS simply for my comfort level and so that I could get the most out of school and have my social network. I really have to credit my parents with "following my lead" in any decisions that impacted my education and growth as a person. In all the decisions that they made, they clearly considered my strengths that could be built upon and did not look at my hearing loss as something to be "fixed." Their decisions were about how to help me succeed, thrive, and function in a way, and in a place, that I could do this comfortably.

For second grade, I transferred to WPS. I loved being in the self-contained class with my former MOSD classmates again. The class was so diverse: Indian, Italian, Portuguese, Jewish, and Chinese students. I remained there for the second through fourth grades and had a very typical educational experience. Our teacher, Penny Packard, who was trained as a teacher of deaf students and affiliated with MOSD, was wonderful about meeting our educational and communication needs. We learned from *Hooked on Phonics*; wore FM systems; and took music, gym, and math class, among others, with our WPS hearing classmates. We also sang in the school choir, where our respective amplification devices allowed us to carry a tune and follow the rhythm. I was the only student in my class with a cochlear implant. My classmates and I were sometimes asked to be on panels for conferences, such as those of the Alexander Graham Bell Association for the Deaf and Hard of Hearing, to share our experiences. We were a very close-knit class; one of our fondest memories is of reading a book together, *The Secret Garden*, following along as each of us read, to build literacy and listening skills.

Not only that, but my mother read to me nearly every night, while I wore the cochlear implant and followed along with the book. We would also make memory books of our family vacations and read them aloud. I have always been an avid reader, and this has helped me academically. Outside of school, I was involved with several community activities. These included activities such as Girl Guides, ice-skating, dance classes, art classes, and piano lessons. This did much to build my self-confidence as I developed several different skills and built relationships with those around me. Like most children, I avoided practicing piano, but my mother insisted I complete the program until I received my intermediary certificate. We still laugh about one of the numbers I played: "The birdlings are singing to me. . . . Of nature so wondrous and free . . ."

Sometime during my years at WPS, Ms. Packard suggested to my parents that I might want to attend summer camp at Clarke School for the Deaf in Northampton, Massachusetts. I must have been about seven or eight years old, and my mother tells me that I was very excited about attending this camp and meeting more deaf friends. Even more exciting was the fact that Stacey would be able to join me, as this program allowed hearing siblings to accompany their deaf brothers or sisters to camp. She and I were close at home, and I depended on her a lot to keep me feeling included in my family. For instance, she would discreetly summarize the family discussion for me at dinnertime, if necessary, or ask if I wanted her to repeat someone's joke that I had missed. Stacey also tells me of times when she would silently wish, "Please look at Lisa, please look at Lisa," if someone was speaking but not looking in my direction. This came very naturally to her; but she also never spoke for me or made me feel like someone to be pitied or "helped." Her comfortable acceptance of my situation as being deaf but in no way deficient or defective is something that I do not take for granted.

Once we arrived at Clarke School that summer, my mother was reluctant to leave me for the two-week session; but I had always been independent, and she often recalls how I told her (as she was lingering), "It's okay, Mommy, you can go now. I'll be fine." I loved this camp, because it was a fun way to meet other deaf people in a different setting. I immediately clicked with my roommate, a hearing girl my age named Lucy, who had an older deaf sister, Suzanne, my sister's age. I continued to attend that camp for two more summers, and I made many friendships that I still maintain today. It was also at this camp that I was first exposed to sign language, as one camper showed Stacey how to fingerspell the alphabet, but I showed very little interest. To me, sign language was a communication tool, and as I already communicated well using my speech and speechreading skills, I did not feel that it applied to me. Looking back, I now realize I did not understand the value of sign language; in my self-contained class, within my family, and at camp, people made conscious efforts to ensure that I would have communication access; I would soon learn that this would not always be the case.

After the fourth grade at WPS, my family and I moved back to Miami, Florida, to rejoin my father, whose business was located there. I reenrolled at the Heritage School of Kendall, where I had attended nursery school, this time as a fifth-grader. Fortunately, because this was a private school, I was able to be in small classes like I was used to. This was essential for speechreading and keeping up with the class. I had a great foundation of skills and knowledge from WPS, and I did well academically, with a few bad grades not due to any factors other than my lack of effort. What helped most through this time was having my parents and sister to continually communicate with as well as praise from my teachers. One experience sticks out in my memory: During a group project, my teacher, Mrs. Cunningham, praised me for speaking up and sharing my ideas with the rest of the group, helping both them and me to realize that I could make a significant contribution, even with my hearing loss. I did so well that I even represented my school at the regional spelling bee in Miami. This proved challenging at the higher level because I was not placed in an optimal position of being able to "hear" the words being called out. Still, everyone—including me—was extremely proud of my achievement.

I graduated from Heritage School of Kendall with an award for Good Citizenship—that is, being friendly with everyone and following rules. I was reasonably outgoing and laid-back at this school. I was invited to parties and had a close friend, Megan. My family relocated again to Montreal, where I began secondary school at Chambly County High School (CCHS). My first day as a seventh-grader was a perfect preview of the years to come. I followed the crowd, looked around at what others were writing down, assessed which teachers were easy or impossible for me to speechread, and smiled a lot. During roll call in each class, I often missed my name, but those who knew me from community activities spoke up for me.

Having my sister at school helped, but there was not much Stacey could do for me in terms of advocating for me in class. Cheryl, my MOSD itinerant teacher from the first grade, returned to see me on a weekly basis, which was great. Of course, being a teenager, it may not have felt great every week to meet her in the early hour before my first class period, but I always appreciated her help and advice. We would work on my class presentations, speech, reading comprehension, and, at times, French. I did not have an interpreter during my first three years of high school, and was not inclined to ask for one. Whether I wanted to blend in with the rest of class, or was not sure how the interpreter would benefit me, I am still not sure to this day. I got by through speechreading and notes from classmates, as well as rereading materials as they related to homework. Looking back, I do regret missing out on many class discussions, school assemblies, and lunchtime conversations. At the time, though, I did not feel unhappy; I was involved in sports, dance groups, and clubs, and would often see my oral deaf friends on the weekends.

I wore my cochlear implant throughout this time. In terms of my personal feelings about the cochlear implant, I was implanted so young that it is just a very natural part of me. Since I was in a self-contained class with other oral deaf kids, and later mainstreamed as the only deaf student during elementary school and high school, it was always a necessity, and I suppose I didn't function as well without it. Especially in high school when I did not use an interpreter: The single-channel cochlear implant was not perfect, but it helped me to get by. I was never able to develop great listening skills without speechreading and "filling in the blanks." I also struggled to learn French, a language commonly used in Montreal, since the class focused so heavily on listening and speaking. But I aced my Latin classes because they only required us to learn to read and write the language. I actually was exempted from the oral component of the French exam and was obligated only to pass the written portion. I also took Spanish at Heritage School since it was in Miami, where so much of the population spoke it. I often wish those languages were taught to me in a way that enabled me to pick them up. I found Spanish easier to learn, as all letters are pronounced, unlike French which has many, many silent letters. In trying to speak it, I often pronounced words as they were written, which then made no sense.

The summer after the ninth grade, I went to Camp Mark Seven in Old Forge, New York. A good friend of mine from Clarke School Summer Camp, Jeremy Gelb, with whom I had kept in touch through letters over the years, had written to tell me about this camp. He was going to attend with his older sister, Jessica. Ever adventurous, I asked my mother if I could attend, and we proceeded to get me registered. We took the five-hour-long drive to upstate New York from Montreal, and I was excited to see my friend and make new ones. Of course, we assumed that this would be another oral deaf camp, because we had not been introduced to signing deaf people, and my friend was oral himself. Imagine our surprise when we walked into the building and saw all these signing hands. My mother and aunt were ready to take me home if I wanted; however, I felt the need and desire to stay. After all, everyone was deaf like me. I registered at the front desk using the limited fingerspelling skills I had, and just took it all in.

Turns out, Jeremy didn't attend camp that summer, but I made many new friends. A few were oral deaf as well, and could relate to me. However, I quickly learned that this was an ASL environment, and I wanted to respect that by picking it up and using it as often and quickly as possible. It was so easy and relaxing to be in this visual environment, to not have to squint to understand what a person was

saying, because they were using not only their lips, but also their entire bodies to communicate information as intensive and detailed as a
sentence in any language I had studied—English, French, Spanish, or
Latin! Three weeks passed by quickly, and I was so happy to have been
there. I not only enjoyed the canoeing, hiking, dances, talent shows, arts
and crafts, laughter, and bonding, but also the fact that all the instruction, lessons, demonstrations, and conversations were all presented
visually, and I did not miss any information. Well, actually, I did, because it was a new language, but I missed a lot less than I did in school.
At the end, I earned the award for Most Improved Signer.

Of course, I was very sad to leave camp because of my new friendships and the fun I had. I decided to sign up to take ASL classes at the
MacKay Center when I returned to Montreal. However, I did not have
a strong desire to use the language for anything other than conversational purposes. At the time, I did not want to adopt the language as
my own, although it is such a beautiful language that I knew I wanted
to improve my skills. I returned to Camp Mark Seven for two summers
after that.

Back at school in the tenth grade, the academic material became too
much for me to handle. We were reading intense books in my English
class, such as Aldous Huxley's *Brave New World*, Timothy Findley's *Not
Wanted on the Voyage*, and Shakespeare plays, with words and sentences
open to multiple interpretations and leading to complex discussion.
While in the past, I had been okay with picking up bits and pieces here
and there, or getting summaries from my classmates and teachers, this
time I wanted to know what was being said as it was being said. I requested an interpreter, but this request was denied due to lack of funds
and the fact that I was not doing poorly in classes. I was consistently
on the honor roll, thanks to my efforts to meet my mother's high expectations, which I had internalized.

At MOSD, we had a teen group, which was so great because my
old classmates could get together and socialize outside of our mainstream schools. If I had a weekday off, I would often go to visit three
friends at their school, which was much bigger than mine. Two of them
had an oral interpreter, who used ASL fingerspelling for support. I considered transferring to this school for two reasons. I was the only deaf
person in my school, and although I was fine with that, I wondered if
things would be better with another deaf classmate. Also, having access to an interpreter would be fantastic. However, the commute, which
would have been over an hour, and the idea of leaving my CCHS

friends with graduation less than two years away, dissuaded me. At that time, I was working with MOSD in making presentations to the government about the importance of having an oral interpreter for deaf students. Myself and a couple of other mainstreamed MOSD students, along with a parent and staff member, wrote speeches and delivered them to representatives of the government, as well as interviewed with them at public hearings. Although I had used them at conferences and MOSD events, I still did not have an oral interpreter at school, so my mother and I pushed harder for one. In response, I was given a special education staff member, who sat in front of me in some classes and mouthed what was being said. I was not happy about this because she was not at all trained in oral interpreting, but she was willing and my only resource.

This "interpreter" was a very nice and fun lady, but she often crossed boundaries and interfered in class, trying to be helpful, of course. I requested to have her only in classes that were discussion-based, such as English and Moral and Religious Education. I remained on my own in my other classes. This arrangement worked out fine, although it was a little embarrassing to have my classmates watching this woman exaggerate mouth movements in front of me. However, they became used to it and maybe even sympathized with me a little.

High school went by fast; I competed in the school public speaking competition, performed in dance shows, had a role in student government, and got along fine both in the classroom and outside. I had also developed stronger self-advocacy skills; I was no longer as timid about asking my history professor for his notes or requesting captioned videotapes for chemistry class. Before my high school graduation, I began thinking about what colleges I wanted to go to. I applied to nearby Dawson College and Champlain College, each a college of general and professional education, called CEGEP (a French acronym for "Collège d'enseignement général et professionnel"): junior colleges attended before one enrolls into university in Quebec. I also applied to Gallaudet University, after researching both Gallaudet and Rochester Institute of Technology/National Technical Institute for the Deaf (RIT/NTID). I was concerned about not being accepted, as I would graduate high school after the eleventh grade (standard in Quebec). Some members of my family encouraged me to attend RIT/NTID, likely due to the fact that there were other hearing students there for me to communicate with in spoken English. My parents and I visited Gallaudet the spring before my graduation, and I fell in love with the campus and programs. Also enticing was the New Signers' Program as well as the city of Washington, D.C. I was accepted to all the colleges I applied to and decided to attend Gallaudet. I envisioned having better access to class content and being able to participate much more in class. At my high school graduation (where, incidentally, I missed my name being called), I was presented with a President's Scholarship from Gallaudet.

My Gallaudet classmates challenged me, as did my entire experience there. During college, I did face a lot of strong opinions about my cochlear implant and was questioned about my "deaf identity" and not making the "right" choice, which to some people there meant to throw away my cochlear implant and make my own decisions. Honestly, I was fascinated with this new perspective from my signing deaf classmates . . . and would always listen and learn. But, they had grown up in schools for deaf students, or they had deaf parents that signed, or they had interpreters while mainstreamed. Their experiences were so different from mine that I didn't let them make me feel bad—I just explained things from my perspective. And, I immersed myself in ASL and discovered another side of myself. Of course, a lot of questions came up at that time in my own head and heart . . . like why my parents didn't choose for me to learn ASL sooner, or what my life would have been like in a school for deaf students. My parents answered these questions openly and honestly, even asking a few questions of their own, since this was also new to them.

My roommate at Gallaudet was oral like myself, with fluent sign skills that I admired. I majored in biology and had big hopes for doing well and developing relationships with friends and professors. My most difficult class, however, turned out to be biology, because I could not understand the teacher's fast fingerspelling of scientific terms. It was too much for me to try reading the text after class to catch up, and I was nervous about seeing the teacher for help because he signed so quickly and complexly. I had avoided a couple of my high school teachers in the same way because they talked too fast or did not move their mouths enough! I ended up, after a few weeks, withdrawing from the class. However, the rest of my classes were wonderful opportunities for me to improve my receptive and expressive ASL, because I was so interested in the topics of psychology and philosophy.

Interestingly, I stopped using my cochlear implant during my year at Gallaudet. Despite all the questions, I did not face much negativity, mainly curiosity. People would continue to ask why I had a cochlear implant, if I no longer considered myself deaf, and whether I liked it or not. Others in my situation may have perceived these questions negatively; but because I was content with my implant, I perceived these questions as opportunities to educate and inform. However, it became evident that my implant was not getting much use in class or outside, as Gallaudet is an exclusively signing community, so I stopped wearing it unless I was visiting my family or going out to a restaurant or the mall.

Having been in a self-contained class with other oral deaf students for several years, I shared with them a cultural bond simply because we had to work harder to communicate and access information, compared to our hearing peers. That may be one of the reasons I did not feel it was too difficult for me to assimilate into the Deaf community. I recall a time when I experienced an eye-opening difference in perspectives. On a weekend trip from college to my hometown in Montreal, I invited two friends to join me for a visit. I introduced them to a childhood friend, who had been my MOSD classmate since nursery school. All three of these friends are extremely smart, funny, and kind individuals; but they did not get along. My oral deaf friend looked down upon the use of sign language, while my signing deaf friends were offended by his acceptance of the term *hearing-impaired*, as if it was something to be fixed. I was fascinated by this, because although they had the same goals of success for themselves as individuals with a hearing loss, they were not able to relate to each other, due to a fear of being different, of having to believe in something other than what their experiences had taught them. I see signing and the oral approach to communication as equal opportunities to be a part of and contributor to the human race, as long as we can all respect each method.

I completed my freshman year at Gallaudet as a President's Scholar and was on the Dean's Honor Roll. Although I enjoyed my experience there, I did not feel that I fit in completely. It helped immensely that I was able to pursue one of my interests, dance, as a member of the Gallaudet Dance Company. Over the following summer, I made the decision to transfer to RIT/NTID, where I might feel more comfortable in a more diverse community of oral deaf, signing, and hearing students. I knew of some friends entering their first year there, because I had graduated at the eleventh grade in Canada, and they were just finishing up twelfth grade. From my very first week, I loved RIT and felt comfortable there—many of my peers were oral like myself and had learned sign language at a later age. We had interpreters in some classes and, in others, hearing teachers that signed at the same time as they talked. And in the classes where I had an interpreter, I had the option of either watching the teacher speak or watching the interpreter sign. I took some classes with a "Deaf section"; all the students used ASL along with the teacher. I had enjoyed my literature classes at Gallaudet as well as the visual discussions of the books we read. I was thrilled to be able to continue this at RIT. It was indeed the best of both worlds. I also joined a cochlear implant support group, which had fun gatherings where everyone could socialize and share their experiences. This is not to say that Gallaudet did not have such a group; I was just not aware of it.

At one point during my college experience, my cochlear implant was not working so well (it was more than fifteen years old), and I just stopped wearing it rather than being annoyed when it would sponta-neously shut on and off or make "crinkling" noises. I think I had gone without it for months at a time when I started thinking about re-implanting—because, while it was not a problem to be without my cochlear implant at school, it was a problem when I would go home. I got frustrated conversing with my hearing family because I could not get some information, and I often was not understood (my speech is definitely lacking when I do not wear my cochlear implant!). Actually, my family was more frustrated with me saying "Huh?" or "What?" over and over, although they did their best not to show it. By this time, my single-channel cochlear implant had experienced a lot of wear and tear. I continued to send in parts for replacement or repair, such as wires and rechargeable batteries. Pretty soon, the company was going to discontinue making these parts, because technology had improved so much. Those in my cochlear implant group had had twenty-two-channel implants for several years already, while I still had a single-channel device. It was time for an important decision: Did I want to wait for my cochlear implant to be useless and then become a true deaf person (meaning no access to sound), or get re-implanted? The inner parts of my cochlear implant would not be compatible with a new ex-ternal device, so surgery would be required. I approached the process of getting a twenty-four-channel cochlear implant with mixed feelings (Shouldn't I forget it altogether and embrace my deaf identity?). But, it really did not make sense to deprive myself of something that makes my life richer and, yes, easier.

I talked this over with my family and with the staff at the Speech and Language Center at NTID. For several months, I believe, my deci-sion was to go without a cochlear implant. I often did not wear it at school, depending on interpreters for communication needs. However, I would soon miss environmental noises, hearing sound at the movies, or conversing more easily with hearing people. Thus, at the age of twenty, I decided to pursue re-implantation. I was fortunate to have my mother go through the insurance process for me. I was re-implanted in 2000 at Jackson Memorial Hospital in Miami, where my parents still resided. My surgeon had done re-implantations in the past, and I went through several weeks of testing in order to be approved. I chose a twenty-four-channel device. I remember sitting and talking with my surgeon on a few occasions—enough to become comfortable with him and know that he was looking out for my best interests.

It is funny to look back on my surgeries and compare them to cochlear implant surgeries today. A few weeks ago, I attended a picnic benefiting children with hearing loss. A baby, under a year old, had had a surgery a few days earlier and was crawling around, playing without a bandage, or stitches, or even staples. Her tiny scar was barely visible, resembling a cat scratch. For my first surgery in 1985, my bandage was the size of a football helmet (at least it seemed that way), and I went through a recovery period of months. I still have a large scar from that surgery. In 2000, my bandage was slightly smaller, and recovery was two weeks. Nowadays, bandages stay on for less than five days, and the scars are so minimal. As with advances in other areas of medicine, I am impressed with how the surgical procedures and rates of recovery have been improved. However, I do fear that with easier and more frequent surgeries, they may not be done for the right reasons. Just because an infant, child, or adult is physically able to be implanted does not always mean that it is the right choice for them. There are other factors to be considered, such as degree of hearing loss, family involvement, learning style, and the individual's strengths and weaknesses.

I also have better memories of the implant being turned on in 2000 than I do from 1985. I recall it being turned on and hearing my mother's voice, and thinking that she sounded like a mouse, high and squeaky. It took time to adjust: Coming home, I could hear all the little things that I could never hear before. I could hear fans, birds, air conditioning, people chewing, all these little sounds that were so annoying. From hearing one range of sound with my single-channel, to a wider range with the twenty-four-channel was a big adjustment. There were a lot of positives; I asked for my first portable CD player for Christmas, because music was a bit clearer to me. On the negative side, I had to request for several of the twenty-four channels to be turned off, because the sounds were causing me pain. These were sharp pains right where the electrodes were implanted, occurring when I would hear a specific sound in a group that corresponded to a particular electrode. I would immediately turn off the external processor when this happened. Having an audiologist turn off the channel easily alleviated the pain; however, I do admit that I was disappointed to lose each sound. It is always an option to turn the channel back on and try again. Currently, eight of my twenty-four channels are turned on. I could turn on more, but I would need to see an audiologist, and that is not my priority at the moment. After all, eight is a definite improvement over one!

I had two types of twenty-four-channel speech processors (the external part of the cochlear implant): a behind-the-ear (BTE) device that I wore religiously and a body-worn processor that I hated because it was inconvenient to wear, but I really liked the sounds I got from it. (Since the body-worn processor is bigger, the sound quality is slightly better.)

When I returned to RIT, the new cochlear implant was a priority, and I scheduled several listening therapy sessions with a very supportive audiologist and coordinator of NTID's Cochlear Implant Program, Catherine Clark, at the Speech and Language Center. I considered her to be very supportive because she focused on my personal growth as a whole person, and our sessions were not limited to my listening rehabilitation. We not only practiced training to hear sounds and talk on the telephone, but she also listened to me vent about other things going on in my life at the time. We also did some reprogramming of my cochlear implant, a process known as "mapping." Mapping refers to setting limits on how much the inner electrodes are stimulated, so that the cochlear implant user is able to hear soft sounds and environmental sounds, as well as to comfortably hear loud sounds. Of course, I was more sensitive to the changes in the "loud sound" limits—too high and it would be very uncomfortable to go to an action movie with lots of explosions! It is important to have frequent mappings, as maps can become weaker, or less clear, over time. I enlisted hearing friends to help me practice listening and discriminating sounds. I improved very slowly. Because I was so used to the single-channel, I did not and still do not get the full benefits of the additional sounds from the twenty-four-channel—I hear them but can't identify them. It appears that I became too "comfortable" with the "map" that my single-channel left in my auditory memory. I began going to fewer and fewer listening therapy sessions, as I also needed to focus on school, my friends, my activities, and my sorority. In the end, I would say that the twenty-four-channel benefits me as much as the single-channel did, although I can hear a bunch more sounds that my brain doesn't know what do to with, not having the proper training. Audiologists have told me that it is a little late in the game to return to listening therapy; I have not really pursued whether this is true or not. With newer technology, I may be able to get a more advanced device, but I wonder how much improvement I would see. Even though I did not devote as much time to the mapping and listening therapy as I should have, I'm pretty satisfied, nonetheless. Only in certain situations—like when my toddler nieces are chattering away—do I wish I could understand things better with the cochlear implant.

After graduation, with my bachelor of science in psychology, I moved to Miami, Florida, where my parents were. I went to the local vocational rehabilitation office for assistance with finding a job in my field. It was a long, hard process, as not many jobs were available. I ended up becoming a job trainer/job coach at a not-for-profit agency that served deaf clients. This job suited me well, because I was able to work with a variety of people. However, it made me more aware of the limited jobs and limited resources available for some deaf people. For example, I sometimes was asked to interpret for clients on job interviews or trainings, simply because there was no interpreter available. Those kinds of situations were not acceptable, and not something that I wanted to continue. I knew I wanted a better job with more opportunities for advancement, so I applied to Gallaudet University's graduate program in school psychology. I had toyed with the idea of becoming a forensic psychologist or industrial/organizational psychologist. What drew me to school psychology was my love for the educational process, the school environment, and children; helping to ensure that they will have chances for academic accomplishment, social success, and opportunities for personal growth. I also knew I could apply my many experiences in diverse educational settings to the field.

My experience in the program was positive due to collaboration with my classmates and trainers, although it was marred by some of my professors' communication modes. However, it was another experience that taught me to adapt to a variety of communication styles and to be patient. I am a strong believer that children (and adults) can adapt to any communication mode if they have a firm language foundation to begin with. Once it was time to look for internship sites, I decided that I wanted to intern at one of the top deaf schools in the nation that followed a bilingual-bicultural (ASL and English—Deaf and hearing) philosophy in their practices. After some research, I applied at the Indiana School for the Deaf (ISD). Some of the staff were resistant to my being hired at ISD, because of my cochlear implant. That attitude was understandable in a school that values ASL, and my equal appreciation for ASL and English worked in my favor.

Interning at ISD, I wore my cochlear implant daily. This was in case I encountered hearing parents or deaf or hard of hearing children using their voices, just to hear what was going on in my environment, and as a way of getting to know deaf people. Sometimes when I can hear a person's voice, it tells me something about their personality or their character. For example, I may get the impression from a Deaf man with a booming loud voice that he is very confident and assertive (although that may not be the case). I also love to hear people's distinctive laughs. Some staff and students used their voices, some did not; it did not make a difference to me either way. The summer after my internship, I took a trip with two girlfriends to Italy and Greece. At some point during the trip, my BTE device died due to static electricity of some kind. I was surprised at how frustrated I was for the rest of the trip; it was fine communicating with my friends, but I did not have a chance to "hear" the voices of the people we met in Greece, especially the family members of one of my fellow travelers. Returning to the States, I stayed with my sister and her family for a while. As I had left my body-worn device in storage in Indiana, I could not hear anything that was being said, but we adapted well. They just had to make sure to articulate more, and my niece, I think, was learning to repeat what she said to me. She was two years old at the time. (Imagine learning such a habit so early!) Although I was not thrilled with the prospect, I adapted to not having a cochlear implant and access to sound yet again.

I returned to Indiana to live and work, and did not bother to wear my body-worn processor that was still functioning. The issue never came up until a couple of months later, when I was invited to attend an event for HEAR Indiana, a chapter of the Alexander Graham Bell Association for the Deaf and Hard-of-Hearing. Until then, I got by with speechreading and using old-fashioned pen and paper. After networking at this event, I was invited to become a board member of this chapter. For the first board meeting one evening, I neglected to bring my body-worn device because I was out of the habit of wearing it. Struggling to speechread and follow discussions in this group setting, I realized how spoiled I had become by having full visual access to information at work on a daily basis! I found myself slightly envious of other oral deaf board members, who were able to follow the dialogue by relying on speechreading much less than I did.

Nowadays in the Deaf community, I would not say there are hostile attitudes toward cochlear implants—only curiosity: When people see me signing, they wonder why I would have a cochlear implant when I can communicate in ASL. I know and understand that it is not for everyone. For people who express themselves beautifully in sign and have good English reading and writing skills, for example, a cochlear implant is not, and should not, be a priority. But even for those people, a cochlear implant might extend their range of opportunities in life if it enhances their ability to hear environmental sounds and, especially, to interact with non-signing people. I'm grateful for the opportunities my cochlear implant offers me, and I see it as completely compatible with being a signing Deaf person.

A Conversation with
Grace Walker: Focus on
Personal Experiences
with a Cochlear Implant

Grace Walker is a resident advisor for high school girls at the Delaware School for the Deaf. We interviewed her in May 2007 about her experiences with a cochlear implant (CI).

EDITORS: Did you grow up in a Deaf family?

GRACE: Yes. My parents are both deaf. I have a deaf brother and sister, as well as a hearing brother. I also have two half-sisters who are deaf and two deaf stepbrothers.

EDITORS: What was your experience with hearing sounds or speech?

GRACE: I went to a residential school for deaf students from kindergarten through high school. We had speech therapy in elementary school, but not in middle school or after. I used an FM system at school when I was small. Later, I got a hearing aid and used it through high school. It helped with environmental sounds, like a truck rumbling by or a door slamming. I'm profoundly deaf, so it didn't help for hearing people's voices.

EDITORS: How old were you when you got your CI? Did you choose to get it on your own, or did family or doctors or friends influence you?

GRACE: I got interested in having a CI through a friend. We had a similar family situation and many friends in common. My friend got it first, and she felt she benefited with regard to environmental sounds. She was also born deaf and is profoundly deaf. But the CI didn't help her for speech. If she was speechreading, it helped some, but not if she wasn't looking at the person.

Because our situations were so similar, it seemed like I would benefit from hearing environmental sounds, too. It would be fun to hear the rain. And it would be helpful to hear fire alarms or warning bells and sirens. I was thirty-nine when I decided to get a CI, and forty when I got it.

EDITORS: Where did you have the surgery done? Did they consider you an optimal candidate?

GRACE: At the time, I was working as a counselor at the Kendall School for the Deaf at Gallaudet University. That was a wonderful and rewarding job. I was there five years. So I went to Johns Hopkins University Hospital, which was nearby.

They looked at the structure of my ear and at my cochlear nerve, which turned out to be promising. And they considered my expectations, which were minimal: I hoped to hear environmental sounds, but I didn't expect to understand what people said. They thought I was a good candidate; they wouldn't have done the surgery otherwise.

EDITORS: How did your family and friends react?

GRACE: My mom was not happy that I was getting a CI. But I was an adult, so it was my choice. My father wasn't forthcoming with an opinion; he's a live-and-let-live type of guy. My sister was upset, though. She was afraid that her son, who is hearing, would become more attached to me than to her, because he'd be able to talk to me like a hearing person. But that didn't happen. My husband (who is now my ex-husband) also didn't want me to get a CI. He thought it would complicate my health in negative ways.

My friends at work (at Gallaudet) were shocked at my decision to get a CI. It was 2001. But they didn't say much about it. In fact, they threw a good luck party for me before the surgery, even though they didn't support it. You know, it wasn't as common then as it is now, so attitudes were different.

EDITORS: Were you counseled by the hospital beforehand about what to expect? Was your family part of the counseling process as well? In hindsight, do you think this counseling was adequate?

GRACE: I already knew what to expect beforehand, and they did counsel me—with a psychological evaluation, as well. For me, what they did was enough. My husband did not get counseled. He wasn't supportive of the idea, so I went alone.

EDITORS: Did you have pre-implant auditory rehabilitation therapy?

GRACE: No, they don't do any of that for adults.

EDITORS: Can you tell us about the surgery itself? What was recovery like?

GRACE: The surgery was really nothing. But I was dizzy afterwards. That was a big negative. Most people do not get this after surgery, but some do. The dizziness lasted about two weeks. Then, a few years later, I experienced dizziness again and I vomited for two days straight, so Mom had to take me to the hospital. They gave me medication and that helped, but then it just came back again. So my mother drove me to Johns Hopkins to figure out what was going on. I had problems with the balance nerves and balance organs of the inner ear—what they call "peripheral vertigo." It caused very serious nausea. So I had to go stay with my mother at her home in Philadelphia for a full week, while I kept vomiting. I was back at work the second week, but I wasn't completely normal for about a month and a half. Four times a day for several weeks, I had to do exercises to reset the balance in my inner ear.

EDITORS: Did you have post-implant rehabilitation therapy?

GRACE: After they attached the external apparatus, they did do some therapy. I went twice a week for an hour at a time to therapists within Gallaudet University. It was difficult. They explained that I only had a few channels that were accessible. I don't really understand the details, and I don't know how many channels hearing people have, but the point was that I didn't have what would be necessary to discriminate speech.

I worked hard at therapy, though. The task was to become familiar enough with the therapist's voice to be able to hear her sounds. But there were some sounds I just couldn't get at all. It took me a long, long time to get most of her sounds. Then I had a change in therapists, and I had to become familiar with a new voice. That's when I realized that the second woman was much easier to understand than the first. Her voice came through better for me.

Editors: Who paid for all this?

Grace: My health insurance paid for the surgery at Johns Hopkins University Hospital. Then the intern students at Gallaudet University were my therapists—that service was free, because I was an employee. But if I had had to go over to Johns Hopkins, I would have had to pay out of pocket after a while, because insurance only covers a limited number of visits.

Editors: How long did you continue the therapy?

Grace: Almost a year. But my schedule was really busy, so I finally quit. I think it's easier for kids to keep it up because they can go to the therapy as part of their school routine. But for me, as an adult with a job, it was just hard to get to the appointments.

Editors: What was your hearing experience like with the CI?

Grace: When the volume was turned up really high, I felt my face vibrate on that side. It was like a continual twitch. But if I turned it down, it was okay. And it certainly helped with hearing the environmental noises I had wanted to hear, but not with human speech.

Editors: Did you use your voice often when communicating with hearing individuals?

Grace: I tried voicing more with the CI, but I don't think I was any clearer. No one ever told me it was clearer, though they told me I was using my voice more. I could hear myself talk with the CI, so I was more aware of pronunciation, but I couldn't judge how well I voiced.

Editors: You're not using a CI anymore. Can you tell us what happened?

Grace: For two years, I was okay using the CI to hear environmental noises. But then something very stressful happened, and I had another attack of vertigo. It was debilitating, as severe as the original vertigo. So then I took off the CI. The vertigo continued, but was much milder.

For about a year, I had this mild vertigo almost all the time. Finally it stopped. But, then, a while later, I had vertigo again, out of the blue. It may well have been because of the CI surgery, because I had never had vertigo before that surgery. But now I do yoga and I don't drink alcohol and I try to avoid stress. If I feel the vertigo symptoms coming on, I take medication. All that seems to have solved the problem. I've gone almost three years without vertigo now.

EDITORS: What benefits do you feel you received from your CI?

GRACE: I definitely could hear environmental sounds when I wore it. I could hear someone coming up behind me. If students were making too much noise or being too loud—turning up the music, for example—I could hear it and tell them to turn it down. I could hear my boxer, Boxy, drinking water. Wow, that was interesting. Slurp, slurp, slurp. It made me laugh. I could hear my two cats meow. I could even hear people speak, but I didn't know what they were saying; I couldn't decipher the speech.

EDITORS: What benefits did you hope for that did not happen?

GRACE: I got pretty much what I expected. Remember, I didn't have high expectations. Probably if I had kept using my CI, I would have gotten better at it.

EDITORS: Are you sorry you went through the process?

GRACE: No, I'm not sorry. I'm glad I went ahead with it. I wish they had a smaller device, because it kept falling off. And I wear glasses, so it was uncomfortable. Even if I wore a hat, it was a problem.

EDITORS: Is there anything else you want to tell us about your experiences with your CI?

GRACE: I wish I had had more training afterwards. I would consider trying my CI again if they could have a smaller external apparatus, so that it wasn't such a burden.

At the hospital, they have a list of risks for CI, but they don't make a big deal about vertigo. I do know one other woman who had bad vertigo, like me. But you don't see a lot of discussion about it.

Editors: What's been your family's reaction to your experience?

Grace: My family has been very nice about it. They didn't say, "I told you so." But my ex-husband did. My family keeps quiet about it. Some people have strong feelings about CIs, but not my family. I didn't even see most of them until a few months after the surgery. They might have had stronger feelings about it if they had seen me through the whole process. But they saw me only now and then—and I'm still the same person I always was—working at the same type of job, acting the same.

Editors: When people find out you had a CI and you no longer use it, do they ask you why?

Grace: Only a few people have asked me about my CI experience. I tell them the positives and the negatives. Expectations are everything. As an older person, you heal more slowly and you don't pick up speech as well as children do. One girl came to me not long ago and said she wanted to be able to talk on the phone—and I told her I had no idea if she'd be able to with a CI. She went ahead and got the CI and she loves it and uses it every day. So for her, it works. Her hopes were a little high—and she now realizes her expectations were not all met. Yet she's still happy with it, even if it causes her some stress in not being able to do all she had hoped for.

Editors: What advice would you offer to someone considering a CI?

Grace: My advice is to have realistic expectations. That way, you can appreciate whatever benefits you receive.

Part Three
Civil Rights

8 | A Conversation with Christy Hennessey: Focus on the Workplace

Christy Hennessey is the program coordinator for Deaf and Hard-of-Hearing Services at Independent Resources, Inc., a center for independent living in Wilmington, Delaware. Independent Resources is a federally funded, private, nonprofit, community-based, consumer-controlled, cross-disability, nonresidential organization. They provide advocacy services by and for people with all types of disabilities.

EDITORS: Did you grow up in a Deaf family?

CHRISTY: Yes, my older brother and I were born deaf, but my parents are hearing. Initially they knew nothing about deafness or American Sign Language. We lived on a farm near Ithaca, New York, but when my parents learned of the New York State School for the Deaf, a residential school in Rome, New York, they moved there so my brother and I could attend the school as day students. When I began school there, at age four, it was an oral school and sign language was forbidden. However, some of the parents got together and petitioned the Board of Education to change this policy, and they won. The school then adopted total communication (TC) methods. My mother played an active role in that change. She also learned sign language and eventually became a teacher at the school. I think my parents passed down their interest in advocacy work to me!

We don't know of any deaf members of our family in earlier generations, but my brother has a deaf son, so deafness may be in our genes. My husband is Deaf, but my five-year-old son is hearing. He's bilingual—he signs beautifully.

EDITORS: Aside from the influence of your parents, how did you get interested in advocacy work?

CHRISTY: After I graduated from the National Technical Institute for the Deaf, I worked in the student loan department at a bank for a few years—long enough to realize it wasn't what I wanted to do. So I decided to go back to school at Gallaudet. That experience gave me a lot of confidence and made me realize I enjoy working with people. After I graduated, the University of Tennessee gave me a full scholarship for graduate work in rehabilitation counseling. That's where I learned about the Americans with Disabilities Act (ADA) and related laws and policies. When I started the graduate program, I was the only Deaf student, but a year later, another Deaf student enrolled. The university provided us with interpreters. It was a good learning environment—the hearing students also signed, as they were preparing to work with deaf clients. I began my career as a job coach at a county college, and later moved to Independent Resources. I love working with deaf people and helping them learn how to advocate for themselves.

EDITORS: When a Deaf or hard of hearing person comes to you for guidance on applying for a job, what kinds of questions do they ask?

CHRISTY: Many times people come in and ask for help writing a résumé. Together we figure out how to describe their work history and their skills on that résumé. We also practice interviewing, because a formal interview is typically a new situation for them. They're not accustomed to being in front of a hearing person with so many questions thrown at them.

Another thing I advise them on is independent living skills. I go over the basics: how to dress for work, making sure you get up on time in the morning, money management, bus schedules, and so on. If someone has just recently gotten out of school, they might not really know how the world works, so I help them. Budgeting is a big issue; my clients are sometimes given credit cards through the mail and then they run up a big debt, because they don't know about managing money and making a budget. I also help them find out about Social Security and whether they qualify for SSI benefits. We talk about housing and how to find a place to live that is conveniently located, so they can easily get from home to work.

I also do a lot of "information and referral." For example, if a person calls, asking about rental assistance from HUD (the Department of Housing and Urban Development), I tell them how to apply. We talk about HUD in general and about Section 8, on housing, in particular. Sometimes under the ADA, a deaf person may be eligible for a discounted rent based on income. And I talk to them about accessibility in an apartment and what they can and should ask for. For instance, they can ask for a visible light instead of a doorbell. The Deaf person shouldn't have to pay the cost of such an accommodation.

Additionally, I provide peer support for Deaf individuals. If they are going through something difficult, I'm there for them. I'm not just an advocate. I pay attention and empathize and help them realize what they need to do in order to get their lives organized. They need a stable living environment if they are going to be able to hold a job and be financially independent.

EDITORS: Do you ask them about their language choices and skills in order to counsel them effectively on job applications?

CHRISTY: I don't ask them explicitly about their language skills, but during our conversation, I assess those skills. I observe whether they use strictly American Sign Language or a form of signed English and speechreading, or whether they are somewhere in between, perhaps with some minimal language and some home sign or gestures.

Usually on a job application, it will say that an applicant must have oral and written skills—so oral skills can be an issue. I encourage the deaf person to use whatever skills they have as much as possible. If a deaf person chooses to use their voice and speechread, I assess how comfortable they are doing this. And I encourage them to rely on an interpreter to assess the quality of their voicing. I urge them, if their voicing skills are not up to the task, to use an interpreter in an interview.

EDITORS: Are there many jobs in which only written communication is necessary? Perhaps jobs in technology?

CHRISTY: No, not really. For many jobs, you may have to use the phone, for example. However, this may change as more workplaces begin to use e-mail for memos and announcements within the office. Also, we encourage employers to install teletypewriters (TTYs) or videophones at a Deaf individual's office, desk, or break room so that a Deaf employee can use the TTY or video relay service.

Whether someone can apply for a technology job depends on their education. Many educational institutions don't meet the needs of Deaf people, so some drop out of school or are somewhat behind with regard to technology.

EDITORS: One of your jobs is to inform people of their rights as a job applicant. Do you find that they are generally already well informed, or is this a major part of your service?

CHRISTY: This is a major part of the job. I ask people if they know about the ADA and if they are familiar with the laws that deal with accommodations. I talk to them specifically about Title I, which includes information about employment accommodations, such as using interpreters for staff meetings.

EDITORS: At the Signs and Voices conference, you said that you advised people to inform potential employers that they are entitled to "reasonable accommodations." Do you find that people are able to do this—or do they have trouble asking for accommodations? Are you ever invited to help a job applicant explain these rights to a potential employer?

CHRISTY: Often someone will give me a contact person's name at the business where they are applying for a job, and I then contact that person to make sure they are informed about the ADA. I tell them how to hire and use interpreters for an interview and for other kinds of meetings. I also explain how to use video relay. When a person already has a job, sometimes they ask me to advocate for them because they're not familiar with the ADA. I strongly urge them to advocate for themselves. But if they truly don't feel comfortable, then I will do this for them. For example, a Deaf person asked me to provide his employer with sensitivity training, and I agreed to offer this training. I talked about Deaf culture and about providing Deaf employees with a TTY or pager, and I explained how the videophone works.

After a sensitivity training session, I find that employers are very good about making the necessary changes to accommodate Deaf employees. But before that, they often have no sense of the challenges involved. It isn't effective just to say to an employer, "Oh, the ADA says you must do something." Rather, employers need to have the sensitivity training before they understand why they must do these things. Then they generally do them willingly.

EDITORS: Do you find that Deaf or hard of hearing people are often not considered seriously for jobs for which they are well qualified?

CHRISTY: Yes, that does happen. Sometimes Deaf people are hired right away. But sometimes the Deaf person is put on hold while the company interviews other people. When that happens, it's hard to know whether the Deaf applicant is not being taken seriously or whether it's just a matter of interviewing everyone. If a person is well qualified for the job, it's very hard for the person to accept that they were not hired.

EDITORS: When a person comes to you complaining of discrimination in hiring or on the job, what do you counsel them to do?

CHRISTY: File an EEOC complaint—that is, an Equal Employment Opportunity Commission complaint.

Once a Deaf person is on the job, I encourage them to document the problems they encounter. For example, if they have any correspondence with the company, they should keep this so that later on, if they have to file a complaint, they've got that record as evidence.

EDITORS: Another aspect of your job is to counsel employers who would like to hire Deaf or hard of hearing people. Do these employers come to you out of the blue—having a desire to hire responsibly? Or do they consult you mainly when a Deaf or hard of hearing person has applied to them and they want to figure out what the ramifications might be of employing the person?

CHRISTY: The first situation never happens. Employers call my agency only when a Deaf person applies and they are looking for interpreters. Sign language interpreters are important, but I explain that we're not an interpreter referral agency, and I give them a list of referral agencies and of freelance interpreters.

Sometimes the Deaf person has a preference for a particular interpreter. In those situations, it's their responsibility to tell the employer and see if the employer can hire that person. This can work out well if they plan at least a week in advance. If it is a last-minute interview, however, the employer just finds whoever is available.

EDITORS: What do you counsel employers to do with respect to their Deaf or hard of hearing employees? Legally, what workplace accommodations must they make? And beyond those, what accommodations should they make just to have well-functioning and satisfied employees?

CHRISTY: Actually, there is nothing legally required unless it's a reasonable accommodation in an individual's job description. But usually employers don't come to me with this sort of question, anyway. Instead, what happens is that the employee will ask me to talk to his employer about accommodations. It is essential that a Deaf person inform their employer about what their needs are. Sometimes I work with someone who's been employed at a job for thirty years, and they don't know that it's their responsibility to tell their employers what their needs are—and what their rights are.

But when I am put in the position of advising employers directly, here's what I say.

First of all, interpreters are important. That way, the Deaf employees get the information they need. Sometimes Deaf people think they are well informed, but then they find out that they were missing something important, and it causes problems on the job. It is a legal requirement to supply interpreters when needed: for staff meetings or any kind of one-on-one meeting (say, with the boss). But interpreters are generally not needed for daily work situations.

Other accommodations would make life easier, but they are not legally required: TTYs, pagers, videophones.

EDITORS: What do you advise employers to do to ensure access to critical information on the job?

CHRISTY: I advise employers to install lights for getting people's attention—as in the case of a fire alarm. A strobe light serves the purpose. If the employer uses a PA system for announcements, they need to have a way to get the information to the Deaf or hard of hearing employee via a pager.

This is really important, both for safety and for common decency. On 9/11, Deaf people didn't find out what had happened until late that night. They were the last to know. That kind of situation makes Deaf people look like they don't know anything. Hearing people don't tend to share information with Deaf people because they don't realize that

Deaf people aren't overhearing information. So Deaf employees should have a pager on the job. It's a necessary expense.

EDITORS: Do you recommend that hearing employers try using facial expressions and gestures to communicate?

CHRISTY: No, not really. Gestures can be misunderstood easily. Sometimes hearing people in the workplace learn some sign, and the Deaf person can teach the employer basic signs—HOME, WORK, SICK—things like that. But it's hard to get across complex ideas with just gestures.

EDITORS: Can you tell us about a frustrating job situation with which you were able to help?

CHRISTY: There was a Deaf person who had been certified to use a forklift. His boss said he couldn't. The man said, "But I just got certified." The boss said, "No." But the man said, "Why not?" The boss said it wouldn't be safe. And he pointed out that you had to follow the yellow painted lines on the ground, and wear a hard hat, and use the light on the forklift truck to let people know you're coming, and on and on, as though the Deaf man wouldn't do that. The Deaf man said that he would definitely follow those procedures. But he couldn't persuade his boss.

So I talked with the boss. I explained that the Deaf man would follow all the safety rules, and that, in fact, Deaf people are better drivers than hearing people because they are more visually alert and less distracted by noises.

We went back and forth and back and forth, and finally the Deaf person filed a complaint. And he won. He's been working there ever since, operating that forklift very well. There have been no problems, no incidents.

In this kind of situation, the Deaf person tries hard to let bygones be bygones and just do the job the best they can. And that seems to work. Everyone gets past it.

EDITORS: In that kind of situation, do you work with a lawyer?

CHRISTY: Yes and no. When a complaint is filed, the EEOC provides an investigator to gather information. Then they provide a mediator, too. Everyone tries mediation first. If that doesn't work out, well, then we go to court with a private attorney.

EDITORS: Do you encounter situations that are frustrating because they can't be resolved well?

CHRISTY: Sure. One of my most common frustrations is dealing with employers who don't want to provide interpreters because of the expense. I tell them that they need to set aside money specifically for interpreters. Employers will say that they have someone on the staff already who knows something about signing—someone who helps out with Deaf people at church or something—or the employers will say they can mouth the words in an exaggerated way so that it will be easy to speechread. They will try all sorts of ineffective things to get out of hiring an interpreter. The employers just don't understand.

Often frustrations build, and employers don't even realize it's happening, because the Deaf person doesn't tell them. The employee nods and smiles even if they don't understand what's going on. I have to urge the Deaf person to speak up and ask for an interpreter so they can get the information they need to do their job fully. I cannot stress that enough: Interpreters are essential in some situations.

EDITORS: In your experience, is the ADA truly effective in protecting the rights of Deaf people?

CHRISTY: Sometimes. Delaware has a weak law relating to accommodations (the Delaware Equal Accommodation Law). The ADA is clear, but the Delaware state law is unclear. And employers will tend to look at the state law rather than the federal law, and then decide they don't have to hire interpreters. They find loopholes. Right now, we are working to draft an amendment to the state law so that it is very clear, particularly with respect to the right to have interpreters. That is the thing to emphasize: Reasonable accommodation must include a qualified interpreter. Right now, the Delaware law refers to auxiliary aids, but it doesn't give specific information about the particular aids.

This is so important. For example, one Deaf person filed a case because he was not provided with an interpreter at places such as doctors' offices, police stations, hospitals, and courts. And the Deaf person lost because the state law did not make it clear that an interpreter is the right of the Deaf person. But we are pushing for the federal law to be followed instead of the state law.

Not just any interpreter will do; qualified interpreters are what the law should require. Unfortunately, even when interpreters are provided by an employer, they may not be qualified. The educational level of interpreters in the mainstreamed programs in schools is not always high. Interpreters need to have proper education and qualifications.

EDITORS: Have employment levels for Deaf people gone up since the passage of the ADA?

CHRISTY: Yes, I believe they have. I don't have the exact figures, but progress has been made.

EDITORS: What do you think remains to be done to help Deaf and hard of hearing people gain full employment?

CHRISTY: They need good role models. Good Deaf leaders. Mentors would be wonderful, so that a Deaf person could learn from a good Deaf role model. Hands-on training on the job by a Deaf mentor would be terrific. Employers can explain how to do something, but actually having a Deaf person there performing a task with you and showing you how to negotiate on the job is something else, something wonderful.

I try to be a mentor in that way, to some extent. I let people see what my life is like. I show them my appointment book and talk to them about my daily activities. Many Deaf people who come into my office get overwhelmed easily and may even miss appointments because they have never had a role model who understood how to manage their time. So I show them that you have to organize all your responsibilities and pay attention to time. These are the people who need independent living skills training.

EDITORS: Is there any final information you'd like to leave our readers with?

CHRISTY: Yes, I'd like to encourage them to use the kind of counseling we offer. My agency, Independent Resources, Inc., is funded with federal money through the Rehabilitation Services Administration. It's a nonprofit organization that works with people with all types of disabilities as well as with deaf and hard of hearing people. All of our services are free. We have an open-door policy; people can come and go as they need us.

Independent Resources was founded in 1994, soon after the ADA passed. There are two of us who are signers in the Wilmington,

Delaware, office. Sometimes I use an interpreter to communicate with other staff or at meetings. While my home office is in Wilmington, I work all over the state of Delaware: Wilmington, Dover, Georgetown. This morning, for example, I was in Dover before I came here for this interview. If a Deaf person comes into the Dover or Georgetown offices, they can confer with me over the videophone. Or I can come down and work with them individually. It depends on the situation. If they are looking for housing, I will take them around in the community to help them find a place to live.

9 A Conversation with Tony Saccente: Focus on HIV/AIDS Counseling

Tony Saccente worked for ten years (ending in 2006) as the coordinator of deaf services for Housing Works, Inc. This conversation with Tony Saccente took place in May 2005. Housing Works, the nation's largest community-based AIDS service organization, is dedicated to providing housing, health care, job training, and other vital support services to homeless people with AIDS and HIV in New York City. Founded in June 1990 by the Rev. Charles King and Keith Cylar of Columbia University, Housing Works is an outgrowth of the Housing Committee of the AIDS Coalition to Unleash Power (ACT UP). Housing Works's innovative approach to providing housing and services, coupled with vigorous advocacy on behalf of its constituents, has made it the national model for attacking the twin crises of AIDS and homelessness.

The Peer Initiative/Deaf AIDS Services Project at Housing Works operates through a contract with the New York State Department of Health AIDS Institute and coordinates peer outreach, education, and related services for, on average, 500 Deaf and hard of hearing clients each month. In addition to working with these clients, they emphasize the education of HIV/AIDS care providers.

EDITORS: Can you tell us about the Deaf Services Program at Housing Works?

TONY: Housing Works was founded in 1990, and I was hired in 1997. The organization has grown enormously, in terms of the services it offers. From 1990 to 1997, there was no Deaf outreach. Some hearing people at Housing Works knew sign, and some knew me through my involvement in the group Big Apple Gay Lesbian for the Deaf. I encouraged Housing Works to develop a program focused specifically on the Deaf community. They turned around and asked me to work with them on HIV/AIDS issues in the Deaf community. The Deaf Services Program at Housing Works offers many types of services, including support groups, harm reduction, needle exchange, adult AIDS day treatment, case management, counseling before and after test results, access to primary medical care, and, of course, housing.

EDITORS: What are some of the barriers to HIV/AIDS care and prevention in the Deaf and hard of hearing communities?

TONY: The embarrassment, the label people would be given, the stigma—all these things hold people back. The communication skills of some people are weak—I'm talking about Deaf immigrants here—so that makes education difficult. Within the community, there are many different types of people, and some of them have trouble dealing with their diagnosis.

Interpreters also have problems because sometimes they are not informed about the subject or comfortable talking about it. When I get together with interpreters, I remind them of the importance of expanding when they interpret HIV/AIDS-related concepts. This allows the Deaf person to ask the right questions and give informed answers. For example, an interpreter cannot simply sign, "You need to get your CD4 done." A Deaf person might think, "What are you talking about? Who cares?" So I have to tell the interpreter to explain that the CD4 refers to a test that counts the T-cells in the body. These cells are like little Pacman creatures, gobbling up the infections. When the CD4 count is low, then there are few T-cells, and they are slow and sluggish. In that case, the person is more open to infection and illness. I show videos of Pacman and pictures of the cells, so that people can understand what's going on. They see the HIV jump from cell to cell, replicating itself and hence destroying T-cells.

Interpreters also have to be comfortable using frank language about intimate behavior, so that the people they interpret for can relax and give and receive information freely. If an interpreter says, "Protect yourself," a Deaf person might think, "What does that mean, 'protect'?" But when I explain it, I'll sign, "When you fuck, your dick needs to be covered." I'll show them a picture of the penis and use very frank language, so there's no possibility for misunderstanding.

I use interpreters all the time, and most are afraid when they see me coming. They know I'm going to demand they be frank. Nothing subtle here.

EDITORS: Have you identified some specific strategies for educating the Deaf community about HIV/AIDS care and prevention?

TONY: I use visuals. I do role playing. For example, I'll get visuals from the medical profession and use them. If a client's T-cell count is 800—well, then, maybe they don't need help. But when someone's count hits 200, that means they're in danger of developing full-blown AIDS, so they need help. They can't fight off infection. Once we know what their viral load is and how many T-cells they have in their body, we know what kind of medical attention they need. So I'll show them a picture that will help them understand what a count of 200 means.

EDITORS: How do you assist clients with AIDS in adhering to their complicated treatment regimen?

TONY: I don't worry, because today, the HIV treatments are so much better. Many people only have to take a few pills a day. In the past, it was different; people had to take so many, and I worried they'd do it improperly. But now there's a combo display that indicates clearly which ones need to be taken and when—in the morning, before lunch, whatever. And on the back, it describes the side effects they might expect. Many people do not understand this, so I explain that if they get a headache or nausea, that's just a side effect and not to worry.

I will also go with them to the doctor to make sure they understand everything that goes on there. An interpreter comes too, of course. I'll typically go to the first three or four appointments. After that, people generally understand. If something special comes up, I can help. But I try to encourage independence. If we have some clients who are lower functioning, then, yes, of course, I go along to help.

EDITORS: There's a large population of Deaf and hard of hearing people in New York City. Is this simply because NYC is densely populated, or do Deaf and hard of hearing people come to NYC in greater numbers?

TONY: The Deaf community is indeed very large. Deaf people come to NYC because there are so many resources here. Queens has no special resources, but Manhattan does, so people flock there to take advantage.

It's hard to say exactly how large the NYC Deaf community is, because folks move around. I would say that the Bronx has a large Deaf Latino population. It's too bad that the United States Census Bureau doesn't keep information on Deaf populations, but it doesn't. I'd say there are about 80,000 deaf people in all five boroughs. But if we're talking about the culturally Deaf—people who use ASL as their primary language—then the number is probably closer to 10,000.

The League for the Hard of Hearing in NYC has collected figures because so many people ask about the numbers. According to Plies and Coles (2002), 34 million people in the United States have hearing loss—which is 10 percent of the national population. This figure, however, includes mild hearing loss and elderly persons with hearing loss.

EDITORS: Do Deaf and hard of hearing people in NYC form a single community, or are there many communities within the larger one? How does this affect your ability to work effectively with them?

TONY: It's a tight community. If you meet someone, they're likely to know the other Deaf people you know. But there are various organizations and subgroups within the community that some people belong to.

People tend to identify first as Deaf, then as Asian, gay, Latino, or African American. I'm an extremely open person—I'm a gay Deaf man, and I'm proud of who I am. But people vary a lot in their self-identification.

I use my good people skills and charisma to relate to different kinds of people. For example, two weeks ago, I went to the Independent Living Center in Harlem where the Deaf folks are what we call "low functioning." I came in very chatty, with street talk, speaking honestly and asking what people were doing with risky behavior, like sex on the street. I work with them at whatever level they are at. I see them as they are and relate to them in a way that can make them relate back to me. I don't sit there and say, "Hmm, okay what behaviors can I put on to make them listen?" Instead, I'm more like a chameleon. I just become more like the people I'm with.

I speak freely, so that helps them speak freely. And that helps them overcome whatever cultural biases they may have. If it's a Christian group, I can go in signing very properly and nicely and politely, asking about "birth control" as opposed to "fucking." And then I leave nicely and politely too.

I recently trained a peer education group—thirteen adults, of whom six were Deaf and seven were hearing. They were all eighteen years old or older. We had a man who moved here from Africa. We had an older Spanish man, who is illiterate, and his partner, another Spanish man who uses gestures and home signs. Lots of variety. I had two interpreters working with me for twelve weeks.

We focused on communication skills, treatment options, networking, and outreach. After twelve weeks, they went out into their respective communities and they educated people there. One Deaf woman who was involved had a high school education and was a Jehovah's Witness. But I was very up front with my teaching. This was not about religion; this was about HIV/AIDS prevention and care. This individual just listened and took it in. She talked about how she had to accept and obey what her religion told her. But I asked her: "If the government told you that as a Deaf person, you couldn't do this, this, and this, how would you feel?" I tried to help her understand that following blindly wouldn't help in this situation. I have to give real-world examples.

Editors: Can you tell us about the survey Housing Works carried out in 2000?

Tony: We conducted a survey at a Deaf Awareness Week festival called Deaf Expo. It was a street fair, and I had a booth with HIV/AIDS information and a bunch of condoms. The survey itself was simple: one page of questions that we handed out. Are you Deaf or hard of hearing? Male or female? Where do you live? Are you working or not? Do you collect SSI (Supplemental Security Income)? Are you a college graduate? A high school graduate? What's the highest grade you completed? Do you receive Medicare or Medicaid? Have you tested positive for HIV? Have you tested and gotten a negative result? When you have sex, do you use condoms? Do you have one partner or multiple partners?

People often ask what "positive" means. Depending on their educational levels, they may be confused. You have to explain that "positive" does not mean good. I ask people what they think "safe sex" means. I show them condoms and other things that can protect them during oral and anal sex.

We learned through this survey that the percentage of HIV-positive Deaf people in NYC is three times the percentage reported for hearing people. We also learned that there were lots of Deaf people going to hearing agencies to find out about HIV/AIDS. So I knew we at Housing Works were seeing only the tip of the iceberg. My guess is that almost 1,000 Deaf people in NYC are HIV-positive. Most of them go to hearing agencies, not Deaf. About fifty come to us. Another agency that works with Deaf people has about thirty HIV-positive clients. But there must be many, many more. And some Deaf people are HIV-positive without knowing it.

EDITORS: Given the intimate nature of the information you offer and the questions you ask, establishing trust must be an important part of your job. How do you go about gaining the trust of the people you work with?

TONY: Recently, I worked on that very point with the peer educators. For example, our clients may be black, white, male, female, butch, femme—and we need to create the best and most natural rapport with each of them. I identify the group I'm working with, and I assign them a peer educator who I think will relate best to that group.

New York State has a law about confidentiality (the Health Insurance Portability and Accountability Act [HIPPA]). If someone breaks that law, that person loses his job. I'm very strict when I work with my peer educators. We are professionals, and we're here for a reason. We have a goal. We expect that they will maintain confidentiality. This is essential for trust.

In the training group, we talk about the do's and don'ts—we have a curriculum. When they finish, they graduate and get a diploma. Then we have biweekly follow-ups. I give them assignments, such as to go to a gay bar and network. Then I watch and give them feedback. And I ask for their feedback. They can recognize their mistakes that way. We develop an ongoing relationship with each other by talking about the sites they visit.

EDITORS: What is the role of support groups at Housing Works? What kinds of support groups do you have?

TONY: I have set up an anger management group, and one on medical issues. Suppose people are saying, "Why me? I'm Deaf and now this?"

They have anger issues, denial. The support groups are all-male or all-female. Sometimes they come together, but that doesn't work as well. They are more comfortable separated by sex. The women's group is run by a woman who is HIV-positive. It addresses women's issues, treatments, and concerns. If there's something the leader can't address, she might write it down and talk with me.

EDITORS: Have you found video relay or other new technologies useful in your work? Do you see any potential problems stemming from them?

TONY: I have video relay in my home, actually. The video relay service (VRS) is perfect—it's exactly what people need—but most can't afford it. A high-speed connection is expensive.

I wish I had it at work to use with my clients; that would be great, but money issues have prevented that so far. We don't have the high-speed line. However, that may change.

I recently went to a public high school where they set up a VRS. People are using it and accessing the service. Sorensen, the company that produces the VRS, will provide a booth, a video camera, and $1,000 a year for a high-speed line. The booth is for privacy, so that if someone else knows sign language, they can't eavesdrop on your conversation.

My agency could do the same thing. And it will. This service is needed by all places that work with Deaf people, and Sorensen will give it to anyone who needs it.

I do see some potential problems with VRS, though. I think Deaf people tend to write less because of VRS, which may affect their literacy skills. I met a school principal who uses VRS, and I asked whether he noticed a change in his own reading and writing skills. And he said yes. He said communicating via VRS was much easier, so why use e-mail? It's better than having to look at your own writing and try to correct the grammar. VRS is the best form of communication for Deaf people across long distances. But literacy skills in a written language may become an issue.

Some have worried about another issue related to VRS use. With this kind of technology, we could stay at home and work from there, not getting together face to face. But Deaf people still get together. The teletypewriter (TTY) helped bring people together at a distance. The VRS does the same. But just as the TTY didn't stop people from getting together in person for the holidays and for Deaf fairs and so forth, the VRS probably won't either. But maybe short visits are fewer now.

Another technology is video interpreting (VI). While VRS is regulated by the Federal Communications Commission and is for general communication, private companies can supply VI for medical situations. For example, if a hospital has an emergency room, and there's a camera set up to access an interpreter, that can help a lot. An interpreter working for VI has to be on-call, and she can do interpreting from her home. It is a twenty-four-hour service.

EDITORS: Can you tell us about some specific projects you're working on now?

TONY: My goal is to improve communication within the Deaf community. Also I want to educate them about testing options. I used to tell them about OraSure, a test that would provide results in three days. Now I also tell them about OraQuick, a newer test that has results in twenty-two minutes. So they can go have a smoke or go to the bathroom, and then come back and get the results. Of course, sometimes they leave and never come back. I still encourage people to get tested using OraSure rather than OraQuick. Every month, I'd say there are about twenty to twenty-five Deaf or hard of hearing people who get tested by us. I'm hoping it will go up to fifty. That's a big push, to get everyone tested.

Also I'm trying to encourage people who are HIV-positive to speak about their status and be more open about it. That's a big struggle. For example, if I could take a friend with me to speak at a Deaf school, someone who is smart and could share his HIV-positive status, that would really help the kids to open up.

EDITORS: Any other new projects you want to tell us about?

TONY: I am working with National Development and Research Institutes, Inc. (NDRI) on a Deaf research project. They came to my office during the summer of 2004 and set up a laptop that allowed us to do a new survey related to HIV. We took this laptop to several states (including Florida, Minnesota, Pennsylvania, and New Jersey) and several locations in NYC to carry out the survey.

The questions had to do with people's general information about HIV and AIDS. On the laptop screen, a person signed the questions, and Deaf people could answer (a), (b), or (c). So the information was in a form accessible to Deaf people. Between 60 and 70 percent of the respondents had a general knowledge of issues related to HIV/AIDS. However, in this survey, 23 percent of Deaf people thought that hearing people—but not Deaf people—could be HIV-positive. But as the survey has continued, we have found that the percentage of people who have that misconception has been going down steadily. I'm curious to know which populations and which age ranges are better informed.

EDITORS: How did you inform members of the Deaf community about this study and get them to take part?

TONY: NYC has a close-knit Deaf community. We got the word out through Deaf News, a website that is updated weekly (http://www.dhisnyc.com). Also, many Deaf people have pagers, and word spreads fast. Getting people to participate was not hard. NDRI gives an appreciation of ten dollars for participating. That raises the number of people who want to get involved. It also makes people more curious about what we're doing. In NYC, people are starving for information. Everyone really wants to know what's going on.

EDITORS: When will final results of this study be available?

TONY: The completed survey was published as Goldstein, Eckhardt, Joyner, and Berry (2006). I'm excited about the statistics we're gathering. We have a good working relationship with NDRI. They will help us to continue the survey that we started together, using this traveling laptop. And I'm hoping that disseminating the results will help us get more funding for our research.

REFERENCES

Goldstein, M., E. Eckhardt, P. Joyner, and R. Berry. 2006. An HIV knowledge and attitude survey of deaf U.S. adults. In *HIV/AIDS and Deaf communities*, ed. C. Schmaling and L. Monaghan, 163–83. Deaf Worlds Special Publication. Gloucestershire, U.K.: Forest Publishers.

Plies, J., and R. Coles. 2002. Summary health statistics for U.S. adults: National Health Interview Survey, 1998. *Vital Health Statistics* 10(209).

10 | HIV/AIDS in the United States Deaf Community

LEILA MONAGHAN

Tony Saccente's interview with the editors of this volume reflects on-going work fighting HIV/AIDS among Deaf people in New York. In the United States, HIV/AIDS has been a problem in the Deaf community since the beginning of the AIDS crisis in the early 1980s. For example, Michel Turgeon, a leading Deaf AIDS activist in Montreal, traces his ac-tivism to a conversation with a Deaf friend in New York in 1985 about the problem of Deaf AIDS (CSSQ 2007). Deaf people from all walks of life have been affected. As in the larger hearing population, the San Fran-cisco and New York Deaf communities were among the first to confront the problem. Prominent Deaf people who have died of AIDS include Sam Edwards, dancer, performer, and sign language teacher, who died in 1989; Bruce Hlibok, actor, activist, and member of the NYC Gay Men's Chorus, who died in 1995; and actor and Deaf rights activist Alan Barwiolek, who died in 1996. These men are just the tip of the iceberg. The disease has affected people throughout the Deaf community—housewives, scholars, laborers, and business people. The *Remember Their Names* Web site (Deaf HIV/AIDS Resources 2006) lists 371 U.S. Deaf people as having died of AIDS, with 28 added in 2006 alone.

Despite these deaths, and as Tony points out, a significant number of Deaf people still think that AIDS is a hearing people's disease. What I would like to do in this chapter is briefly review studies of Deaf atti-tudes toward HIV/AIDS, look at the very limited information available on the extent of HIV/AIDS in the U.S. Deaf community, and review the kinds of AIDS awareness and treatment programs available today for Deaf people. The good news is that there are programs such as the peer education program described by Tony, as well as Deaf-oriented case management, that have been shown to be effective in the fight against HIV/AIDS. The bad news is that funding for many of these programs is limited, and even successful programs are threatened.

Information about HIV/AIDS in the Deaf Community

While there were a number of studies in the 1990s about the knowledge and attitudes of various groups of Deaf people in the United States with regards to HIV/AIDS (see Gaskins 1999 for review), I would like here to focus on a few more recent studies, including quantitative work by Goldstein, Eckhardt, Joyner, and Berry (2006), and two qualitative studies by Eckhardt (2005) and Mallinson (2004).[1] I will supplement this review with information from two other studies: a qualitative study done with focus groups (Bat-Chava, Martin, and Kosciw 2005) and a quantitative study of the effectiveness of HIV training (Perlman and Leon 2006). Goldstein et al. (2006) conducted the NDRI (National Development and Research Institutes, Inc.) study mentioned by Tony Saccente in his interview. Elizabeth Eckhardt's dissertation analyzes in-depth interviews done in conjunction with this larger quantitative NDRI study. Goldstein et al. surveyed 452 Deaf adults in eight states—California, Colorado, Maryland, Massachusetts, Michigan, New Jersey, New York, and Pennsylvania—while Eckhardt analyzed sixteen interviews from the New York and Philadelphia areas. R. Kevin Mallinson (2004) did in-depth interviews with five gay men in the Washington, D.C.–Baltimore area. Particularly with these two small qualitative studies, we need to keep in mind that findings may not be representative. These varied sources, however, will allow us to build a more complex picture than any individual source could present.

One commonality among the three studies I am highlighting is that they were sign language–oriented. As Eckhardt (2005) points out, most previous studies were paper-and-pencil questionnaires, which "have been shown to give inaccurate results for deaf persons whose main communication modes are manual languages" (4). Goldstein et al. (2006) used an American Sign Language (ASL) video questionnaire on the laptop computer mentioned by Tony. The videotaped interviews Eckhardt analyzed were in-depth personalized follow-ups of individuals who took the computerized survey in New York and

Table 1. Top 5 States/Areas: General AIDS Case Rate
per 100,000 Population (2003)

District of Columbia	170.6
New York	34.8
Virgin Islands	31.2
Maryland	28.5
Puerto Rico	27.5

Source. Adapted from Kaiser 2005: 1.

Philadelphia, and were conducted and preliminarily translated by a native ASL/English bilingual. Participants in Mallinson's (2004) small-scale study varied in communication style. Three were comfortable enough with Mallinson's signing skills and their own oral skills to be interviewed by only Mallinson; two were interviewed in the presence of a professional interpreter. All interactions were audiotaped and later transcribed.

All three studies focus on areas with significant rates of HIV/AIDS in general. Washington, D.C., New York, and the Baltimore area have some of the highest per-capita rates for AIDS in the general population (table 1).

While Pennsylvania, home state of Philadelphia, has a lower per-capita rate, it still has high numbers of cumulative AIDS cases.[2]

Although Mallinson's (2004) study is small, he worked with gay men in the Washington, D.C.–Baltimore area, a particularly vulnerable general population.[3] His interviewees were five Deaf gay males. They were either employed full time or college students, between the ages of 24 and 49, and could communicate fluently in ASL, spoken English, or both. Four were white, one Latino; four were HIV-negative, one HIV-positive.

The interviews he collected are searing.

Interviewer: What do you think would happen if you became HIV-positive?

Participant: I don't think about "if" I will get HIV. It's more like "when" I get it. . . . You can have HIV for more than 10 years before you get AIDS and die. It wouldn't be so bad to die at 40 years old. I am 26 years old now and, with medication, it would be a long life.

Interviewer: It wouldn't be so bad to die at 40?

Participant: No. . . . It's OK to be lonely when you are young.
. . . I know that many of my friends will probably have died by
that time. It wouldn't be so bad. (Mallinson 2004, 30)

Mallinson (2004) continues: "Although this man was all too familiar with AIDS-related infections, debilitation, and death ('I know too
much about it.'), he had little information on how to cope with his dis-
tress or negotiate safer sex" (30). This man's experiences were reflected
in other interviews. A forty-nine-year-old participant estimated "about
9 out of 10 of my friends have HIV" (2004, 30).

A major complaint among the men was the difficulty in getting
information.
    Words, words, words. Many Deaf don't understand and
    the reading is not easy. . . pictures are better and not boring
    . . . to show what to do and what not to do with sex to pre-
    vent having HIV come into your body . . . and make you sick.
    (Mallinson 2004, 31).

In general, many Deaf individuals who rely on ASL can have difficulty reading medical material. The education system for Deaf students
has left many with a comprehension level that has limited their ability
to access written prevention and health information (Perlman and Leon
2006, 143; Phillips 1996; McEwan and Anton-Culver 1998; Rudd 2003).
    On the other hand, Mallinson's (2004) interviewees emphasized
that they could understand when information was presented correctly, particularly when presented in their own language, ASL. As
one man commented about a videotape at a Deaf workshop, "It's a
good tape. You can understand a hell of a lot better because the ASL
really pulls it together for them, better than English written" (31). This
reflects the Deaf cultural preference, discussed by Tony in his interview, for direct, explicit, and visual communication. As Tony explains,
he uses "very frank language so there's no possibility for misunderstanding" (chapter 9).[4]
    Mallinson (2004) points out that Deaf gay men face particular
challenges as a minority within a minority. The Deaf gay community
is small and has been decimated by AIDS, and the larger Deaf community may stigmatize gay members for their sexual orientation.
Interviewees "described being ridiculed, belittled, or socially
marginalized by heterosexual Deaf persons who thought they were
weak and effeminate" (Mallinson 2004, 32; see also Eckhardt 2005).

In the larger gay community, hearing gay men usually lack the communication skills to successfully communicate with Deaf people. Eckhardt's (2005) study provides a view of HIV in the Deaf community from a mainly heterosexual perspective. She focused on sixteen New York- and Philadelphia-area Deaf adults, eight women and eight men, and does not explicitly discuss the sexual orientation or HIV status of the interviewees. Based on the interviews, the majority of the respondents seem to be heterosexual, and none admits to being HIV-positive. Male-with-male sexual activities, however, are referred to by one man when he discusses the importance of using condoms when receiving anal sex.

While some of Eckhardt's (2005) respondents know people with HIV, none report the decimation of their social networks experienced by Mallinson's (2004) interviewees. Those that did report knowing people with HIV had a range of reactions.

> . . . a friend from the same background has it. This person had sex without thinking about it and found out he had HIV. I thought, "It just happened with two friends of mine who have the same upraising as me. I better be safe about what I am doing." (Eckhardt 2005, 47)

> Well, I know a person that has HIV, he continues to sleep around and that makes me angry. I'm angry with that person because I believe he himself is angry too of getting it so he's like "who cares, I'm gonna die." . . . Maybe because he is young and he has this macho ego and he wants to enjoy it before other people get the word out and he's not able to have such access to the community. (Eckhardt 2005, 49)

With respect to the need for accessible preventive materials, however, Eckhardt's (2005) respondents made comments similar to those made by Tony Saccente and the men that Mallinson (2004) interviewed. There is a general sense that Deaf people do not have the information they need to protect themselves. "We lag behind on information on a daily basis. I feel like it's a constant catch-up game with the hearing community, we just have a lack of up to date information" (Eckhardt 2005, 55). There is also a specific desire for accessible information. As Eckhardt (2005) points out, "Fourteen of sixteen individuals mentioned that HIV information must be disseminated in ASL" (39). One example of such a response is

Just lectures is not enough, there's got to be graphic pictures. I saw a picture of an [sexually transmitted disease] and man that made an impression on me. The pictures were graphic and it made an impression so when you teach about AIDS you can do the straight language narrative but you MUST give pictures of the potential consequences or show people a picture of some one who is healthy and has HIV and this is what a full blown AIDS attack can look like. There's got to be a ton of visuals. . . . they need images in their mind that would make them stop and that image needs to be done frequently. (Eckhardt 2005, 40)

Interactive group presentations were particularly well received by the respondents. One person even specifically mentioned programs at Housing Works, where Tony was working.

We had a workshop at "Housing Works" . . . I thought it was awesome I learned so much. I mean of course I've been learning about HIV and AIDS through television and literature but boy this in person explanation increased my knowledge so much and then I got to meet people with HIV and who have AIDS and found them quite human and they let me ask them personal questions and they shared their own stories. (Eckhardt 2005, 37)

Meeting people with HIV in a formal setting such as a workshop or school-sponsored activity was mentioned as an important way to learn about HIV/AIDS by a number of respondents. Interviewees also stressed that information should be widely accessible. One person suggested that information should be disseminated at schools, workshops, and at "events among the deaf community" (Eckhardt 2005, 41).

Bat-Chava, Martin, and Kosciw's (2005) work, based on focus group discussions conducted in 1999 and 2000, indicates the importance of general community knowledge about HIV/AIDS. They compared groups in four cities in New York State: New York City, Rochester, Albany, and Buffalo. The best-informed participants were from Rochester, home of the National Technical Institute for the Deaf (NTID).

Participants interviewed in this area believed that the presence of a college for deaf students . . . made the local deaf community better educated and better able to comprehend written information about HIV/AIDS risks and prevention. In turn, greater understanding of HIV/AIDS triggered local community efforts at HIV/AIDS education programs by the Rochester Club for the Deaf, targeting non-college community groups. (Bat-Chava et al. 2005, 628)

Participants from New York City (home of Housing Works) were also moderately well informed, particularly if they were from high-risk groups such as Deaf men who have sex with men (MSM; MSM is the formal designation used in health studies for all men who have sex with other men, whether they identify themselves as gay or not) or ex-drug users, but even these people still had some incorrect information. In contrast, considerable confusion about HIV/AIDS was evident in focus groups in Albany and Buffalo. Although most studies of knowledge of AIDS focus on individual knowledge, these city-specific findings show that social networks or communities might be a better unit of analysis in some cases.

The kind of trained peer networks discussed by Tony Saccente in his interview (see chapter 9 in this volume) are one excellent way to get correct information to a social group, particularly for people that might not attend Deaf events on a regular basis. Peer information networks have also been shown to be effective in a range of Deaf and hearing settings. Gwendolyn Roberts (2006) documents the success of one peer network designed to spread information about HIV/AIDS at Gallaudet University. A combination of workshops and peer educators also can help address the difficult issues surrounding what one of Eckhardt's (2005) respondents called the "less educated deaf folks" (46).

Two other issues Eckhardt (2005) points out as problems connected to accessing correct information are the enormous stigma attached to HIV/AIDS in the Deaf community and related fears about breaches of confidentiality. Deaf people prize their contacts with the Deaf community. As one interviewee put it,

We have our own original language and unfortunately hearing people do not understand our culture. I cherish my language and our culture. It is the ability to sign easily with each other that makes me feel so comfortable. There is an ease of communication, it's just free and open. Anything you want to say you can say. It's not that way when I am in the hearing world. (Eckhardt 2005, 65)

This feeling of being able to say "anything you want to say" paradoxically leads to fear about the stigma of HIV/AIDS and fears about losing access to this cherished community. These fears are heightened by a sense that the Deaf community is small and that news travels fast.

One person even listed fear of stigma before fear of HIV as an illness.

> If I just ignored what I learned about HIV prevention, I just couldn't imagine it. I think about the stigma of my family, my desire to live, I don't want to waste my life so I would just avoid everything not to get it. (Eckhardt 2005, 43)

Closely connected with the stigma of HIV is the stigma of being gay.

> Out in the hearing world if you are gay people stay away from you and if they found out you had HIV they'd stay away from you as well, even more so it's the same in the deaf world. If they found out you are a gay man they would shun you and if you had HIV they would shun you even more. (Eckhardt 2005, 56)

One of the most dangerous aspects of the stigma of HIV is that people will ignore the issue of having HIV at all (as did the man referred to above who continued to sleep around despite knowing he had HIV), or they will avoid testing and treatment in places designed to serve Deaf people in order to avoid being seen by others in the Deaf community. Even interpreters may be suspected of passing on information. One respondent put it this way:

> I know three deaf men who have HIV and who won't participate in the deaf community. They go to hospitals, they refuse the interpreter, and they write notes back and forth because they are so dreadfully frightened that their secret will get out to the deaf community. (Eckhardt 2005, 57)

Others in Eckhardt's (2005) study echoed similar sentiments. All of this makes the job of Deaf outreach all the more important. Not only do HIV educators need to combat misinformation about AIDS, they need to combat the stigma that prevents Deaf people from getting help when they need it.

Although these interviews vividly illustrate some of the concerns Deaf community members have about HIV/AIDS, they don't give a sense of the extent or proportions of attitudes. For this information, let me turn to Goldstein, Eckhardt, Joyner, and Berry (2006), the quantitative NDRI study referred to by Tony.

Goldstein et al. (2006) is the largest study of HIV attitudes of Deaf people ever done. The survey included a mixed group of 452 participants. Background information on the participants included gender, age, ethnicity (whether Latino or not), race (African American, white, Asian American, Native American/Pacific Islander, or other), level of and type of education, whether they self-identified as Deaf or hard of hearing, and whether they used the full ASL or highly contextualized (referred to as HC below) and simplified version of the survey. The full ASL version had 135 questions; the HC version had 48 questions in a highly contextualized ASL. Abstract concepts were explained by concrete examples or stories on videotape. Grounding abstractions with commonplace examples is something Tony also found effective, as illustrated by his use of the idea of a Pacman to explain the effect of HIV on T-cells. English subtitles were also easily available for both versions of the survey, if participants wished. Which version was used was decided by fluent ASL project staff members at the time of the survey after a short conversation with participants; 58 percent took the full ASL version, 42 percent took the HC version. Another characteristic that proved important was whether the individual had a source of information about HIV, be it from a friend, media, or medical sources, or not. (See table 2.)

These survey-taker characteristics were then correlated with the number of correct answers to seven specific questions designed to judge knowledge about HIV, including "Can a pregnant woman who has HIV pass it on to her newborn baby?," "Can a man give HIV to a woman if

Table 2. Where Survey Participants Get HIV Information
(more than one source possible) (n = 452)

Friends	55%
Doctors	50%
Family members	35%
School or training programs	60%
Print or captioned media	77%
No source of HIV information listed	10%

Source. Adapted from Goldstein et al. 2006: 172.

they are having sex without a condom?" and "Can I get HIV from kissing someone with HIV?" (Goldstein et al. 2006, 172). These questions yielded a 0- to 7-point score for each participant that was used to judge statistical significance. After calculating significances for characteristics including gender, age, ethnicity, education, Deaf identity, knowledge of a person with HIV, HIV information source, and version of the survey, Goldstein et al. then ran multiple regressions on them.

> [The variables that] remained significant in the equation when all other variables were controlled were: attendance at a deaf school (lower score), knowing (of) a deaf person with HIV (higher score), ASL version of the interview (HC ASL, lower score), identifying any source of HIV information (higher score). (Goldstein et al. 2006, 175)

One troubling statistic in the Goldstein et al. (2006) study is that those who attended Deaf schools did significantly worse than those who attended a hearing school, even if briefly. Since Deaf school education is often associated with strong Deaf community values and fluent signing skills, this result seems to contradict the findings that those who took the full ASL version of the survey did better. Past studies, however, point to weaknesses in Deaf education. Two studies in the 1990s (Luckner and Gonzales 1993; Baker-Duncan, Dancer, Gentry, Highly, and Gibson 1997) of students at Deaf high schools showed that these youth had substantial gaps in their knowledge about HIV/AIDS, larger than those documented in this study by Goldstein et al. Given the seriousness of the AIDS problem in the Deaf community, Deaf schools should emphasize thorough and accurate sex education. Bat-Chava et al. (2005), working with adolescent focus groups from New York State Deaf schools in 1999 and 2000, found these Deaf students learned about AIDS regularly throughout their high school education: "Most students had good basic knowledge about HIV/AIDS and its prevention" (628–29). This gives hope that the current generation is better educated about HIV than their older counterparts.

The Bush administration's conservative attitude towards sex education in general, however, is probably not helping the situation. During an interview with Harry Vrenna (personal communication with author, January 2007), a long-term advocate for HIV education in the Deaf community, he discussed his frustration with the recently appointed principal of a well-known East Coast Deaf school. While the previous principal had invited HIV educators to the school, the current religiously conservative principal had banned all such visits and forbade even adult staff members from having educational literature at school.

On the positive side, personal knowledge of someone living with HIV increases overall knowledge about HIV by almost a point on average. Given the great stigma attached to HIV in the community, the courage of these HIV-positive people in agreeing to share their stories is remarkable. The experiences of the one self-identified HIV-positive man in Mallinson's (2004) study reinforces the value of HIV-positive members of the community. "As a Deaf man with HIV who had significant education, this participant felt an obligation to help fellow Deaf persons navigate the health care system" (Mallinson 2004, 34). In Bat-Chava et al. (2005), the older adults of the Albany-area focus groups trace their knowledge about AIDS to one of their peers who had become infected in the early 1980s. The work of these openly HIV-positive individuals is particularly important, given the "lack of funding and diminishing resources" (Mallinson 2004, 34) available for Deaf outreach and treatment.

This lack of funding is all the more frustrating because research suggests that community outreach does work. In a study of the changes in knowledge that a mixed group of Chicago-area and other midwestern Deaf people (n = 81) experienced after a comprehensive AIDS workshop conducted in ASL by experienced Deaf educators, Toby Perlman and Scott Leon (2006) found

> . . . that a culturally and linguistically sensitive presentation of HIV/AIDS prevention education materials can significantly increase a Deaf person's level of knowledge and can significantly strengthen a Deaf person's attitudes towards proactively reducing one's risk of becoming infected with HIV. (2006, 157)[5]

The finding that Tony refers to in his interview, that "23 percent of the Deaf thought that hearing people—but not Deaf people—could be HIV positive" (this volume, 167) is another example of community stigma. Goldstein et al. (2006) discuss the implications of 23 percent of their participants holding this view.

> It may be that some deaf people regard HIV as having a source outside of their own community, even though deaf people can become infected. This is analogous to members of the general

public viewing HIV as a "gay disease" even though they know that heterosexuals can also be infected. Another possibility is that this is a form of "community denial". After decades of discrimination, deaf culture has only recently been recognized as a distinct subculture by other Americans and deaf persons may not want to admit that a stigmatized medical condition also affects their community. This possibility is supported by the significant association found between this item and other items designed to measure stigma (e.g., "I would refuse to work with someone who has AIDS"). (2006, 178)

These qualitative and quantitative studies confirm the importance of the work done by Tony Saccente at Housing Works. His insights about how and what to present and the format that these presentations should take are confirmed by the responses of the variety of Deaf people presented here. In light of stigmas around HIV in the Deaf community, Tony's type of outreach work is particularly vital. Teaching about HIV is not just a matter of giving people the information they need but also addressing deeply held cultural notions.

The Extent of HIV/AIDS in the Deaf Community

One of the problems connected with HIV education in the Deaf community is that there is little information available on the extent of HIV/AIDS. There are no comprehensive studies of the incidence of HIV/AIDS in the U.S. Deaf community. One reason is that the Centers for Disease Control (CDC) does not recognize Deaf people as a cultural group, so it does not require states to collect information on the hearing status of people being tested for HIV. Tony's New York-based study showing that deaf people are three times more likely to be HIV-positive than hearing people is echoed by Connecticut figures (Harry Vrenna, personal communication with author, January 2007).[6] The Maryland testing figures discussed below point to a range between two and ten times more likely. Both the health of deaf people and the funding for often shoestring outreach programs are endangered by the lack of national statistics on this matter.

Maryland is the only state that keeps statistics on the hearing status of its HIV population, and then only at public testing sites. A Maryland Department of Health and Mental Hygiene (MDMHD) official estimated that, each year, 25 percent of HIV-positive people are identified at such public testing sites (personal communication with author, May

2007 [MDMHD forbids the use of specific names]). For the years information is available (2003, 2005, and 2006), deaf people were, on average, about twice as likely as hearing people to be HIV-positive. When
these numbers are adjusted for the comparative numbers of deaf and
hearing people taking the test, this ratio varies from almost eleven
times as likely in 2003 to more than five times as likely in 2006.[7] The
large inferences from small numbers and uncertain deaf population
size estimates make these numbers less reliable than the plain testing
data, but they do point to a very troubling trend. (See table 3.)

At the time of this writing, specific breakdowns for the 2005 and
2006 testing data were not available. In Monaghan (2006), however, I
analyzed the HIV figures made available by MDMHD for 2003 for patterns according to gender, ethnicity, age, and other factors. This analysis showed important differences between the deaf and hearing
epidemics. Although hearing men were substantially more likely to be
HIV-positive than hearing women (2.8 percent to 1.5 percent), deaf
women were almost as likely as deaf men to be HIV-positive (4.3 percent to 4.7 percent). Although among the hearing population being
tested, 91 percent of people in Maryland (a state with a large African
American population) testing positive were African American, among
the deaf population, 82 percent were African American. This decrease
in the proportion of African American HIV infections reflects an increase in the proportion of white cases. Although only 7 percent of
hearing cases are white, 16 percent of deaf cases are white (Monaghan
2006).

As in the hearing population, the group most at risk was the 40–49-
year-olds—4.7 percent of the hearing people in the study tested HIV-
positive while 6.7 percent of the deaf people in this cohort tested
HIV-positive.

This is an apparent contradiction to the predictions of Eckhardt's
(2005) participants, who saw young people at particular risk. Interviewees emphasized the active sexuality of teenagers.

> If you are talking about high school students, oh my God, yes,
> obviously because ya know it's the crazy days, sex is no big
> deal and that's why I think people get into the most trouble.
> (Eckhardt 2005, 61)

If one compares the age range to the progress of the HIV epidemic,
however, we can see that those ages 40–49 in 2003 were in their twen-
ties during the height of the epidemic in the 1980s. One hypothesis is

Table 3. Maryland 2003, 2005, and 2006 Public HIV Testing Results

Year	Hearing Status	HIV Negative	Indeterminate	HIV Positive	TOTAL	Percent Testing HIV+	Ratio Deaf to Not Deaf HIV+	Population Adjusted Ratio
2003	Deaf	794	0	38	832	4.5%	2.1	10.9
	Not Deaf	37,789	0	813	38,602	2.1%		
2005*	Deaf	740	1	25	766	3.3%	1.9	6.8
	Not Deaf	51,759	27	875	52,661	1.7%		
2006**	Deaf	415	0	10	425	2.4%	1.8	5.4
	Not Deaf	34,181	7	458	34,646	1.3%		

* No 2004 figures were available.

** Positive figures from 2006 include preliminary and non-confirmed positives.

(Chart adapted from figures from Monaghan 2006 and from new information provided by the Maryland Department of Health and Mental Hygiene, July 2007.)

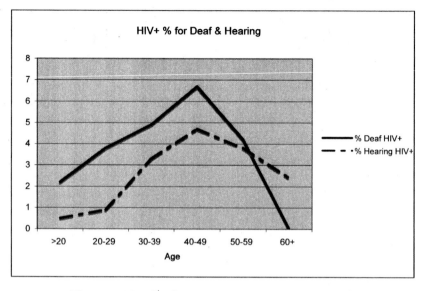

Figure 1. Maryland 2003 HIV testing figures by age.

that HIV entered this cohort before much was known about it (the first serious fights against HIV in the Deaf communities started in the 1980s) and has remained a danger to this cohort ever since.

If we look at comparative risk between hearing people and deaf people of the same age cohort, however, quite a different picture emerges. The 2 percent absolute gap between deaf and hearing HIV populations leads to quite different ratios of infection rates between different age cohorts.

If we look back at Figure 1, we can see that the epidemic decreases for both hearing and deaf people in the younger cohorts. When we compare these rates, as in Figure 2, however, we can see that proportional danger increases dramatically for young deaf people. While the risk in the 50–59 age group is comparable for deaf and hearing people, in the youngest age groups, deaf people are over four times more likely to test positive than their hearing peers. If this information is connected to the HIV knowledge surveys of Goldstein et al. (2006) and Perlman and Leon (2006), one hypothesis is that this 2 percent gap in infection rates parallels the knowledge gap between deaf and hearing people.

The 2 percent risk gap that shows up between age groups may or may not show up in other parts of the survey. The 2 percent risk gap is not visible between deaf and hearing MSM, but between deaf and

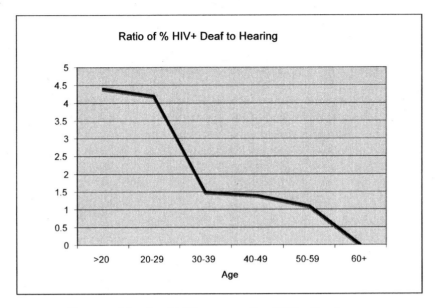

Figure 2. Maryland 2003 comparative HIV ratios by age.

hearing intravenous drug users (IUDs), the risk is double this, more than 4 percent (this holds even if you add the MSM IUDs into the figure). The 2 percent gap is evident between hearing and deaf partners at risk—a 1.1 percent versus 3.1 percent risk of partners being infected. One hypothesis is that deaf drug users and people with indirect risks of HIV are less likely than MSM to be aware of the potential threats of the disease, and are, therefore, less likely to be able to protect themselves.

The 2 percent gap is not reflected in the preliminary figures for 2005 and 2006, but an almost 2:1 ratio remains consistent across all three years. These Maryland figures are slim data on which to base a general understanding of the extent of HIV infection in the larger Deaf community, but they do indicate a serious problem that needs much further investigation.

Testing and Treatment

Not only is getting information about HIV/AIDS problematic for Deaf people, but so are testing and treatment. One of Eckhardt's (2006) female.participants stated, "I admit that many of us are clueless and many of us have not been tested because we don't know where to go. We have no information, it's just not there" (54). While outreach efforts such as those run by Tony Saccente can inform Deaf people about testing opportunities, it is often hard to come by this information outside such settings.

Gaskins (1999) lists the CDC teletypewriter (TTY) phone line (800-243-7889) as a place to get information about seventy-one organizations that serve the Deaf community. When the author called the TTY in February 2007, however, someone answered; but there was no response after I identified myself as doing research on resources available for Deaf people. Someone answered the National Testing Resource TTY line (888-232-6348) but was not able to give any testing sites near area code 11215—Brooklyn, New York—and when asked about 90210—Los Angeles, California—named only a hospital that served disabled people in general. The database this operator was working from seems to have been the same one available on the National HIV Testing Resources Web site: http://www.hivtest.org.

The National HIV Testing Resources Web site makes it relatively easy to find a testing site by entering a city or zip code, but difficult to find information about which sites provide services in ASL, particularly in large cities like New York and Los Angeles, which have hundreds of sites. Although languages available at a clinic are listed as part of the information page for each site, there is no specialized search function that lets you look for sites that provide specific language services; ASL users and Chinese speakers alike have no easy way to find accessible services. Users of this site have to individually check all nearby clinics separately.

The CDC keeps statistics about cities with significant AIDS populations. In a survey I did using the National HIV Testing Resources Web site, looking for all ASL testing sites within twenty miles of forty-four of the forty-nine cities designated a "Ryan White CARE Act eligible metropolitan area of residence" (CDC 2006), I found that twenty-eight of these forty-four cities had no sites listing ASL as one of their languages, including three of the top ten cities for AIDS: Philadelphia, Miami, and Ft. Lauderdale (and no sites listed for the rest of Florida either).[8] The information on the testing sites is both incomplete and inaccurate. There are, indeed, services available for Deaf people in both Philadelphia and Florida (sites of significant—but undocumented—numbers of deaf AIDS cases); on the other hand, some places listed as ASL testing sites did not, in fact, provide even interpreting services.

The services directory Web site of the AIDS-related *POZ Magazine*, http://directory.poz.com/, is more useful, listing twenty-one organizations that work with Deaf people; but the Web site can be difficult to negotiate.[9]

Given that the Americans with Disabilities Act makes it a requirement that all medical facilities be accessible, these figures are particularly distressing. The Connecticut Office of Protection and Advocacy for Persons with Disabilities had to sue Connecticut hospitals to make sure interpreters were available when needed (Department of Justice 1998), and the National Association of the Deaf (NAD) recently announced a settlement for lawsuits against Baltimore Washington Hospital.

> The agreement stems from a lawsuit filed by Alma Andrews against Baltimore Washington Medical Center (BWMC) in the United States District Court in Baltimore. . . . Under the agreement, BWMC reaffirmed and strengthened its policy of providing video interpreting services to deaf and hard of hearing patients. As they have done in the past, the hospital will provide on-site interpreters when using the video interpreting technology does not result in effective communication for a particular patient. BWMC agreed to implement additional procedures to facilitate the provision of on-site interpreters. (NAD 2007, 1)

As mentioned above, participants in Eckhardt's (2005) study repeatedly mentioned the stigma attached to receiving AIDS services. Most of the Deaf people who responded to Tony's New York survey went to mainstream facilities for their medical services. But as Alma Andrews found, these services are often unequipped to help Deaf people. People who want accessible communication with their medical providers are often frustrated. One of Mallinson's (2004) participants described being ignored after testing HIV-positive.

> When I was first diagnosed HIV [sic], they informed me of that and I felt pretty awful. And it was an awful experience. It was a lot of grief for me. Well, number one, there's no support. I had no support there. During my grief, the doctor, you know, the doctor left. (2004, 33)

Harry Vrenna, HIV rights advocate and counselor (in a personal communication with the author, January 2007) described one man diagnosed with HIV sitting in his office, with tears streaming down his face, crying "Why, why, why?"—why couldn't he, as a Deaf man, get the same services as hearing people, the easy access to testing, treatment, and other services that was offered to the general hearing public. Vrenna described another man spending five days dying in a large hospital with no access to an interpreter and therefore no explanation for what was happening to him.

The Ryan White CARE Act is at the center of AIDS treatment and care in the United States. It provides money to designated cities and to each state. Under one part of the act, the federal government provides money for case managers. These case managers shepherd clients with HIV or AIDS through the maze of medical and social institutions they need to deal with to get proper care. Certain large cities, including New York and Atlanta, have signing case managers who can help Deaf patients navigate the system. In other instances, case managers work closely with interpreters to make sure their clients get the care they need. Unfortunately, even with this system, Deaf people may fall through the cracks, particularly if they are not aware of their rights. One situation where this may occur is when a person's deafness is caused by AIDS. Bat-Chava et al. (2005) described a patient who was deafened by AIDS, got a cochlear implant, and then got no follow-up speech therapy to help him. Although he could speak to his case manager, this man's case manager and doctors had no idea of what was needed to make a cochlear implant successful.

Other federal and local state and city money has been available for outreach and related activities. In 2000, the federal Health Resources and Services Administration (HRSA) "took a leading role in the National Meeting on HIV/AIDS and the Deaf and Hard of Hearing Community," bringing together a meeting of Deaf AIDS providers and advocates and government officials (HRSA 2006). In the closing statement of the meeting report published by the Office on HIV/AIDS Policy (2000), Eric Goosby, then-director of HIV/AIDS policy at the Department of Health and Human Services, promised further government action on the issue.

We intend to specifically react and respond to the issues that you have brought before us. Dr. Satcher [the Surgeon General] is committed to incorporating your message to us into our programs, and we are going to bring these issues before our colleagues and create a subgroup that will focus on the unique needs of the deaf and hard of hearing. You absolutely need to stay in our face. (Office of HIV/AIDS Policy 2000, 17)

Since this report was published, however, the amount of money available for projects, particularly vital outreach projects, has diminished rather than increased. Deaf AIDS programs and projects in California, Connecticut, Illinois, New York, and Washington, D.C., have not been refunded and have been eliminated. Other programs, including a long-term one in Maryland, are threatened.

Conclusion

There is an AIDS crisis in the Deaf community, and so little information is kept by federal and state authorities that we do not even know the true extent of the disease. Direct testing figures in Maryland point to deaf people being twice as likely as hearing people to test HIV-positive. When adjusted for the fact that deaf people are more likely to get tested for HIV, this raises the infection rate to perhaps five to ten times as likely; these estimations could be overestimates as deaf people might be overrepresented at public sites compared to other testing sites, but they still point to a major epidemic. Tony Saccente's figures echo these rates and point to deaf people being three times more likely to test HIV-positive.

While the risk factors vary for different groups within the Deaf community, and the Maryland epidemic shares many of the same general trends as that of the larger hearing community, the epidemic is different among deaf people than it is among hearing people. As in the hearing population, the 40-49 age group is most at risk, but the proportion of deaf people compared to hearing people infected increases in younger groups. There seems to be a serious risk gap between deaf and hearing people across age groups. For example, whereas 4.7 percent of the 40- to 49-year-old hearing cohort tested were HIV-positive, 6.7 percent of the deaf cohort tested positive. This risk gap parallels a knowledge gap that shows up in qualitative and quantitative studies like Mallinson (2004), Eckhardt (2005), Bat-Chava et al. (2005), Goldstein et al. (2006), and Perlman and Leon (2006). The kind of outreach that Tony Saccente discusses in his interview with the editors saves lives by decreasing the knowledge gap, in turn reducing the risk gap facing the Deaf community. The people of New York City and Rochester know more because of programs like Housing Works.

Reducing risk is made even more important because health care is not easily accessed. Despite the legal requirements of the ADA, medical treatment is often not available in an accessible form. People have died with no interpreters to help explain what was happening to them, or have had to sue to get the treatment that they are entitled to. There are also internal community issues, including stigmas about being gay or having HIV, and privacy concerns that prevent some people from getting the access they need to maintain their health. Although video relay technology offers some hope as an interpretation method that won't compromise privacy, it is still a clumsy system with potential for misunderstanding, according to even hospital administrators interviewed during my survey of HIV testing service facilities (Monaghan 2006). Far better to prevent the spread of HIV in the first place, yet HIV programs are being cut across the country. Unfortunately, many in the general population do not know that HIV/AIDS in Deaf communities is a problem at all, and the CDC does not recognize deaf people as an at-risk category. This lack of recognition has led to limited funding that threatens the very programs that help the most.

ACKNOWLEDGMENTS

Thanks to the editors for their invitation to join this volume and their support throughout the process, to Tony Saccente for the use of his important interview, and to Douglas McLean of Forest Books, publisher of *Deaf Worlds*, for permission to reprint many of the tables cited here. Many thanks as well for proofreading, bibliographic suggestions, and help in understanding this complex issue to Constanze Schmaling, Amy Wilson, Harry Vrenna, Deborah Karp, Andy Bartley, and Michel Turgeon.

ENDNOTES

1. These 1990s studies include Bares 1992; Luckner and Gonzales 1993; Peinkofer 1994; Doyle 1995; Kennedy and Bucholz 1995; and Gaskins 1999. See Eckhardt 2005; Goldstein, Eckhardt, Joyner, and Berry 2006; Perlman and Leon 2006 for general reviews; and Roberts 2006 for a review of issues as related to Deaf adolescents and college students.
2. Philadelphia, with 29,988 cases, is seventh in ranking among states with accumulated AIDS cases between 1981 and 2003. New York tops the list with 162,446 cases (Kaiser 2005, 1).

3. Baltimore had the highest general rate of new infection in the United States among MSM. An 8 percent infection rate was found in Baltimore. The next two highest rates in the nation were found in Miami, with a 2.6 percent new infection rate, and New York City with 2.3 percent. These figures are from HIV tests conducted from June 2004 to April 2005 ($n = 1,767$ men), which are cited in Murphy 2005.

4. This preference for frank talk is not just a trait of the American Deaf community. Norine Berenz (2006) discusses the importance of an explicit Canadian-produced ASL safe sex video, "Hot and Safe," in Brazil, as it provided visual information on safe sex and "broke the barrier of silence around Gay sex" (187).

5. The methodology of the study involved both written English and ASL. "The surveys were printed in English for purposes of collecting the data but the presenter, one of three native signers formally trained in HIV/AIDS education, converted each question into ASL" (Perlman and Leon 2006, 148).

6. As the testing procedure reflected a medical rather than a cultural assessment (the people giving the test were trained to check a box marked "deaf" or "not deaf"), in this section, "deaf" will be used.

7. The population-adjusted ratio is based on calculations in Monaghan (2006) on the different rates between deaf and hearing people being tested. The same 2003 population statistics were used for all years. Monaghan (2006, 102) describes the procedure used to calculate these numbers.

> According to July 1, 2003 U.S. Census Bureau estimates, Maryland had a population of 5,508,909 people (U.S. Census Bureau 2004), and according to MD 2003, 39,434 of these people had themselves tested for HIV/AIDS, 0.72% of the population, and 851 were found to be HIV+. . . . The crude estimate of the population over 16 'who can't hear normal conversation' in Maryland was 17,089 (Harrington 2004). If the number is adjusted to add the approximately 24% of the population that is 16 and under, . . . we get roughly 22,600 people. Using these adjusted figures, we get 3.7% of the Deaf population being tested (832 people), and 0.17% testing HIV+ (38 people). When compared to the MD 2003 hearing people tested, this gives us the very sobering figures of Deaf people in the testing results being 5.1 times more likely to be tested and 10.9 more likely to be HIV+ than the general population. Problems here include the general unreliability of the estimate and that the definition of deafness is not clear. (Monahan 2006, 102)

8. To do the survey, I searched for the zip codes for each city on the list and then chose the lowest ordinary zip code for each city, estimating that it would reflect some center of population—for example, for New York, I used 10001, Houston 77002, and Minneapolis 55401. I then checked every testing site in each city, making note of what languages were available in every clinic. I have since called some, but not all, of the listed clinics. Four cities, three in New Jersey and Oakland, California, were within twenty miles of New York City or San Francisco so were not separately tabulated. No information was available about Portland, Oregon.

9. To find sites serving deaf people at http://directory.poz.com/, click on the "search by service" menu, scroll down for "Deaf," and then press "search." I found twenty-one sites when I searched on May 14, 2007.

REFERENCES

Baker-Duncan, N., J. Dancer, B. Gentry, P. Highly, and B. Gibson. 1997. Deaf adolescents' knowledge of AIDS: Grade and gender effects. *American Annals for the Deaf* 142(5): 368–72.

Bares, B. 1992. Facing AIDS: How prevalent is this deadly disease in the deaf population? *Hearing Health* 8: 12–16.

Bat-Chava, Y., D. Martin, and J. G. Kosciw. 2005. Barriers to HIV/AIDS knowledge and prevention among deaf and hard of hearing people. *AIDS Care* 17(5): 623–34.

Berenz, N. 2006. HIV/AIDS in the Brazilian Deaf community. *Deaf Worlds* [Special issue: HIV/AIDS and Deaf Communities, ed. C. Schmaling and L. Monaghan] 22(1): S184–88.

CDC. 2006. Centers for Disease Control and Prevention's AIDS Cases by State and Metropolitan Area Provided for the Ryan White CARE Act, June 2005. Table 2 at http://www.cdc.gov/hiv/topics/surveillance/resources/reports/2005supp_vol11no1/default.htm (accessed May 14, 2007).

CSSQ. 2007. Notre historique. Coalition Sida des Sourds du Québéc. http://www.cssq.org/pages/accueil/historique.htm (accessed August 8, 2007).

Deaf HIV/AIDS Resources. 2006. Remember Their Names. http://www.deafaids.info/remember/index.html (accessed May 14, 2007).

Department of Justice. 1998. Connecticut Hospitals Settle Suit to Provide Sign Language, no. 303 06-26-98. http://www.usdoj.gov/opa/pr/1998/June/303.html (accessed May 14, 2007).

Doyle, A. G. 1995. AIDS knowledge, attitudes and behaviors among deaf college students. *Sexuality and Disability* 13(2): 107–34.

Eckhardt, E. 2005. An exploration of HIV/AIDS perceptions, knowledge, and beliefs among individuals who are deaf. Ph.D. diss., New York University.

Gaskins, S. 1999. Special population: HIV/AIDS among the deaf and hard of hearing. *Journal of the Association of Nurses in AIDS Care* 10(2): 75–78.

Goldstein, M. F., E. Eckhardt, P. Joyner, and R. Berry. 2006. An HIV knowledge and attitude survey of deaf U.S. adults. *Deaf Worlds* [Special issue: HIV/ AIDS and Deaf Communities, ed. C. Schmaling and L. Monaghan] 22(1): 163–83.

Harrington, T. 2004. Statistics: Deaf population of the United States. Gallaudet University Library Deaf-related resources, frequently asked questions. http://library.gallaudet.edu/dr/faq-statistics-deaf-us.htm (accessed February 5, 2006).

HRSA. 2006. The Deaf and Hard of Hearing and HIV/AIDS in the United States. A publication of the U.S. Department of Health and Human Services, Health Resources and Services Administration, HIV/AIDS Bureau. http://hab.hrsa.gov/history/deaf/ (accessed August 8, 2007).

Kaiser Family Foundation. 2005. The HIV/AIDS epidemic in the United States. http://www.kff.org/hivaids/upload/Fact-Sheet-The-HIV-AIDS-Epidemic-in-the-United-States-2005-Update.pdf (accessed August 8, 2007).

Kennedy, S. G., and C. L. Bucholz. 1995. HIV and AIDS among the Deaf. *Sexuality and Disability* 13(2): 111–19.

Luckner, J. L., and B. R. Gonzales. 1993. What deaf and hard-of-hearing adolescents know and think about AIDS. *American Annals of the Deaf* 19(8): 338–42.

Mallinson, R. K. 2004. Perceptions of HIV/AIDS by deaf gay men. *Journal of the Association of Nurses in AIDS Care* 15(4): 27–36.

McEwan, E., and H. Anton-Culver. 1988. The medical communication of Deaf patients. *Journal of Family Practice* 26(3): 289–91.

Monaghan, L. 2006. Maryland 2003 HIV infection statistics for hearing and deaf populations. *Deaf Worlds* [Special issue: HIV/AIDS and Deaf Communities, ed. C. Schmaling and L. Monaghan] 22(1): 83–110.

Murphy, D. E. 2005. A good report on AIDS, and some credit the web." *New York Times*, August 18, 2005. http://www.nytimes.com/2005/08/18 /health/18aids.html (accessed May 14, 2007).

National Association of the Deaf. 2007. NAD settles complaint against Baltimore Washington Medical Center. Press release. www.nad.org/contactus (accessed May 2, 2007).

Office of HIV/AIDS Policy. 2000. *Conference proceedings: National meeting on the deaf and hard of hearing*. Washington, D.C.: U.S. Department of Health and Human Services.

Peinkofer, J. 1994. HIV education for the deaf, a vulnerable minority. *Public Health Reports* 109(3): 390–96.

Perlman, T. S., and S. C. Leon. 2006. Preventing AIDS in the Midwest. Special issue, HIV/AIDS and Deaf Communities, *Deaf Worlds* [Special issue: HIV/ AIDS and Deaf Communities, ed. C. Schmaling and L. Monaghan] 22(1): 140–62.

Phillips, B. A. 1996. Bringing culture to the forefront: Formulating diagnostic impressions of Deaf and hard of hearing people at times of medical crisis. *Professional Psychology: Research and Practice* 27(2): 137–44.

Rainbow History Project. 2006. Heroes: Remembering Those We Lost to AIDS. http://www.rainbowhistory.org/chronAIDSlosses.pdf (accessed February 5, 2006).

Roberts, G. S. 2006. Sexuality and HIV/AIDS education among deaf and hard
    of hearing students. *Deaf Worlds* [Special issue: HIV/AIDS and Deaf Com-
    munities, ed. C. Schmaling and L. Monaghan] 22(1): 111–39.
Rudd, R. 2003, Improvement of health literacy. In *Communicating health: Priorities
    and strategies for progress*, 35–60. Washington, D.C.: U.S. Department of
    Health and Human Services, Office of Disease Prevention and Health
    Promotion.
U.S. Census Bureau, Population Division. 2004. *Annual estimates of the popula-
    tion for the counties of Maryland: April 1, 2000, to July 1, 2003* (CO-EST2003-
    01-24). Washington, D.C.: Author.

11 ▍ DPN and Civil Rights

Gregory J. Hlibok

Since childhood, I have understood and asserted my civil rights as an individual—something instilled in me by my parents. Their passionate involvement with Deaf advocacy matters, in pursuit of the betterment of deaf people's lives, has contributed to where I am now. For example, I have a letter posted on the wall in my office from Senator James L. Buckley of New York, which was dated August 13, 1976. This letter was written in response to my oldest brother, Bruce. He wrote the senator, asking him about the possibility of having television programs displayed in captions. (This was back when there were few captioned TV programs.) However, nowadays, most TV programs are captioned, thanks to the tireless and enduring efforts of Deaf community leaders who fought for our rights to have full access to them.

My childhood experience taught me that good things do not magically happen by themselves. It has been embedded in my mind that you cannot take things for granted, and you should always be conscious of how things came to be. My parents encouraged me to be an independent thinker, and to think out loud, especially during dinnertime, when my parents, two brothers, and one sister ate together every day.

Growing up in a Deaf household, I experienced absolutely no communication or attitude barriers. Going out on the street, we would use gestures with our hearing peers. I did not really experience frustrating communication barriers until I was enrolled in public school as a first-grader.

That first-grade year, I staged my first civil rights protest. I had gone to kindergarten at the Lexington School for the Deaf, which was an oral school, but which presented me with no communication barriers, nonetheless. Because of my speaking ability, Lexington recommended placing me in a local public school as a first-grader, which my parents did. It was a drastic change for me: The first-grade class was filled with forty hearing students, whom I could not communicate with, including the teacher, who had no idea of how to communicate with a deaf child. I came to call it the "hearing" school, and I waged a silent protest against my parents, trying to get them to transfer me back to Lexington. To understand how much of a shock that public school was, take a look back at where I grew up.

There were no communication barriers in my family; I grew up with deaf parents and three deaf siblings—two brothers and a sister. I did not recognize any communication barriers until 1980, when closed captioning was first introduced. It was then that I realized the benefits of watching a closed-captioned program. Now, I get frustrated when I see a program without captioning, because I understand the difference. I grew up with a black-and-white TV, but never really paid attention to it until closed captioning became available.

My family communicated entirely in sign language, and we always ate dinner together at the same table regardless of our hectic schedules. This table still exists at my parents' house. It's wobbly and unstable, but my parents kept it for its sentimental value, as it reminds us all of intriguing dinnertime conversations about many subjects, but mostly about deaf education and advocacy issues. We would bang our hands on the table, trying to win everyone's attention, just like when a hearing person tries to talk louder in order to win another hearing person's attention. We would talk about current events, which made me very conscious of daily political issues.

My parents were involved with various community and advocacy activities at the local, state, and national levels, such as the Empire State Association of the Deaf, which acts solely for the betterment of deaf people's lives. Their involvements influenced me and my siblings to become active in the community as well. They instilled a sense of responsibility to assert our rights outside of the home. It was during these formative years that our household instituted a "free communication zone"—a place where we could all be entirely open about our viewpoints.

SOURCE OF SUCCESS FOR CIVIL RIGHTS PROTESTS

It was this chapter of my life growing up—this civil rights in practice—that inspired me to become an activist. People often want me to talk about my involvement as a student leader with the Deaf President Now (DPN) movement of March 1988 that led to the selection of Gallaudet University's first Deaf president. But I often find it intriguing to discuss civil rights issues. This is because I like to look forward to something, to look into something that can be done or ought to be done rather than resting on my laurels. However, talking about DPN always gives me goose bumps, as it is a reminder of how much we can truly achieve together as a team, large or small.

After the week-long DPN protest concluded, those of us involved in DPN received a lot of requests from a variety of student body governments at colleges and universities across the country, asking for a "tool kit" in leading a successful protest. From the Vietnam era on, student protests typically had an ugly ending. So our DPN protest was rare in that it was relatively non-violent. However, I was unable to provide an answer because the protest was not preplanned but, rather, purely spontaneous. Civil rights is not an academic matter, based on textbooks. Rather, for a civil rights protest or movement to succeed, it must be based on an individual's life experience, which ignites a sense of purpose. This sense is inherent. The more an individual experiences some form of oppression and frustration, the greater desire that individual will have to succeed in such a protest. Thus, success depends on the circumstances the individual is in. Different circumstances produce different outcomes, and there is no particular formula for this. However, you can look at certain successful aspects of the DPN movement that brought us to where we are now. Those aspects are, essentially, the strengths of the people involved in the movement.

The history of civil rights provides us with clues in learning how to develop the confidence to get what it takes to succeed. Primarily it is the combination of an individual's experience and character that allows him or her to successfully crack through the oppressor's paternalistic attitude. In other words, a child who grew up in an oppressed environment is inclined to become a civil rights activist like Dr. Martin Luther King, Jr. This is why I tend to view a d/Deaf person as a more effective civil rights activist for our cause than a hearing person, especially for those who were born deaf or became deaf during early childhood.

EFFECTS OF THE DPN MOVEMENT

The effects of the DPN movement upon Deaf and hard of hearing constituents are gigantic and immeasurable. Here I will sum them up in three major positive groups of outcomes: (1) greater awareness, (2) increased job opportunity, and (3) greater access to communications technology. There is evidence of a significant increase in attendance of American Sign Language courses across the country, and the horizon for job opportunities has widened from traditional occupations for deaf people, such as teachers, printers, and postal workers, to business owners, lawyers, journalists, and so on.

I will concentrate, however, on the effects of DPN on access to communications technology. In the years following the DPN protest, a number of laws protecting the civil rights of people with disabilities were passed. I testified in support of the Americans with Disabilities Act (ADA), which was passed in 1990. Congress also passed the TV Decoder Circuitry Act, soon thereafter, in 1990, as well as the Telecommunications Act of 1996, which contained Section 713 mandating closed captioning in nearly 100 percent of all television programs. In 2001, I started at the Federal Communications Commission (FCC) as an attorney advisor in regulating telecommunication relay service (TRS) matters and captioning.

The most important message that came out as a result of the protest was that deaf people should be given the opportunity to control our own destiny, because deaf people can do anything except hear. This is as straightforward as it can be. We were not asking for a free lunch but, rather, the opportunity that enables us the same inalienable rights that hearing people have been afforded. We have fought all of our lives for opportunity; it was discrimination that we were fighting against.

Justin Dart, the father of the ADA, never failed to remind me how instrumental DPN was in the passage of ADA legislation. He always thanked me for this since I served as spokesperson for DPN. The importance of his remarks did not really sink in for me until I attended a memorial service for Dart in July 2002 at the historical New York Avenue Presbyterian Church in Washington, D.C. President Clinton, in his eulogy, referred to Justin as "the father of the ADA" and spoke about the law as if it was the most sacred piece of legislation to him. He also spoke about the DPN and how it brought tremendous awareness among people all over the world about the capabilities of Deaf and hard of hearing people. Indeed, we can take pride in living up to the intent of the DPN movement and ADA. The intent of the DPN movement was simply to assert that Deaf people shall control their destiny because, regardless of their hearing capabilities, Deaf people can do anything.

It is interesting to note that the term "civil rights" is often perceived negatively because it implies that the disadvantaged are "complaining" for their rights and that the disadvantages are perpetuated as a result of their choice of career and lifestyle, rather than by the society's oppressive actions. It sounds as if the protestors simply want their civil rights because they feel some special sense of entitlement rather than because they, like all people, deserve them. That cannot be true for d/Deaf and hard of hearing persons, as they did not choose their disability.

This particular perception of civil rights and its terminology is very much implied, especially where the FCC is concerned. The FCC receives and reviews complaints. The term "complaints" by itself is misleading, because it appears that you are dependent on others in solving your personal issues, which certainly does not have a positive connotation and is in conflict with the fact that a great majority of deaf people are self-reliant. Rather than seeing a submission to the FCC as a complaint, we need to look at it as a problem which has to be resolved or as an indication of a broader issue which has to be addressed. There needs to be a better word to replace "complaints," a term that conveys a more proactive and positive response instead of a negative one. It requires attitude adjustment among all of us that complaints be treated as an indication of an underlying issue. For example, complaints showing a trend toward increased problems with the HDTV captioning issue is, in fact, a sign that the industry is not adequately addressing the problem of a lack of, or the poor quality of, captioning on HDTV. Consumers get frustrated when they purchase a pricey HDTV that displays flawless captioning at the retail store only to find out that the captioning quality decreases significantly at home. The problem is that the retail store uses taped or closed-circuit programs that show pre-captioned programs which are usually flawless.

Congress delegated to the FCC the jurisdiction to oversee regulatory responsibilities related to the TRS, television captioning, hearing aid compatibility, accessible telecommunications services and products, and access to emergency information. Nearly all of these issues are handled in the Disability Rights Office (DRO), a division of the Consumer and Governmental Affairs Bureau at the FCC.

I come into my office each day wearing two hats, one as an attorney and another as a deaf consumer. Folks have been telling me that it will be difficult to wear my attorney hat because I must have to strictly interpret certain regulations that may not promote deaf consumers' telecommunications needs. After working here for several years, I have reached a level of maturity where it is no longer an issue to wear both hats. I have learned to wear my hats interchangeably. I find it is entirely possible to interpret the rules appropriately and write a new requirement in a way that would be consistent with the intent of the statutory rule. For example, Title IV of the ADA states that the TRS must be provided in a way that is functionally equivalent to a voice-to-voice telephone call. The phrase "functionally equivalent" is a moving goal, where providers must constantly ensure that relay service is improving whenever new technology arrives, enabling them to reach a higher level of functionality. For example, the standard of a functional equivalent relay call in the 1990s was a teletypewriter (TTY)-to-voice call that could be relayed in a time lag that ranged from five to ten seconds or longer in some instances and such as navigating through an interactive voice response menu. Back then, it took me an average of twenty minutes to complete a TTY relay call because I had to navigate through several menu selections. Today, the standard for relaying a call is three seconds or better through the use of the video relay service (VRS), which features a video connection with a sign language interpreter. This new form of TRS has enabled me to complete the same call in three minutes. Because of advances in technology, both consumer expectations and the bar for functional equivalency have been raised. Deaf consumers have been dropping TTYs like hot potatoes in the last few years because they are not interested in dealing with a ten-second lag time with a TTY relay call. Lag time can be more than just an annoyance, as in the case of 911 emergency calls (see chapter 2 in this volume).

There is another bright spot in Title IV of the ADA (amended as Section 225 of the Communications Act of 1934), which states that the FCC shall ensure that regulations encourage the use of existing technology and do not discourage or impair the development of improved technology. This dovetails with the functional equivalency principle. Is it fair for a deaf person to be glued to her chair for a VRS call while a hearing person can talk on his cellular phone with a live video function out in the street? No, it should not happen, because once the portable video functionality feature becomes available, a deaf consumer should be able to place a VRS call using this video-enabled portable device from anywhere.

With regard to universal access, it has been the perception among some that certain legislative items appear to be designed solely for the benefit of certain constituents at the expense of the general public. For example, a greater social service for a certain group translates into a greater burden on the public, since the public would have to foot the tax bill. Although increased social services may appear to be just for certain constituents, they benefit nearly everyone. This is true for technology. The purpose of universal access is to make technology as accessible as possible for everyone. We need to ensure that technology brings everyone on board while not creating a new division between the haves and have-nots. Deaf people appreciate the new technology tremendously, but they are constantly reminded about the invention of the telephone, which historically proved to be a bittersweet milestone because it widened the gap between the deaf and hearing in terms of communications access and opportunities.

One excellent example of unintended consequences is that of ramps on curbs, required by Title II of the ADA and designed to benefit targeted groups (i.e., those in wheelchairs). Those ramps benefit mothers pushing strollers, people on bicycles, people using dollies, the elderly, etc. This is also true for the closed captioning of TVs. The TV industry lobbied against requiring TVs to be built with a decoder chip that costs a measly few dollars. However, the Television Decoder Cir-cuitry Act of 1990 required that all TVs, thirteen inches or larger, must contain a built-in decoder chip. As a result, millions of TV viewers set up the captioning feature while watching, including many hearing people who rely on captioning in noisy areas, such as bars, airports, and train stations. Also, many senior citizens have come to appreciate this feature when they lose their hearing.

The FCC rules required that nearly all TV programs be captioned by January 1, 2006. This benefited not only deaf people but also more than 100 million other Americans, including 28 million individuals with hearing loss, 30 million people who use English as a second language, 27 million illiterate adults who are trying to learn to read, 12 million children learning how to read, and 4 million remedial readers.

When TV captions are turned on in public places, this greater exposure brings greater awareness, which eventually helps hearing people unconsciously adjust their attitude to becoming more accepting of captions. The general attitude has improved over time, but without much exposure to people with disabilities, ignorance is usually an excuse for this attitude. Also, the public is slow to understand deaf people's needs, including the need for closed captioning. So increasing the visibility of captions can actually raise awareness. Furthermore, we need to increase awareness, which will, in turn, raise consciousness about the needs of people with disabilities. Ignorance is simply no longer an excuse in this day and age.

We need to emphasize that there should be no exceptions when it comes to equality for opportunity and accessibility. The Bill of Rights did not hold any exceptions to this and is simply straightforward in its language. We need to be forthcoming with the technology industry and applaud innovations, but not those that present barriers for some people.

We need to constantly ask ourselves whether we are on equal footing with the American mainstream. In my capacity as an FCC attorney, I ask myself whether Deaf and hard of hearing consumers are experiencing a functionally equivalent telephone service, that is, whether the quality of a relay service is equivalent to a voice-to-voice telephone call. This is a moving target for us because of the emerging telecommunications technology. The bar keeps on going higher and higher as long as new technologies are introduced. Our work is never done.

Contributors

H. Timothy Bunnell received his Ph.D. in experimental psychology from the Pennsylvania State University in 1983. From 1983 to 1989, he held the position of research scientist at Gallaudet University. In 1989, he accepted the position of director of the speech research program at the Alfred I. duPont Hospital for Children (AIDHC). He now directs the Nemours Center for Pediatric Auditory and Speech Sciences at AIDHC and participates in the AIDHC cochlear implant program as a research advisor.

Maggie Casteel is a late-deafened adult with a cochlear implant and a hearing aid. She is passionate about the use of hearing assistive technology and has been advocating for the accessibility rights of persons with hearing loss for fifteen years. She is a recent graduate of the University of Pittsburgh, where she earned an M.S. in rehabilitation counseling and a certification in rehabilitation technology. She is a certified rehabilitation counselor currently working for the Veteran's Administration Pittsburgh Health Care System. In her role as a vocational rehabilitation specialist, she is able to continue pursuit of her passion for assistive technology while serving disabled veterans.

Doreen DeLuca is a nationally certified sign language interpreter in the Philadelphia region. She has a B.S. degree in elementary education and is a certified deaf education teacher. Her professional experience includes work with the Deaf community in educational, theatrical, conference, legal, and Deaf-Blind settings. Doreen has been teaching American Sign Language at Swarthmore College in Pennsylvania since 1999. She is a co-editor for the companion book, *Signs and Voices,* published in 2008 and is the co-author of a storybook for deaf children and their hearing peers, soon to be published by Gallaudet University Press.

Jami N. Fisher is the American Sign Language Program coordinator at the University of Pennsylvania. She has a B.A. in English and education and an M.S.Ed. in education, culture, and society with a concentration in deaf cultural issues in education. Her current research interests focus on second-language acquisition methodology for teaching ASL.

Christy Hennessey is the program coordinator for Deaf and Hard-of-Hearing Services at Independent Resources, Inc., in Wilmington, Delaware. She received an associate's degree in business from the National Technical Institute for the Deaf in Rochester, N.Y., a B.A. in ASL studies from Gallaudet University, and an M.A. in rehabilitation counseling for the deaf from the University of Tennessee. Christy has worked at Independent Resources since 1998, and she also teaches American Sign Language courses at the University of Pennsylvania.

Lisa Herbert is a Black Deaf adult who has worked at the Indiana School for the Deaf since 2005. She has an M.A. in developmental psychology and a specialist degree (Psy.S.) in school psychology with specialization in working with Deaf and hard of hearing children. Her goal is to pursue her Ph.D. in the area of psychology, linguistics, or school administration. Lisa is a former Miss Deaf Florida, and her platform focused on forming bridges between Deaf students in the mainstream and those in residential schools.

Gregory J. Hlibok is a senior attorney at the Federal Communications Commission's Disability Rights Office. He has taken a lead on several crucial rule-making proceedings that resulted in an unprecedented growth in video relay service and Internet protocol relay service. He comes from a second-generation Deaf family and is a Gallaudet University alumnus with a law degree from Hofstra University School of Law. He is known for his leadership role during the Deaf President Now movement at Gallaudet in 1988 and is a leader in Deaf Pride events.

Irene W. Leigh, a deaf psychologist who holds a Ph.D., has done high school teaching, psychological assessment, psychotherapy, and mental health administration. She has been a professor in the Gallaudet University Clinical Psychology doctoral program since 1992. In addition to conducting numerous presentations, she has published more than fifty articles and book chapters, edited *Psychotherapy with Deaf Clients from Diverse Groups* (1999), and co-authored *Cochlear Implants in Deaf Children: Ethics and Choices* (2002/2005) and *Deaf People: Evolving Perspectives from Psychology, Education, and Sociology* (2004). She is a fellow of the American Psychological Association and associate editor for the *Journal of Deaf Studies and Deaf Education*.

Kristin A. Lindgren directs the Haverford Writing Center and teaches in the Writing Program at Haverford College. She holds an M.A. in English literature from Bryn Mawr College. With Donna Jo Napoli and Doreen DeLuca, she co-edited *Signs and Voices: Deaf Culture, Identity, Language, and Arts*, the companion volume to *Access*. She teaches courses in literature, writing, and disability studies, and has taught at Bryn Mawr and the University of Pennsylvania as well as Haverford. Her recent work appears in *Disability/Teaching/Writing: A Critical Sourcebook* (Bedford/St. Martin's Press 2007), *Illness in the Alchemy* (Purdue University Press 2007), and *Gendering Disability* (Rutgers University Press 2004).

Amanda J. Mangiardi has worked with deaf children as a certified teacher of deaf students and a certified auditory-verbal therapist for fourteen years. She is currently the coordinator of the Cochlear Implant Program at A.I. duPont Hospital for Children. Amanda's son, Adrean Mangiardi, is a film and animation student at the School of the Art Institute of Chicago and has bilateral cochlear implants. Adrean's short film, *Equilibrium*, was featured on a recent PBS documentary titled *History through Deaf Eyes*. Adrean's film portrays both the joys and the frustrations of relying on technological devices to connect to the hearing world.

Philip J. Mattiacci was born in Philadelphia, Penn., and attended the Pennsylvania School for the Deaf and Abraham Lincoln High School. He obtained his B.A. in government from Gallaudet University in 1998 and his M.A. in political management from George Washington University in 2003. Philip is the program coordinator at the Office of Advocacy and Outreach Services for the Deaf and Hard of Hearing at Temple University. Since 2006, he has been Gallaudet University's presidential fellow as a doctoral candidate in political science at Temple University. His research focuses on voting behavior and the political participation of Deaf and hard of hearing Americans.

Leila Monaghan teaches anthropology at the University of Wyoming. She has a Ph.D. in linguistic anthropology from UCLA and has worked with Deaf communities in New Zealand and the United States. She is the co-editor of the books *Many Ways to Be Deaf* (with Constanze Schmaling, Karen Nakamura, and Graham Turner) and *HIV/AIDS and Deaf Communities* (with Constanze Schmaling) and is currently doing further research on the issue of HIV/AIDS as well as more general studies on the development of communities, ranging from parent groups in Brooklyn to the field of linguistic anthropology.

Donna Jo Napoli is professor of linguistics at Swarthmore College. She completed undergraduate and doctoral degrees at Harvard University and then taught at several universities before settling at Swarthmore. She has published heavily in theoretical linguistics and in the past decade has worked on American Sign Language morphology, sign language humor, and developing reading materials to enhance literacy skills, including materials designed specifically for Deaf and hard of hearing children. She is the mother of five and also publishes fiction for children. For more information, see http://www.donnajonapoli.com.

Robert C. O'Reilly, M.D., is director of the Pediatric Cochlear Implant and Auditory Rehabilitation Program at the A.I. duPont Hospital for Children in Wilmington, Delaware, and head of the Pediatric Balance and Vestibular Disorders Laboratory: Center for Pediatric Auditory and Speech Sciences, Nemours Department of Biomedical Research. He is clinical associate professor of otolaryngology and pediatrics at Jefferson Medical College and a staff otologist/neurotologist at A.I. duPont. He completed his residency in otolaryngology/head and neck surgery at Thomas Jefferson University Hospital and his fellowship in neurotology at the University of Pittsburgh Medical Center. His publications involve topics in pediatric auditory and vestibular function.

Tony Saccente was a special education teacher and instructor of American Sign Language at the Lexington School for the Deaf for ten years. He was also coordinator of deaf services for Housing Works, Inc., for nearly ten years. Tony founded Big Apple Gay Lesbian for the Deaf.

In 2003, he was a finalist for the New York Post Liberty Medal Award in Education. In 2005, he received a special commendation from New York City for his education and support work for Deaf people with HIV/AIDS. He's been featured in *Time Out New York* and *Deaf Life* and is a leader in Deaf Pride events. He comes from a second-generation Deaf family.

Alfred Sonnenstrahl attended the Lexington School for the Deaf and P.S. 47 in New York City. He received a B.S. in mechanical engineering from New York University and a M.A. in administration and supervision from California State University, Northridge. He has also done postgraduate work at Gallaudet University. Former positions include, among others, engineer in the Department of the Navy, job placement consultant in Michigan, director of state vocational rehabilitation services for the Deaf in Massachusetts, and executive director of TDI. He is presently doing telecommunications consulting.

Michael Stinson is a professor in the Department of Research and Teacher Education, National Technical Institute for the Deaf, Rochester Institute of Technology (RIT). He teaches courses in the graduate program that prepares teachers of deaf students and has taught in the program in school psychology at RIT. He received a B.A. in psychology and a Ph.D. in educational psychology. Stinson has presented and published extensively on the instruction and social integration of deaf and hard of hearing students in general education classrooms, as well as the effects of technology and interpreting upon access.

Grace Walker graduated from Gallaudet University in 1985 in home economics. She worked at Columbia Maryland School for the Deaf as resident advisor with special needs children from 1985 to 1990. She then returned to Gallaudet and earned her master's in mental health counseling in 1992. She worked for the next six years as a full-time intern and counselor at Deaf Reach. In 1998, she went to Kendall Demonstration Elementary School for the Deaf as a school counselor. Since 2003, she has been working as a resident advisor for high school girls at the Delaware School for the Deaf.

Index

Figures and tables are denoted by "f" and "t" following page numbers.